ASHLEY RHODES-COURTER

Three Little Words

The heartbreaking true story of
an abandoned little girl

EBURY
PRESS

5 7 9 10 8 6

This edition published 2014 by Ebury Press, an imprint of Ebury Publishing
A Random House Group company
First published in the United States by Atheneum, an imprint of Simon & Schuster
Publishing in 2008

The Random House Group Limited Reg. No. 954009

Addresses for companies within the Random House Group can be found at
www.randomhouse.co.uk

A CIP catalogue record for this book is available from the British Library

The Random House Group Limited supports The Forest Stewardship
Council® (FSC®), the leading international forest-certification organisation.
Our books carrying the FSC label are printed on FSC®-certified paper.
FSC is the only forest-certification scheme supported by the leading
environmental organisations, including Greenpeace. Our
paper procurement policy can be found at
www.randomhouse.co.uk/environment

Printed and bound in Great Britain by Clays Ltd, St Ives plc

ISBN 9780091958305

To buy books by your favourite authors and register for offers visit
www.randomhouse.co.uk

Contents

I hear and I forget; I see and I remember;
I write and I understand.

—Chinese proverb

Dedicated to all children who are still waiting for safe,
permanent homes.

May they find one much more quickly than I did.

May they also find as much love and happiness.

Preface

I have had more than a dozen so-called mothers in my life. Lorraine Rhodes gave birth to me. Gay Courter adopted me. Then there are the fillers. Some were kind, a few were quirky, and one, Marjorie Moss, was as wicked as a fairy-tale witch. No matter where I lived, I waited impatiently to be reunited with my mother. Sometimes we had frequent visits, but other times—for some unexplained reason—I did not see her for years at a stretch.

I remember the rush of joy as I fell into her arms after one of those interminable separations.

"Sunshine, you're my baby and I'm your only mother. You must listen to the one taking care of you, but she's not your mama. Never forget, I'm the only mama who will love you forever and ever." She pledged that we would be together soon. Soon! How often I heard that word. It was soft, soothing. "Soon, I'll be back," she promised. "I'll bring more presents, soon. We'll go home—soon."

Soon, soon, soon . . . I would croon the word to myself like a lullaby when I would try to sleep, a mantra when nobody would listen to me, a chant to block out doubts that surfaced when it seemed too long between visits. My mother loved me. I was her special Sunshine. She would be back soon. Soon! Yes, she would. Naïve and trusting, I always believed her, and in some very small way—even now—I still do.

1

The day they stole my mother from me

Two days compete for the worst day in my life: The first is the day I was taken from my mother; the second is the day I arrived at the Mosses' foster home four years later. Three weeks before I lost my mother, I had left South Carolina bound for Florida with her, her husband, and my brother. I was three and a half years old and remember lying on the backseat watching slippery raindrops making patterns as they plopped down the car's windows.

My infant brother, Luke, was in a car seat, which nobody had bothered to belt in, so it squished me into the door when his father took a sharp turn. Luke had a heart monitor, but it must not have been on him all the time because I remember using it on my favorite toy: a Teddy Ruxpin bear.

Until Dustin Grover came along, we shared a trailer with my mother's twin sister, Leanne, who had dropped out of school to help support me. Even though the twins looked completely different, they were interchangeable to me since Aunt Leanne spent almost as much time with me as my mother, and I never minded when one left and the other took over. I loved to nestle by Aunt Leanne's side. She would rake my curls with her fingers while talking on the phone to her friends.

My mother was only seventeen when she gave birth to me. If she and my aunt were anything like most teenagers, they probably were more interested in hanging out with friends than changing diapers. Nevertheless, they worked different shifts and took turns caring for me. Their trailer became the local hangout because there was no adult supervision.

"Turn that down," my mother yelled one afternoon. I was watching cartoons, trying to drown out the teen voices by raising the volume higher and higher. "I said, turn that down!"

"Well, if you would shut the hell up, I could hear the damn TV," I said. My mother and her friends burst out laughing.

I was an intuitive two-year-old soaking up language and behaviors from a crew of rowdy adolescents who were trying on adult attitudes and habits. I got attention by acting grown up, and my mother bragged about how early I was toilet trained and how clearly I spoke.

My mother had a carefree attitude. She was too self-absorbed to fuss about my safety. Although she always strapped me in my car seat, her battered truck did not have seat belts. Driving down a bumpy South Carolina road, the unlocked door popped open. I tumbled out, rolling a few times before landing on the shoulder. My mother turned the truck around and found me waving at her. I was still buckled into the seat.

When my mother began living with Dustin—whom everyone called "Dusty"—the whole mood in the house shifted and Aunt Leanne wasn't around as much. Dusty was like an ocean that changed unexpectedly with the weather. One moment he could be placid, the next he turned into choppy waves that broke hard and stung. I cowered when he yelled. Since my mother was busy with me, she did not always have the perfect hot meal her boyfriend expected ready the moment he walked in the door.

"Can't you even bake a damn biscuit right?" he yelled after he saw the burnt bottom on one, sending the pie tin flying like a Frisbee.

I hid under my blanket as I always did when the fighting started, hoping it would protect me from their nasty words or physical brawls. I peered through a hole at a single object—like a shoe—and tried to make everything else disappear.

I remember when my pregnant mother awoke from a nap and found my aunt and Dusty sitting close together watching television. She caught them tickling and laughing. My mother screamed at my aunt, "How could you? He's the father of my baby!"

"You sure of that?" my aunt screeched back before she slammed the screen door behind her.

After that, she was gone for weeks, and I missed her so much that I would curl my hair around my own fingers and pretend it was her doing it.

Not long after that, there was a new baby: Tommy. My mother brought him home in a yellow blanket and let me kiss his tiny fingers. I don't remember much else because he came and went in less than two months. Sometimes I thought that I had dreamed him or that he was merely a doll I was not supposed to touch. The last time I saw him, he had suddenly stopped moving and turned from pink to gray. We all sat in a room and everyone passed him around. He was lying in a box that was padded with a pillow.

My mother got pregnant again shortly after Tommy disappeared. A few months later she married Dusty, and for a short time we seemed like a happy little family. But only nine months after Tommy was born, Luke arrived premature. Before my mother was even twenty, she had managed to have three children in less than three years.

At least Luke—unlike me—came into the world with a father. At birth my new brother weighed only two pounds. My mother had to come home from the hospital without him.

"Did you really have a baby?" I asked my mother.

"He has to stay with the nurses until he gets bigger," she explained.

A few days later I awoke to her sobbing. Dusty was trying to comfort her, but she pushed him away. "It's all your fault because you hit me!" she yelled.

I tried to understand how Dusty's hitting her could harm the unborn baby. I rested my head on her belly. It felt like a balloon that had some of the air let out. "When can I see my brother?" I asked.

"They had to take him from the hospital in Spartanburg to the one in Greenville where they can care for him better," my mother explained. "We'll drive up there as soon as we can."

In the meantime, my mother went back to work. Dusty was supposed to watch me while my mother worked the late shift. One night neighbors found me wandering through the trailer park alone and kept me until my mother returned home.

The next day she packed a bag and we moved into a Ronald McDonald House near the hospital.

We went to see Luke every day. Most of the time I had to wait outside in a room where there were little tables, coloring books, and crayons. Sometimes they would let me put on a mask and come into the room where the babies were kept in boxes—not like the wooden one that had held Tommy, but a plastic one that I could peek through when my mother lifted me up.

"Is he ever getting out of there?" I asked.

"Oh, yes," my mother promised. "He's strong like his daddy."

When Luke came home seven months later, he was not much bigger than one of my dolls. He sometimes wore a doctor's face mask instead of a diaper.

Aunt Leanne came by to help and called often. "Where's your mama?" she asked when I answered the phone.

"In the kitchen cookin' dope," I replied.

"I'm coming right over," she said, but when she did, Dusty refused to let her in.

Dusty worked as a framing subcontractor. After an argument over money, his partner stormed over to our trailer. Dusty locked him out, but he busted down the door and then started tearing up the house. A chair hit the wall and a table flew in my direction. I ducked, but my mother started screaming, "You almost hurt Ashley!"

"I'm okay, Mama," I said as I crouched in a corner.

"We need to move," my mother announced to Dusty while they cleaned up the mess. "There are too many bad influences on you around here."

"And you're an angel?" he shot back. "Besides, all my work is here."

"There's plenty of work in Florida." She kicked the broken chair into a corner. "I wish I had never left there after Mama died."

Her mother—my maternal grandmother, Jenny—had her first child when she was fourteen, but she put that baby up for adoption. Over the next six years she had Perry; followed by the twins, Leanne and Lorraine; and finally, Sammie. Then, at twenty-one, Grandma Jenny was diagnosed with cervical cancer and had a hysterectomy. Sick, poor, and battered by her alcoholic husband, she decided she could not raise her kids any longer and turned them over to a Baptist children's home. My mother did not have much to do with either parent for many years, but when Jenny was about to die in Florida, my mother went to see her for the last time. Jenny was thirty-three.

Using her small inheritance, my mother enrolled in cosmetology school. Before they would allow her to train with the hair treatment chemicals, she had to have a physical checkup. This is how she found out she was pregnant with me. My mother thinks she conceived me when she partied the night of her mother's funeral. In any case, I was born thirty-nine weeks later. While she was in labor, she was watching *The Young and the Restless*, and so she named me Ashley after one of the soap opera characters.

When Dusty agreed to move to Tampa, my mother

cheered up. As she packed, she hummed "You Are My Sunshine" and explained to me, "We're moving to the Sunshine State to live happily ever after."

I do not remember much about the long car trip except singing along with Joan Jett on the radio. When we first arrived in Florida, we stayed at a motel, then a trailer that smelled like low tide. I have memories of walking around that trailer park carrying Luke's bottle and begging for milk.

Our car always smelled of pickles and mustard from all the fast food we ate in it. I was enjoying my usual kids' meal in the backseat when my mother shouted, "Shit, shit!" A flashing red light made the car's windows glow rosy, and I liked the way my hands looked, as though they were on fire.

A siren blared. Dusty banged the steering wheel. "Ashley, you keep saying you gotta go potty, okay?" my mother ordered.

A police officer asked where our license plate was.

"Mommy, gotta go potty!" I called loudly.

"Where're you headed?" the officer asked.

"To my stepfather's house," my mother said in her most genial voice.

"We're just in from South Carolina. We're moving here," Dusty continued rapidly, "so I'll get a new Florida plate tomorrow."

"Welcome to Florida," he said, glancing at me and Luke before arresting Dusty for not having a license plate on the car or a valid driver's license.

My mother alternately cussed and cried while we waited for Dusty to be released. It was several hours before we could go home to our apartment. The shoebox-style building was on tree-lined Sewaha Street. "We're living in a duplex now," my mother explained, and I sensed that we had come up in the world. Three days later I encountered more police officers—the ones who broke up our family forever.

I was sitting on the stoop dressed only in shorts when the police cars pulled up. "He's not here," my mother said when they asked for Dusty. One of the men kept coming toward her. My mother, who was holding Luke, screamed, "I didn't do anything!"

"Mama," I cried, reaching both hands up for her to lift me as well. A uniformed man pushed me away and snatched Luke out of her arms. I tried to rush toward my mother, who was already being put in the backseat of a police car. The door slammed so hard, it shook my legs. Through the closed window, I could hear my mother shouting, "Ashley!" Someone held me back as the car pulled away. I struggled and kicked trying to chase after her.

"It's okay! Settle down!" the man with the shiny buttons said.

I sobbed for my Teddy Ruxpin. "Winky!"

"Who's that?" The officer let me run inside. I pulled Winky out from under a blanket on my bed. "Oh, it's your teddy. He can come too." He grabbed two of my T-shirts and told me to put one on and to wear my flip-flops. My Strawberry Shortcake T-shirt ended up on Luke, although it was way too big for him.

At the police station a man in uniform handed Luke to a woman in uniform. Luke tugged on Winky's ears as I sat beside him and the female officer. In the background I could hear my mother yelling for us, but I could not see her. Two women wearing regular clothes arrived. One lifted Luke; the other's rough hand pulled me in her direction. The woman who held Luke also took Winky.

"No!" I cried, reaching for Winky.

"It's just for a little while," the first woman told me.

"Winky!"

My mother came into view for a few seconds. "Ashley! I'll get you soon!" Then a door slammed and she was gone. I turned and Luke was no longer there. I was pushed outside and loaded into a car.

"Mommy! Luke!" I cried. "Winky!"

"You'll see them later," the woman said as our car drove off.

Thinking about that moment is like peeling a scab off an almost-healed wound. I still believed everything would return to normal. Little did I know, I would never live with my mother—or see Winky—again.

2

They're nice to you ... until you're naughty

When they ripped me from my family, nobody told me anything. I completely expected that I was going to end up wherever my mother and Luke were. I might have been too young for an explanation, but years would pass without anyone answering any of my questions. I went to live with complete strangers. I was shuffled like a hand-me-down toy for the next nine years. The first anguished hours away from my mother are clearer than the next few years.

Speed bumps slowed the car. I glimpsed a tree with blue blossoms as big as teacups. "Here we are!" the driver said, as though I should be delighted with the destination.

The front door opened, and a woman bent over and patted my head. "Hello there. I'm Mrs. O'Connor and I'm going to take care of you."

"Mama?"

"She can't come tonight," Mrs. O'Connor said. Two toddlers clung to her legs.

She put me to bed in a room where other small children were sleeping in a crib, playpen, and bunk beds. It was crowded, but I felt utterly alone. I sobbed for my mother. When nobody soothed me, I started to whimper "You Are My Sunshine" until I fell asleep.

In the morning I asked, "Is my mama here yet?"

"No, but you're going to be with your brother," Mrs. O'Connor replied.

That afternoon another worker moved me to the home of Benedict and Annabelle Hines in Seffner. Luke was there, which made me happy, but they kept him downstairs with another baby while I had to sleep upstairs in a room with a slanted ceiling that frightened me.

If I couldn't be in the same room with my brother, like in the South Carolina trailer, I wanted to be with my mother and Dusty. I did not care that this was the nicest house I had ever seen. There was a tire swing, a mini-trampoline, and a wading pool. But instead of waiting my turn to use any of these toys, I took my frustrations out on a younger girl who was also named Ashlee.

"You're my little pumpkin," Mr. Hines said to make me feel special, but I knew they preferred the younger children. They especially fussed over Luke, who was so tiny, they could not believe he was almost a year old. Mrs. Hines cooked special food for him and claimed he was growing so fast because of her pureed beets.

I kept asking for my mother, but nobody ever explained why she did not come for me. Once, I handed Mrs. Hines the phone. "Call my mama and tell her to pick me up!" I demanded.

"I don't have her number." She sighed. "But I'll see what I can do."

A few days later they dressed Luke and me in our best clothes and Mr. Hines took us to the Department of Children and Families building.

My mother hugged me, then examined my arms and legs. "How did you get all those red spots?" she asked with an accusing tone.

"Bug bites."

"What do they do, leave you out in the woods?" My mother directed her question to the worker who was standing in the doorway.

"I don't like it there! Take me home with you."

"Sunshine, not today, but soon."

"When, Mama, when?"

She looked to the waiting worker and back to me. "As soon as I have a better apartment and a job."

When we went for the next visit, we waited for a long time; but my mother never arrived.

"Where is she?" I asked every few minutes, getting whinier each time.

"Doesn't look like the M-O-M is going to show," the worker said.

"How can she do this to her children?" Mr. Hines fumed. Switching to a cheerful voice, he said, "Time to go."

"But Mama—"

"We can't wait any longer. Mrs. Hines will wonder what happened to us."

"Please!" I begged. "She's coming! She's coming!"

He pushed Luke and me into the corridor. "I'm not putting these children through this again," Mr. Hines said to the worker.

I wanted to tell them that they were making a mistake, that they had the time wrong, because my mother would never miss a chance to see us. I pulled away from Mr. Hines and rushed back into the visitation room.

"Let's go," Mr. Hines said in exasperation.

I ducked under a worker's desk to stall the departure. My mother could be running late—she sometimes had problems with her car or not finding her way. Mr. Hines let go of Luke and lunged toward me. "Ashley! Enough of this nonsense. We aren't waiting any longer." He reached under the desk, but I kicked his arm away. *They* had the time wrong; *they* weren't patient enough; *they* weren't giving her a chance. Eventually, they dragged me out flailing and crying and took me back to what they called "home."

They couldn't keep me from thinking about my mother all the time—her smiles, her songs in the shower, the way she painted her eyes and lips with colors. I would say, "Mama, you look so beautiful," and then she would kiss my cheek to blot her lipstick. I loved the mark it left. I was jealous that she had so many hugs and kisses for Dusty, and I often spied on them when I was supposed to be asleep in a motel room or the small space of one of our trailers.

I was playing with two teddy bears from the Hineses' toy chest. "Want to see all the ways my mommy and daddy have fun?" I asked the other girls. I pressed the bears' fronts together. They squealed with laughter. "And they can do it this way, too." I had one hump the other's back. Their giggles encouraged me, so I put one's head between the other's legs. I added the grunting noises I had heard in the dark.

"What's going on here?" Mrs. Hines chided when she checked on us.

The other children dispersed, but I gave Mrs. Hines the same demonstration. "Why don't you put the bears back and go out to play?" she said in a voice that left no room to disagree.

I stormed outside, slamming the screen door behind me. "It's my turn!" I shouted to Ashlee, who ignored me and pedaled off on the tricycle. Enraged, I caught up, reached around her neck, and choked her. Luke came over to join the fray. He grasped my leg and tried to pull me down. To shake him off, I kicked him. When he screeched, Mrs. Hines came running. She gripped my arm, steered me in the house, and gave me a stern time-out on a stool.

A while later I heard her complaining about me on the phone. "I do believe this child is hyper. She breaks all her toys, is really mean to the little ones—even her brother— and isn't still for a minute." Her voice changed to a whisper as she recounted how I had played with the bears. When she mentioned that I had started wetting the bed, I went to where the others were watching TV and started to mimic what was on the screen.

One of the older children shooed me away, but I did not listen. "Hey, Ashley, we can't see through you," he said.

If my mother had been there, she would have applauded my antics; but here, I was nobody's special Sunshine.

Then, after only four months, Mrs. Hines announced that Luke and I were going to live with my grandfather. "Won't that be nice?" she said as she packed my clothes.

I went around the house piling up Luke's toys and bottles, but they kept ending up back in their original places. I was oblivious to the fact that Mrs. Hines was packing only my possessions.

When the worker arrived, Luke was napping. I was bundled into the car. "What about my brother?"

"He has to take his nap," the worker said. "You'll see him later."

It took several days before I realized Luke was not coming to my new foster home, which was nowhere near my grandfather's house. I wondered what was so horrible about me and why I had been rejected again. Then there was my perpetual question: What had I done that was so terrible that I had to be taken from my mother? I had no idea why she hadn't been able to get me back. You would think someone would have explained it in words a child could understand. Yet nobody did. I believed they were keeping secrets from me—but supposedly, they thought they were protecting me.

Now I know that—in the beginning at least—my mother never did anything seriously wrong. She never hurt us. She loved us and I adored her. Originally, the police had arrested my mother for writing a bad check; but Dusty admitted he had stolen the checks, and she was released six days later. When my mother returned home, she found our duplex padlocked. Three weeks after Dusty was let out of jail, they arrested him again for attempting to steal cigarettes from a food store. My mother moved to a new apartment but had lost most of our possessions. Although she submitted applications for food stamps and aid for dependent children, the welfare officials told her that she was ineligible because her children were no longer living with her. When she tried to get us back, the caseworker said she had to be able to provide food for us.

Two months after we were placed in temporary shelter care, Judge Vincent E. Giglio officially ordered us into foster care. We were now state property. Our legal guardian was the executive branch of the Florida government, an entity that would rather pay strangers to care for us than offer any economic help to my mother to care for her own children.

My fourth mother was Yolanda Schott. Other than running around in some orange groves, I have no memory of my time with her. I would still like to know why the Schotts took me in—and why they let me go after such a short time. Maybe it was a temporary placement until the state could find something better; or maybe the Schotts did not like me either. The blankness bothers me, as does the fact that there is not a single person who can fill in that part of my story.

Next, I moved to the home of Julio and Rosa Ortiz and stayed with them for thirteen months. They lived in a Tampa neighborhood where the houses were only a few feet apart. Their small backyard included an aboveground pool as well as a chicken coop. The Ortizes had three teenage birth daughters and four adopted children, plus a constant stream of foster children. Some were there for only a few days; some came before me and stayed longer. At least twenty children cycled in and out of the home while I was with them. There were so many of us that we ate in shifts. It was hard to feel alone, but still I missed Luke.

"Can you go get my brother?" I asked Mrs. Ortiz, who looked like a Hispanic Mrs. Claus, one day during dinner.

"Okay," she said to hush me.

"When?" I demanded, and kicked the table leg.

"Ashley, go to your room until you can calm down," she said.

I turned my back to her and stormed down the hallway to the bedrooms. As I got closer to the babies' room, I smelled something putrid. Peering in, I could see that a toddler had smeared poop all over the wall. I slammed the door to the room, which caused the baby to wail.

Hearing the baby's piercing screams, Mrs. Ortiz came rushing. "Ashley, what did you do to the baby?"

"I shut the door because he stinks."

Mrs. Ortiz opened it and rushed to comfort the child. Her shoe slipped on something soft, and she wheeled around and gave me an accusing look. "Ashley, how could you do something so disgusting?"

"I didn't do anything!" I screamed, which only got me a longer time-out in my room.

Since I had been blamed for the mess, a few of the other children came to check on me as if I were a sideshow. I stuck my middle finger up—the way Dusty did when he was mad at someone. Some of the others copied me and went around the house showing everyone what I had just taught them.

Mrs. Ortiz barreled into my room. "Why are you teaching the little ones to shoot birds?"

"I did not!" I retorted.

"Ashley, you are going to have to stop your lying," she said, and marched off. I had never seen her so furious and did not understand why I was blamed for hurting birds when there had not been any in the house.

I soon realized that if Mrs. Ortiz yelled at me, I could stare just above her head and she would still think that I was looking directly at her, hanging on her every word. I would purposely let my mind wander to take me far away from the current confrontation.

"Chicken pox!" I overheard Mrs. Ortiz on the phone. "Yeah, three of them—two of them foster." I wished I could tell my mother that I had a chicken disease that made me itch all over.

Mrs. Ortiz put me in a bathtub with her daughter Trina and a blond foster girl. The spots bloomed on each of us.

"Don't scratch," Mrs. Ortiz said. "This special soap will help you feel better."

She pushed my hand away from a cluster of pox. "If you don't stop, you'll have ugly marks forever."

I sulked. "I don't want ugly marks!"

"Of course not—you're too pretty for that," Mrs. Ortiz said kindly.

Her older daughters took turns picking out outfits for me that looked good with my red hair. I loved my aqua shorts and matching socks with lace trim and a yellow dress with a flounced skirt. I came out and twirled around to show it off.

"Here comes my prissy girl," Mrs. Ortiz complimented.

Every day when the older children went off to school, I asked to go as well.

"You have to be five," Mr. Ortiz said in his slight Cuban accent.

"I *am* five!" I insisted, although I was just about to turn four.

Mrs. Ortiz tilted her head. "I don't think so."

"Ask my *real* mother!"

"Ashley is smart enough to go to kindergarten," Mr. Ortiz admitted.

"It would do her good to be in school," Mrs. Ortiz agreed. "She's the brainiest kid I ever had."

DeSoto, the neighborhood primary school, had a pre-K program, so they enrolled me. I was so overjoyed to leave the house with the older kids that I raced to beat the others to the school on the edge of the bay.

My teacher called Mrs. Ortiz and asked her to come in because she had concerns about my adjustment. She said, "Ashley is a good student, but she does five times as many papers as the others."

"What's the problem?" Mrs. Ortiz threw up her hands and shrugged. "Give her more papers."

While I liked school, I thought church was boring. They liked to dress Trina and me in matching frilly dresses and hats—hers were usually white and mine were pink. As Mrs. Ortiz dropped us off at Sunday school, she would say, "Ashley, if you don't mind the teacher, you can't watch *Alice in Wonderland* or any of your other movies later."

Mrs. Ortiz often fostered infants, so she spent many hours bottle-feeding them. This was a good time to snuggle against her; and as long as the baby was sucking, she did not mind. When I was comfy, I would ask, "When can I see my mama?"

Mrs. Ortiz dodged the question as best she could because she probably knew that a few weeks after I came to live with her, my mother had been charged with possession of cocaine and drug paraphernalia as well as offering to commit prostitution.

When Mr. Ortiz took me to a family visit, I asked, "Will Mama be there?"

"I don't think so," he said. "You'll see your daddy and your brother. Won't that be nice?"

"Are you sure my mother isn't coming?" My birthday had been the previous week and I had been certain she would come with my gifts.

"Well, you never know," he said to appease me.

Luke arrived with Mr. Hines, who called me "Pumpkin" and ruffled my hair. "His father is coming from South Carolina . . . out on bail . . ." were words I caught, but they did not mean much to me. When nobody else appeared, our worker took us back to our respective foster homes.

There was at least one time while I lived with the Ortizes that my mother did show up. The moment I saw her, I felt my heart would leap out of my chest. She wrapped her arms around me and told me everything would be all right—and I believed every word. Luke had not made it to this visit, so I asked, "Is Luke at your house now?"

"No, not yet," she replied.

"Oh." I thought about my other brother. "What about Tommy?"

My mother startled. "Who?"

"The one in the box."

"You can't ever tell anyone about him."

"Why?"

"Because—" She checked to make sure we were alone. "He's our secret. If anyone knew, they might not let you come to live with me again."

"Why?"

"They might put me in jail."

"Why?"

"Honey, you are too young to understand, but someday

I'll tell you all about it." She gave me her sweetest smile. "Now, what shall I bring you on my next visit?"

All too soon, we separated, both of us in tears.

When I returned to the foster home, I started spinning to make myself dizzy. "My, aren't you all wound up!" Mrs. Ortiz remarked. "Did you have a good visit with your mother?"

I stopped twirling and said, "My mommy told me that I have to keep our secret or she'll go to jail and I'll never see her again."

"Oh, really?" Mrs. Ortiz arched her bushy eyebrows.

A baby cried and she went to tend to her. When she was giving her a bottle, I cuddled against Mrs. Ortiz and laid my head on her bosom. "Do you want to know my secret?" I asked.

"Only if you want to tell me."

"My mommy put my baby brother in a box, and if I tell anyone, she'll get in trouble and go to jail and I'll never see her again."

Mrs. Ortiz dropped the baby's bottle. "Your little brother is in another foster home and he's fine."

"No, another baby," I tried to explain.

She handed her husband the bottle to wash off the nipple. He brought it back and said, "I'll call the worker and arrange a sibling visit," he said.

"And check whether they know about another one," Mrs. Ortiz added.

That summer I splashed in the pool and waited for more family visits—but none came. I was happier when I returned to the pre-K classroom with the fenced play yard and tubular slide.

Mrs. Ortiz asked, "Do you remember your grandpa in South Carolina?"

"Yep," I said, even though I mostly remembered Aunt Leanne and Dusty.

"Wouldn't it be nice if you and your brother could visit him?"

"Yep," I agreed, and went back to coloring my school papers.

A few days later Luke and I met at the Department of Children and Families, supposedly to see our mother and Dusty, but Dusty arrived alone. He whirled Luke in the air, and then he got down on the floor and played with us both.

Our caseworker, Dennis Benson, asked, "How do you feel about them going to their grandfather's?" he asked.

"You know my mother has put in for them too," he said.

"She also withdrew the papers once before," the worker replied, "and she is only related to your son."

"If they're with my wife's father, my family can still visit them, can't they?"

"I don't see why not," Mr. Benson said. "They live close by, right?"

"Yeah, but there's been some bad blood, if you know what I mean."

"We can arrange regular visitations for you and them at the county offices," the worker replied. He checked his watch. "Is their mother coming?"

"Don't you know?" Dusty asked with a lopsided grin. He pantomimed a key turning in a lock, which meant she was back in jail.

A few days later Mrs. Ortiz gave me a bath and dressed me in clean school clothes instead of pajamas. "Aren't I going to bed?" I asked.

"Yes, but you're getting up very early to go visit your grandfather."

Before dawn Mrs. Ortiz awakened me from a deep sleep, hugged me against her pillow-soft chest that had a lavender scent, and whispered, "Don't forget us!" Dennis Benson carried me to the car and placed a plastic bag with all my belongings beside me. Luke was in a car seat sound asleep. The next thing I remember is a uniformed woman lifting me into an airline seat and cinching a belt over my lap. Someone handed me a little white pillow. As the plane whooshed up and away, I fell asleep trying to memorize Mrs. Ortiz's face because I had already forgotten my first foster parents, and I feared I would not remember my grandfather, my aunt Leanne, or worse, my mother.

3

Papa fall down

Daylight and strangers greeted us when I stumbled sleepily into the South Carolina airport terminal. A woman lifted Luke and a man took me by the hand, but I pulled it away. "Don't you recognize your grandpa?" the woman asked. I shook my head. "I guess it's been too long a time." She bent close and explained that she was Adele and the man was my mama's daddy.

Mr. Benson passed over some papers and our plastic bags. Grandpa did not say much, but Adele cooed over Luke, who clung to her neck.

As we drove off, I started with my questions. "Where are we going?"

"To our house," Adele responded.

"Is Luke going to stay with us?"

"Of course, darlin'." Adele laughed.

"When do I go to school?"

"Not till you're five."

"I'll be five soon."

"I know that, hon, and next year you'll ride the big yellow bus."

"Wheels on the bus go round and round!" Luke clapped.

I cupped my hand over my brother's mouth. "Will I have a birthday cake?"

"Sure, hon. Do you prefer chocolate or vanilla?"

"Vanilla!" Luke chimed in.

"No, chocolate." I shoved him to be quiet. "Where's Mrs. Ortiz?"

"Who?" Grandpa asked as we turned down their dirt lane.

"That foreign lady who had her," Adele said in a disapproving voice.

While Adele fixed lunch, Grandpa took us to see the cow named Moe, the chickens, the goat, and the pigs.

There was almost no conversation while the four of us ate grilled cheese sandwiches, pickles, and potato chips. I was wistful for the commotion in the Ortizes' home. "It's too quiet here," I announced.

"Peace and quiet are priceless," Grandpa said.

I would soon learn that when he wanted peace and quiet, he had to have it; but when he wanted to raise a ruckus, it was best to stay out of his way. I sometimes held as still as a statue and pretended I couldn't hear or see when my grandpa squabbled with Adele and called her mean names.

Luke and I shared a bedroom. Sometimes he would climb into my bed when he was scared. If he wet my bed, he would sneak back into his dry one.

"I never wet the bed!" I protested.

Adele grumbled. "Liars get soap in their mouths," she said, and even made me lick a bar a few times. Still, I refused to take the blame for Luke's mess.

Adele was a registered nurse and also had an associate degree in commercial art. She had decorated the mobile home with her paintings. She taught me how to color inside the lines and the proper ways to shade an object. While we were working on a project, Luke would follow Grandpa around like a baby duckling behind its mother.

Our life fell into a routine that—for once—usually centered on us. There were warm chocolate chip cookies and my favorite video, *Fantasia*. Grandpa built a two-story playhouse in the backyard, where I played house and Luke took the roles I bossily assigned to him. In the evenings we would watch whatever television show Grandpa wanted to see while Adele crocheted or sewed. Even though we arrived the last week in October, Adele made Halloween costumes for us. I was an angel with stiffened wings strapped on my back with a gold harness. She filled my closet with handmade dresses with puffed sleeves and made dolls' outfits from the scraps. I had a basin where I would scrub my dolls' clothes and hang them with tiny clothespins on the wash line Adele strung at my height next to the playhouse.

Adele tucked us in with prayers and kisses. Soon Luke was calling Adele "Mama" and my grandpa "Papa," but I kept my promise to my mother and called them "Grandpa" and "Adele." After a few weeks I let my guard down. I stopped worrying about someone coming to take me somewhere else.

The state authorities had only approved the transfer "with reservations" because Grandpa had never provided a stable home for his own children. He had had a tumultuous childhood and quit school in the seventh grade. By the time I was returned to South Carolina, their oldest son, Perry, age twenty-four, was in prison for murder. The twins, Leanne and Lorraine, were twenty-two; and their youngest, Sammie, had just turned eighteen and was still in foster care. My grandpa had been in and out of jail for crimes he committed while intoxicated, and my grandmother had divorced him because he abused her. Perhaps the authorities believed that Adele, who was twelve years older than my grandfather and had been his live-in companion for two years by that time, would make sure that nothing happened to us. She had three grown children, four grandchildren, and a clean record.

Two weeks after we arrived, Ava Willis, a local caseworker, came to check on us. Adele showed her my drawings and some of my make-believe schoolwork. "This child is itching to go to school."

"You know I had concerns about this placement," Ms. Willis replied, "but I always say that it's best for children to be with their family, so I am delighted at how well everything is going."

"Who wants to go for a ride?" Grandpa asked while Adele was napping. We rarely rode in his beat-up car because it did not have doors or seat belts. He joked that it had "all-natural air-conditioning." The junker was so rusty that I could see through the floor.

We stopped at the country store, and Grandpa told us to wait in the car while he shopped. When he came out of the store, he was yelling at a man. He got in the car muttering obscenities, floored the gas, and the car lurched forward. I clutched the seat as we whizzed past our dirt road. The tires screeched as Grandpa did a 180-degree turn. Coming directly toward us in another car was the man from the store. "Let's see who's boss!" Grandpa shouted. He hit the accelerator even harder. The gap was closing between the oncoming car and us. Terrified, I looked away. The pavement rushed by like a river. When I glanced to the side, ribbons of flickering green flashed by the nonexistent door.

"Fassa!" Luke laughed with manic delight.

"Stop, stop!" I yelled.

The other guy swerved around us at the last second, but not before he clipped our rear fender. I smashed my face into the back of the front seat. By the time we got home, my lip was swelling. Dust blanketed our clothes. "What in the world?" Adele asked.

Grandpa gave Adele a don't-you-start-with-me look, marched into the kitchen, grabbed a can of beer from the refrigerator, planted himself in his favorite chair in front of the television, and lit a cigarette. Blue smoke curled into the air like an exclamation point. Adele herded us into the bathroom and shut the door with an incensed slam.

Two weeks later, Ava Willis was back and she was furious. Grandpa had taken Luke to town and had been arrested for drunk driving.

When Ms. Willis confronted him, he was belligerent. "I only drank apple cider. Those deputies were out to get me."

"You know I was worried about your stability," she chided him, "but I hoped that Adele's strengths would compensate for your shortcomings."

"I haven't had a single drink in three years!"

"The police tested you, sir."

"Sometimes I have a taste, just to be social."

"It's my fault," Adele said as she wept. "I should have been more protective. I won't let them go with him ever again."

"I have to report this to Florida," she told Adele and Grandpa.

"Are you going to send them back?" Adele moaned.

"The authorities in Florida are still in charge of the case," the caseworker said. "Personally, I don't think the children are at risk based on this single incident, but my supervisor is probably not going to want to accept further responsibility."

All the commotion caused Adele to cancel my fifth birthday party. She still gave me two dolls: Lilly, a Cabbage Patch doll; and a life-size baby doll I named Katie. I wrote my initials—A. M. R.—on her bottom with permanent black marker.

"Christmas is my favorite time of year!" Adele said. She decorated the whole trailer before Thanksgiving. We went to the mall and sat on Santa's lap, and I wore my angel costume again in a holiday pageant at church.

There were many phone calls about our placement, and Adele pleaded with the authorities not to move us before the holidays. "We'll do anything you say," she promised Ms. Willis, who had stalled our return after Adele and Grandpa had agreed to undergo psychological examinations.

On Christmas morning I received a pink bicycle with training wheels and Luke got a red tricycle. Grandpa gave me a battery-powered Barbie car that I could drive down our long road, and Adele made me a red dress with a white pinafore that had strawberry appliqués and matching outfits for my dolls. After we opened our presents at home, we visited Adele's relatives and played with her three grandchildren, who were close to my age.

A few weeks later Adele woke me up early. "We're going to drive up in the mountains so you can see snow."

I slept in the car until Adele nudged me awake. Huge flakes whirled around and the ground looked as if it were coated with shiny pearls. When the car stopped, I ran outside, opened my mouth, and curled my tongue to catch snowflakes. I thought that they would taste like vanilla. Instead, they had a rusty-nail flavor. I wanted to make a snowman, but the thin layer was melting into mud.

After our trip to the mountains, I asked when it was going to snow at our house so I could build a snowman. "It's very rare around here," Adele said, and made me a cup of cocoa with a marshmallow bobbing in the middle.

"But could it happen?"

"Only the weatherman knows."

From then on, I listened to weather reports for any mention of snow. When I finally heard the word, I kept checking for the predicted snow, but it never came. "That weatherman is a liar!" I said.

"It's snowing in Colorado," Adele said with a laugh.

"Take me there!" I demanded.

"Maybe someday," she replied offhandedly.

A few weeks after Christmas my grandpa was arrested again—this time for nonpayment of child support for his youngest son. Adele bailed him out, and in his attempt to deflect the heat from himself, he told the police that Adele's heart condition made her unfit to care for us.

"Yes, I had a problem with my heart muscle, but it's in remission," Adele explained to Ms. Willis when she came to investigate. "Anyway, caring for the kids isn't too hard."

"You're judging me because of my past," Grandpa argued. "People have always been against me. Why should the system take my own flesh and blood?"

"I went to bat for you," the caseworker reminded him. "We wouldn't have a problem if it hadn't been for these recent arrests."

"The last arrest was unfair," Grandpa scoffed. "Why should I have to pay child support when I gave all my children up for adoption?"

"If you gave them up, then you are no longer Lorraine's legal father," the worker responded. "That means you have no legal basis to have your grandchildren."

"What about me?" Adele said in a timid voice.

"The children were placed with a relative, and you're no kin to them."

Grandpa left the room several times. Each time, Adele lowered her guard and cried. "He doesn't care about the children the way I do. I'm the one who will suffer if they leave."

Ms. Willis shook her head. "Because Mr. Rhodes assumes no responsibility for his actions, we have no other choice but to send them back to Florida."

"Like hell she will!" Adele screamed as the caseworker drove away from the house, a trail of dusty fumes in her wake.

I had never seen Adele so furious. She made a series of phone calls ending with one to Ms. Willis. "I've spoken to our attorney," she said. "We will not relinquish the children without a court order."

Adele had gotten good advice, because the South Carolina Department of Social Services would have to get a Florida court order to force the issue. What she did not know—and I discovered many years later—was that someone in Florida had neglected to get the court's permission for us to live with our relatives in the first place. Now they had to figure out how to ask for an order recalling us when no judge had approved sending us to South Carolina.

Adele kept the appointment with the psychologist and took me along. I sat in the waiting room coloring, but then the therapist called me inside. After admiring my drawing, she asked, "What do you think of what's been going on at your house?"

I leaned back in my chair, propped my feet up on the coffee table, and sighed. "These social services people want to send me back to Florida, but I'm not much in the mood to go."

"What do you think about your mother and Dusty?"

I refused to look directly at her when I replied, "I like them okay, but my mama did bad things, so social services had to take me away for my own good."

The psychologist gave me some tests and said, "You are doing far better than most children." Then she showed me some pictures and asked me to make up a story about each one. My replies involved ghosts, witches eating people, and monsters swallowing parents alive. "She's very bright," she told Adele, who preened at the news. "Her level of verbal expression and her ability to grasp her total situation are way above her age level." She then whispered something I could not quite hear about showing signs of being disturbed by all the upheavals in my life.

There was no further talk of moving us, but the legal staff in Florida scurried around trying to figure out how to redo the paperwork so it would look like we had been sent to South Carolina legally. They filed a motion to send us to Grandpa as though we'd never left Florida. The judge signed this document five months after we were already in South Carolina.

We had visits with Dusty in January and March. He brought toys, candy, and clothes to each visit. I loved the pile of pretty dresses, each wrapped in a plastic bag like the kind you get from the dry cleaner. I sat on his lap and sang songs with him, but Luke—who really had no memory of him—would not join in. We went to a scheduled third visit in April; but after waiting more than an hour, Adele, who had little patience with the Grover clan, took us home. I know Dusty showed up eventually because Ms. Willis brought our gifts to us a few days later.

My South Carolina interlude has a dreamlike quality to it. I know it existed because I have more photos from that time than from any other placement in foster care. They depict Luke and me snug in new pajamas, splashing in a bubble bath, and hugging a hound dog whose head is twice as big as my brother's. There are snapshots of us having a picnic in the park, posing in new outfits, and floating in a plastic kiddie pool. Despite the fact that this interval was doomed not to last, we are always smiling in the pictures and they evoke only warm feelings in me.

That summer Luke stayed home while I went to the beach with Leanne, her boyfriend, and his daughter, Savannah, who was about my age. We built sand castles, ran in the surf, rode a merry-go-round, a miniature train, and bumper cars. Savannah and I slept together in a double bed, wearing T-shirt nighties and hugging matching dolls.

Adele made a big fuss over Luke's third birthday in July with a homemade cake, balloons, and fancy hats for us and her grandchildren.

"Why didn't I have a party?" I complained.

"You had just arrived." Adele did not mention Grandpa's arrest a few days before I turned five. "But when you are six, you can invite children from your class."

Sometime later that summer, Ava Willis dropped by. "The report from the mental health center shows that Ashley has bonded with you and is relatively well adjusted." She paused. "How are things going between you and Sam?"

Adele admitted that Grandpa sometimes spoke to her cruelly. "But don't you worry, he would never hurt me or those children."

"It must be hard for you," the caseworker said sympathetically.

"Yes, sometimes I think about leaving him, but since I'm not kin, I'd lose the children, right?"

"If you got a foster parent license, they could stay with you."

Luke ran up to Adele. "Mama!" He slipped into her lap. She kissed his forehead. After wiggling around a bit, he slipped down, crawled under the table, and started grunting like a pig.

"How long has he been calling you 'Mama'?" the caseworker asked.

"Almost right away," Adele said. "He doesn't remember anyone else."

"What about Ashley?"

Adele chuckled. "One time I said something like 'You mind your mama,' and she stuck out her tongue and said, 'You're *not* my mama!'" She sighed. "I do love them as much as if they were mine."

"Is she still seeing the therapist?"

Adele nodded.

"Then give her some time."

"It would be better for all of us if this was permanent. How can we get custody?"

"It might help if you two were married."

"I'm working on that!" Adele laughed. Then she lowered her voice and said something about wanting to make sure the Grovers were ruled out as placements.

A week later it did not matter who loved us or who wanted us. It did not matter whether Adele and Grandpa were married. It did not matter whom we called "Mama" or "Papa." It only took a few seconds for everything to blow apart.

Someone had come to see my grandfather about buying a car. He let Luke and me tag along while Adele did the dishes. Almost at once the men started shouting. Grandpa placed his beer bottle on the hood and told us to go back to the house. I heard cussing, and then there was a strange popping, like a car backfiring. Then another. And another. Luke turned and shouted, "Papa fall down!"

Grandpa was facedown in the dirt. He howled more like an animal than a man. Terrified, I took off toward the house. Adele was running in our direction, and I pressed myself into her outstretched arms. She collapsed on the porch steps, crying with her hands clasped over her mouth. The other man had shot Grandpa four times—twice to his head.

"Of course he's home," Adele said when Ava Willis called four days after the shooting. "I'm a registered nurse and I can take care of him better right here." Ava Willis's voice was so loud, I overheard her shrill questions. "No need for you to come over. Everything is back to normal. Sam always said he came from the strongest stock in this county, and I guess he proved himself right," Adele said with a forced laugh. After a pause her tone became more challenging. "He's already agreed to attend Alcoholics Anonymous, what more do you want?" She began to pace, squeezing the coiled phone cord in her hand. "I've told you before that I am willing to leave him if that's what it takes to keep my kids. Sure, I'll become a foster parent, but I can't do that until Sam's better. Besides, he can't get in any trouble in the shape he's in!" She slammed down the phone.

It rang again about an hour later. "Lena who?" Adele asked. Apparently, a new Florida caseworker, Lena Jamison, had just taken over Dennis Benson's job. Adele's expression went from irate to crestfallen. "You're coming when?"

She hung up, went to her room, closed the door, and sobbed loudly. I put my head on the hound dog and snuffled into his salty fur.

4

Waiting for mama

"I don't want to go!" I wailed.

"It's just for a little while," Adele promised. She told us we would be back in a few days and convinced me to leave behind my dolls and dresses.

She packed only one small green suitcase for the both of us. "We'll leave your school clothes here 'cause you'll start kindergarten as soon as you get back." She hugged me close. "Besides," she added as an afterthought, "your mama's in Florida. Won't it be nice to see her?"

At the airport we met Lena Jamison, a stocky woman with a no-nonsense voice. She shook my hand and then inspected Luke's speckled arms. "What are those red marks?" she asked accusingly.

He started to cry as though he had done something wrong. "They're just mosquito bites." I kneeled next to him. "Don't worry, Lukie, we're just going to visit Mama, and then we are coming back when Grandpa is better,

38

right?" I looked up for some confirmation, but the worker avoided my eye.

Fourteen hours later we swayed sleepily in a car that wound down a twisting road back to Seffner, where Ms. Jamison deposited us on Paula and Milton Pace's doorstep.

From the exterior, the ranch home did not appear large enough for the dozen or so residents, and I quickly learned that it wasn't. Five of the children, including Luke and a set of fraternal twins, were three years old. In the boys' room miniature bunk beds were stacked three high, while the girl twin and I shared a room with the biological daughter.

If I counted living with my mother, this was my seventh home in a little more than two years and the worst place I had been—so far. A few years later, when I moved into the Mosses' home, I would be reminded of the cramped quarters and zooey smells I first encountered here. In a few weeks four more children joined the fray, for a total of eleven foster children between the ages of two and six.

At first I refused to unpack. "I'm going back tomorrow," I insisted.

After a few days I took out my toiletries but kept the rest of my belongings in the suitcase. I did not want to settle in, and I also did not want the rug rats messing with my few possessions. Mrs. Pace always seemed to be yelling at someone and often it was Luke. I was disgusted by the piles of dirty diapers, the snotty noses, and the screeches of children vying for any sort of attention. As I stared out the picture window that looked across a horse pasture, I wondered where Adele and Grandpa were and why I hadn't seen my mother yet. Beyond where the waving grass met the sky was South Carolina, but how could I get back there?

"Why are we here so long?" I asked Mrs. Pace when I had worn many times over all the clothes Adele had packed. She mumbled something that made no sense. "When can I see my mama?" I stamped my foot. "Adele said I would visit her, so where is she?" My demands resulted only in time-outs, where I anxiously bit my fingernails.

Luke would not let me out of his sight. "Sissy!" he would shout if I was in another room. He even tried to follow me into the bathroom. "I wanna sleep in Ashley's room," he begged at bedtime.

"Boys stay with boys, girls with girls," Mrs. Pace said, as though that would satisfy him.

Even at that age, I knew what he needed more than the professionals did. I was the one who comforted him when he was scared or lonely. At the Hines', he came to me for everything and even at Grandpa's, he ended up in my bed most mornings. When Mrs. Pace told Lena Jamison that she had found him sneaking into my room, the caseworker noted in our files that a psychologist needed to evaluate us for sex abuse. If any worker had bothered to review our case, they would have realized that at the age of three, Luke already had lost his biological mother—whom he had barely known—then Mrs. Hines, and now Adele. Seeing Grandpa shot or our hasty removal might have traumatized him. Now he was in a congested home with strangers. He received no loving, individualized attention from a parent figure. I was his security blanket—nothing more—and none of this had anything to do with sex. However, sex was a hot-button topic and I think caseworkers liked to gossip about it, even if the accusations were ridiculous.

The Paces ran the Perfect Angels day-care center in Plant City, where the younger children went while the older ones attended school. I wished I could wear my angel wings that Adele had made, but of course they had been left behind. In the afternoon the school bus dropped the school-age kids off at the day-care center; and then we all went home when the center closed. We were a needy bunch of baby birds who had fallen out of our original nests and were desperate for any scrap of attention. We each found ways to be noticed. Luke hid under the bed at bath time, threw food on the floor, and bit other children. When Mr. or Mrs. Pace swooped down flapping parental wings, he was getting precisely what he wanted.

In early September, Adele wrote me a long letter saying that she had washed my dolls' clothes and that my "babies" were doing fine. *I miss you both something awful, but I know you are well and taken care of.* She said her granddaughters were enjoying school, that her grandson had started pre-K, and that Ms. Hurley was holding a spot for me in her class. Adele went on to tell me that Uncle Sammie and his girlfriend, Courtney, had stopped by after visiting with Uncle Perry. When I was there, we had gone to see Uncle Perry in prison as though it were a typical family outing. She closed with, *I love you both so much . . . always and always. Love, Mama.*

The letter made me miss Adele but also wonder what had become of my mother. I convinced myself that she was coming for us, which is why we had to stay in Florida. She was somewhere out there . . . nearby . . . I just knew it!

It turns out Mama was in the women's state prison and Dusty was in another jail in Florida. In the meantime, Adele was making good on her promise to become a licensed foster parent. Grandpa had moved out and she was getting the property in shape. Adele wrote that the hen with the feathers on her feet was sitting on seven eggs. I was desperate to be there when the chicks hatched. I could not understand what was taking so long for Adele to get us back. Adele had my dolls, dresses— everything that mattered—so I was confident I would be leaving any day. In a corner of my mind I had realized that my mother was unreliable, but Adele was a loving grandmother who had always done what she said. My mother, my grandfather, and Adele detested the state people, so I did too. If they would stop meddling in our lives, we would be fine.

Lena Jamison came to Perfect Angels for a visit. "I have your inoculation records, so you can go to kindergarten," she said in a singsong voice. "Won't you like that?"

"No, I'm supposed to be in Ms. Hurley's class."

My first day of kindergarten at Lopez Elementary School should have been a special event, but since it was already October, nobody fussed. The class was busy coloring *P*s for "pumpkin." Adele had promised to make me a princess costume for Halloween, and I kept hoping I would get back in time—just as we had the year before. Unfortunately, the holiday came and went with only some candy at the day-care center.

On my birthday the school bus dropped me off at Perfect Angels. Ms. Jamison was waiting with a big box from Aunt Leanne. I ran to claim my gifts. The box contained a new doll with matching clothes and a Chutes and Ladders board game. "Where are Lilly and Katie?" I asked.

"Who?"

"My favorite dolls!"

"These are new presents, honey." The caseworker stroked my red curls and turned to Mrs. Pace. "How's she settling in at school?"

"She's a very good student—way ahead, even though she missed the first nine weeks." She indicated Luke with her chin. "He's *finally* stopped wandering around the house at night."

"When am I going home?" I whined.

"Honey, you just go play and enjoy your birthday," Mrs. Pace said. "Why don't you show the other kids what you got?"

I repacked the gifts in the box and vowed I would not let anyone else near them because the other kids destroyed everything they touched.

Adele received her South Carolina foster care license on my sixth birthday, but she was told it would take several more months before the interstate paperwork would allow us to travel. She begged the officials to return us in time for Christmas. When it looked like that was not possible, she promised to send us some warm clothes and my dolls.

Then, to everyone's surprise, the documents were ready in early December, and we shuttled back to South Carolina.

"Look, I lost a tooth!" I crowed when Adele met us at the airport.

Grandpa was no longer there, which made life easier since there were no more raised voices or slammed doors. I felt comfortable in Adele's loving embrace. On Christmas, I received a pink Barbie radio and a Precious Moments sleeping bag. I liked the way we did everything the same as we had the previous year, including opening one gift on Christmas Eve and the rest before breakfast the next morning. Then we had crisp bacon and biscuits before going to open more presents and have lunch with Adele's grandchildren.

"I want to do this next year too!" I said to Adele when she tucked us in that night.

"Of course you will," she assured me. "How else will Santa know where to find you?"

"But what if they come to take me away again?" I asked.

"They tricked me last time, but I'll never let you go again."

"Promise?"

She kissed my forehead. "You are here to stay."

By the time spring came, I had lost both front teeth. Adele made her granddaughters and me Easter outfits in pastel colors, and we celebrated with an Easter egg hunt and picnic in a park.

Fresh flowers popped out of the grass every day like all the new lessons I learned in school. I couldn't wait to see my teacher's welcoming smile, open to the next page in a book, or start marking a clean work sheet with a sharpened pencil. I tried to keep these thoughts in mind as I made the scary walk down the long, rutted dirt road all by myself each morning. If it had rained, I had to try to balance on the high part to keep my shoes clean. If it had been dry for a spell, dust swirled around, and I had to breathe through my nose to keep from eating grit. Adele was always busy with Luke, so mostly, I had to plod along on my own. One morning I waited and waited, but the bus never came. I sat on the grassy shoulder and wrote my name in the dirt with a stick. I saw a rabbit scamper into a hole and wished I could follow him like Alice in Wonderland would have. After several hours the man who ran the mom-and-pop shop in town sauntered up to me. "What are you doing out here?"

"Waitin' for the school bus."

"Honey, there ain't no school today. Didn't Ms. Adele know that?" I shrugged. "Well, it's a good thing someone told me about a little girl out here. Are you hungry?" I nodded.

He led me to his store and gave me a Coke and a sandwich. While I was eating, his wife called Adele. When she arrived, Adele was flustered. "I told Ashley that I thought this was a holiday, but she insisted." Adele had trouble catching her breath. "I never did see a child who liked school so much."

"When are you going to listen?" she shouted when we were in the car. "And you missed lunch."

"I ate at the store."

"Did you pay?"

"I didn't have money."

She took a few dollars from her purse. "You go back up there, pay the man, thank him, and tell him you're sorry."

"By myself?" I asked. Seeing her stern face, I did not complain any further.

I was furious that I had to walk up that hated road and then back again. As I kicked stones along the way, I had no idea that I would be living with her for only another week. I have never been able to find any official reason why we were returned to Florida a second time. Perhaps someone reported my being alone by the side of the road and that is what led to our removal. Maybe the neighbors reported something. Grandpa had started coming around again while we were still there—he did live with Adele again after we left—and maybe the authorities found out. Adele did receive foster care payments from Florida during that time, which is unusual, so money might have been the issue. All I know is that at the end of April, Luke and I were back at the airport. This time I carried Katie wrapped in her pink blanket. Nobody was ever again going to talk me into leaving without my precious dolls. Adele kept wiping away tears as she snapped pictures.

Lena Jamison led us onto the plane. I was so upset, I was shivering, so she wrapped her sweater around me. "I didn't know you were afraid of flying," she said, completely misunderstanding me.

She folded her hands across a manila envelope in her lap. "What's in there?" I asked.

"Your papers."

"Does it say where we're going?"

"No."

"Are we going back to the Paces' house?"

"I don't know."

"Why can't we stay with Adele?"

Ms. Jamison puffed out with annoyance. "Honey, we need to keep you safe."

Again, she missed the point. Adele had fussed over us even more than our mother had. She gave us more attention, food, and affection than anyone ever had. It seemed logical to me that Luke and I would be safest with someone who actually loved us.

When we arrived in Florida, Luke and I went our separate ways—he ended up at another congested baby farm, while I "lucked out" and got to be the only child in the home of Boris and Doreen Potts, an older couple who lived in a double-wide mobile home surrounded by a chain-link fence that seemed to buckle into itself like a Slinky. The strawberries in the field next door smelled so ripe that I would press my nose through a diamond of wire to sniff the fragrant fruit.

The Pottses had a revolving wash line in the backyard that I enjoyed spinning when it was empty. I often sat in the shade of their tangerine tree and played with my dolls. I had my own room, and I folded my Precious Moments sleeping bag at the end of the bed. Sometimes they would leave gifts on my sleeping bag, like a pair of jelly sandals with silver sparkles that I thought were the greatest shoes I ever had.

Mr. Potts barely talked to me, but I was always questioning him. When he dumped ketchup on his eggs, I asked, "Why are you doing that?"

"I like it that way."

I wrinkled my nose. "That's disgusting!"

"It isn't polite to comment on someone else's food," Mrs. Potts chided.

Mostly, though, Mrs. Potts liked me because I entertained myself.

"Could you turn the sprinkler on?" I asked on a blistering summer day.

"It's going to rain," Mrs. Potts said, but then she relented because she knew it would keep me amused for a while.

I put on my bathing suit and jumped around as it sprayed back and forth. A dark cloud hovered nearby, but I kept playing until I was forced to stop. I felt rain on my shoulders and looked up to see if I would be called inside. The sun still baked the yard near the driveway, but it was pouring near the house. I skipped between the wet and the dry side of the yard a few times, calling for Mrs. Potts. "Come and see the miracle!"

She said, "If it rains when the sun is out, it means that the devil's beating his wife." This scared me, so I came inside.

After dinner I would sit on the porch swing and wait for the first star so I could make my eternal wish: to be with my mother. My yearning was like an insect bite. If I left it alone, I would stop noticing it; but if I focused on it, it would drive me crazy. I had sucked on my fingers as a baby, so when something bothered me, they still fluttered into my mouth. The more anxious I was, the more intensely I gnawed on my fingernails, sometimes making my fingers bleed. Then I could concentrate on that rather than the feelings inside.

I could not help worrying about Luke. He lived only about twenty minutes away, but we rarely saw each other. His foster parents had a three-bedroom mobile home on a property that also had a plant nursery. On one visit there were eight foster kids, and my brother shared a room with five other boys.

"We have more room at our house. Why can't he come and live with us?" I asked Mrs. Potts.

"That's not my decision." She closed off all further discussion on the matter.

My favorite activity was watching a television that I did not have to share with other children who hogged the remote control. I would get up early and flip to *Care Bears* or *Adventures in Wonderland.* I wished I could go through the looking glass so I could find my mother.

Then there was the video.

The last time I had watched a movie, it had been a Disney tape, so I pressed the play button on the Pottses' VCR remote. This was not a cartoon, but I could tell it had something to do with history. Thinking it was educational, I curled up in Mr. Potts's chair. A female Nazi commandant was torturing some of the prettier female prisoners with electric dildos because she was jealous of them. I knew I should turn it off, but I kept hoping that the good guys would prevail so I wouldn't have to go to bed with the frightening images etched in my mind. I shuddered as the story became even more gruesome. The commandant forced guys to make love to her, and she castrated those who did not satisfy her insatiable lust. An American prisoner was the only one who was able to pleasure her, so she spared him. In other frightening scenes she tortured women sexually and drunken German men doused women with beer and then raped them.

I wished that one of the Pottses would catch me so I would not have to watch it until the end, but they had gone to bed and left me on my own. The worst scene in the movie came when the commandant gave a dinner party. A woman was ordered to stand on a block of ice with a noose around her neck. By the end of the meal the ice had melted and she had hanged herself.

For years scenes from that movie have haunted me, and the images still bubble to the surface whenever I remember my time at the Pottses' house. I eventually learned the name of the movie, *Ilsa, She Wolf of the SS,* and I learned something else, too: Mr. Potts had been accused of molesting children.

I saw that movie only a few weeks before I entered first grade. Walden Lake Elementary was the most beautiful school I had ever seen; it even had a fountain in the courtyard. My only friend in the neighborhood was an older boy named Fernando. He promised he would not let anyone harass me on the school bus, which I appreciated until he showed me a knife he had hidden in his backpack. I was afraid we both would get in trouble. I liked some of the girls in my class, but—without any preparation—I was moved from the Pottses' foster home to live with Irma and Clifford Hagen in October. I already knew Mrs. Hagen because she was Mr. and Mrs. Potts's daughter, but I begged to stay where I was because I did not want to leave my new school friends.

"You'll be happier living with other girls," Mrs. Potts insisted.

"Can't I go to Luke's house?"

"They don't have enough beds for the ones they have."

I knew it was hopeless to ask about my mother or Adele. I flung my arms around Mrs. Potts's waist and looked up pleadingly. "Please, can't I just stay?"

"*They* won't let you," she sputtered angrily. Something had happened, but I would not find out until much later why they took me away.

According to my tally, Mrs. Hagen was my eighth so-called mother in three and a half years. To cope, I pretended I was destined for a different life, just like Cinderella, Sleeping Beauty, the Little Princess and, of course, Alice. I had only to fit in the shoe, be kissed by the prince, come into my rightful inheritance, or find some other through-the-looking-glass way out of foster care, and I'd enter the life I was meant to live. Each time I moved, I cheered myself with a little rhyme: *Heigh-ho! Heigh-ho! Down the rabbit hole to another place I go!* I always believed that my happily ever after with my real mother was just over the next horizon.

To my annoyance, the Hagens asked me to call them "Mom" and "Dad" right away, but I resisted. Adele had drilled into me the correctness of addressing my elders as "sir" and "ma'am," so I could pretty easily say "ma'am," which sounded close enough to "Mom" and sounded respectful enough to satisfy Mrs. Hagen. Plus, the Hagens were suckers for my stare into space. As long as I pretended to listen and said I was sorry for any infractions, I got off without much punishment. The important thing, I had learned by now, was not to get on a foster parent's bad side, because certain incidents trailed you like dog poop on your shoes.

The Hagens lived in the nicest home I had been in so far. There were four bedrooms, two baths, and a breezy family room. In the back there was an inground pool and a combination basketball and tennis court. Even though there were nine people in the house, it did not seem crowded. The Hagens' daughter, who was around seventeen, had her own bedroom, while the six foster girls (the five others ranged in age from ten to fourteen), shared two bedrooms. I unfolded my Precious Moments sleeping bag, arranged Katie and Lilly on the shelf, put my jelly sandals in the closet, and tested my new bed, which smelled mustier than the sunshine-dried sheets that had flapped on Mrs. Potts's line.

I did like having others to play with and enjoyed girly activities, like having my nails polished or my hair done and dressing up like a princess. My imaginary prince's name was Jonathan Rodriquez. He looked like a grown Fernando and he wore a blue uniform trimmed with gold braid. Someday he would whisk me to his kingdom, where I would be safe forever.

My new school, Seffner Elementary, was overcrowded. My teacher's name was Ms. Port, which I thought was a funny coincidence since her classroom was in a portable trailer.

The day I started there, Mrs. Hagen dropped me off and said, "You'll have to find your own way from now on, so remember where your classroom is."

"I will!" I said in my most chipper voice. When I looked back, she had disappeared. Other children were hugging their parents good-bye, but I was alone. My fingers flew to my mouth, and I bit off my thumbnail as I forced myself up the first metal step, then the next.

"You must be Ashley Rhodes." Ms. Port greeted me with a wide smile. As a way to welcome me to the classroom, she asked the students to make new name tags for our desks. "You can write your name any way you want," she told me. I drew my name in bubble letters. When we finished, we each stood to show off our artwork and say our names. When the other students saw my creation, they clapped.

I loved school, but I was envious of the children whose parents walked them to the classroom door in the morning and were waiting outside when the bell rang each afternoon. Like the older girls in the foster home, I rode my bike to school. Pedaling uphill on Kingsway Road during the morning rush hour could be scary because so many cars were passing me, but the downhill ride was exhilarating.

On class picture day I chose my fanciest dress with a hoop skirt. When I got on my bike, I sat on the wire to keep the skirt from tangling in the greasy chain, but then the front popped up and I could not see over the top. Even worse, my panties were exposed. If I sat on the front of the dress, my butt hung out in the breeze. I was so frustrated that I had to walk the bike. I got grease stains on the hem and arrived after the bell.

When I walked in the classroom, Ms. Port saw that I had been crying, so she did not fuss at my tardiness. "Are you okay?"

"My bike—"

She assumed I had fallen off. "Are you hurt?"

"No, but my dress is ruined!" My sobs rolled in heaves.

"Honey, the bottom won't show in the pictures and the spots will wash out," she said, then sent me to wash up for the photographs.

I had moved in with the Hagens only six weeks before my seventh birthday, but I do not recall any special celebration or recognition. Christmas, though, was a big deal in foster homes. The foster parents' associations provided plenty of gifts. Adele had promised me an Easy-Bake oven, but I had not heard from her since April. The Hagens said it was their tradition to open a single present on Christmas Eve. One of the girls asked if we could have a second. Mrs. Hagen relented. Someone asked for "just one more," and somehow we ended up unwrapping all the gifts. I lay in bed that night feeling that Christmas was ruined. I no longer believed in Santa, so I knew the holiday was all over. The next morning we awoke to find one more gift under the tree for each of us! Although it was only a puzzle, it had been important to receive something—even if it wasn't from someone who loved me. Since I had left South Carolina, I had not felt special to anyone in the world.

At the end of January, Clayton Hooper, my latest caseworker, visited me at the Hagens' house. He watched me coloring valentines, then went to talk to Mrs. Hagen in a whispery voice on the other side of the room.

When I overheard Luke's name, my ears alerted. I held up a valentine. "Can you take this to Luke?"

"Sure," Mr. Hooper said.

I wrote *Mama* on the prettiest one. "Do you know where my mother is?"

He hesitated. "I believe she's in South Carolina."

"With Adele!" I felt giddy and sighed deeply several times. It was perfect. If Adele and my mother were together, they would figure out how to get us back. My face flushed with excitement. "Can you send this to her?"

"I'll try," he said.

I had not seen my mother since before our first trip to South Carolina—more than two years earlier—but now she would know where I was and could come back for me.

"I knew she would come! I knew it!" I danced around the Hagens' home, hugging my doll when I heard that I would be seeing my mother. The closer we got to the downtown office, the shorter my already-stubby nails became. By the time my mother walked into the room, the cuticle on my thumb was bleeding.

"How big you are!" my mother exclaimed. Tears streaked her makeup. She fussed about a mark on my chin. "Did you bump yourself?" Using her spit on her finger, she wiped my face and was relieved when the smudge came off.

I pressed myself to her. "I missed you so much!"

"Oh, me too, Sunshine." She rumpled my curls and sniffled into my hair. "*They* kept me away from you for so long! I would have done *anything* to see you."

I did not doubt that it was "them" against "us."

"I'm getting all A's and I can read, Mama!"

Her eyes narrowed. "You're not calling anyone else 'Mama,' are you?"

I shook my head. "No, Mama," I promised.

"That's my Sunshine. You were always my good girl."

She stroked my hand. "Luke is Dusty's boy, and you are *my* girl." She drew me onto her lap. "Do you want to live with me in South Carolina?"

I gulped. "Today?"

"I wish." She bit her lip. "They won't let me have you until I—" Someone peered through the doorway. "First, I have to find us a nicer place to live, but I'm getting my act together. Anyway, we won't have to worry about Dusty anymore."

I was confused. "But you said that Luke belonged to him."

Mr. Hooper took a chair and listened while my mother tried to explain that Luke was not going to be my brother any longer.

"Is he my brother now?"

"Yes, for a while longer."

A blurry vision of the baby in the box tried to surface, yet I could not express my confusion. Seeing that I still did not understand, my mother took a deep breath and tried again. "He's just going with his daddy."

"Dusty's his daddy?"

"Yes."

"Who's my daddy?"

"Oh, he went away."

Tommy had gone away, and Luke had arrived not too long after. Maybe if Luke wasn't around, I could be with my mother. "I can get another brother."

When it was time for my mother to leave, we hugged so tightly, the worker had to pry me from her neck. "Be good," she said with heaving sobs. "You're my good girl. You're my Sunshine. I'll see you soon."

I started to chase after her, but someone tugged me in the opposite direction. As we rounded the corner, I turned for a last view of my mother. She looked over, and her strangled voice called, "Good-bye, my Sunshine!"

I was still at the stage where I did not question anything she said. While I was already dubious about many of the foster parents and caseworkers, I do not remember being angry or resenting my mother. If she said she would return soon, then she would. I ignored her broken promises and pretended to be unaware of elapsed time when it came to her.

As the weather warmed, I could not wait to go swimming. I began with inflatable swimmies on my arms, which Mrs. Hagen deflated a little at a time. When I could swim the width of the pool without them, I was allowed to jump off the diving board. I loved to float on my back and try to find my mother's face in the cotton-ball clouds.

The Hagens, who had been foster parents for more than twenty years, had decided to close their foster home. They prepared us by telling us that we would be moving at the end of the school year.

I was elated. "I'm going to my mother!"

"Not yet," Mrs. Hagen explained. "But you are going to live with your brother."

I was confused. I thought I was supposed to live with my mother and Luke would live with Dusty. I worried that my brother was somehow keeping me away from my mother. I tried to imagine the perfect foster mother for us both. She would have Adele's melted-butter voice. She would prepare tea parties with a blue-flowered pot of hot tea, cinnamon toast cut into triangles, and cream-filled cookies on minia-ture plates. That would be an agreeable way to while away the time until our mother took us home. She would arrive in a red convertible, and we would drive with the top down all the way to South Carolina. When we got there, I would start second grade. Every day my mother would drive me to school, and in the afternoon she would be waiting to pick me up and give me huge hugs. Then we would go out for strawberry milk shakes and sing along to Joan Jett on the radio. My mother was coming to get me. So it did not mat-ter where I lived for the next few weeks. Besides, how bad could it be?

5

The wicked witch

My caseworkers changed more frequently than my placements. Miles Ferris was fairly new when he arrived at the Hagen house to take me to my next foster home. He had a gentle smile and puppy-dog eyes. Mrs. Hagen helped stuff my clothes, dolls, and sleeping bag into large plastic garbage bags. The hoopskirt of my favorite dress kept popping back up like a child who refuses to lie down.

Mrs. Hagen lifted it out. "Why don't you leave this here?" she asked. "It's too snug anyway."

"But it's mine!"

She relented. "Maybe they have younger girls who can fit in it."

"Oh, they have plenty of friends for Ashley," Mr. Ferris said in a slick tone that didn't match his friendly face. "And her brother is so anxious to see her." I would soon learn that behind his gentle appearance was a careless and uncaring man.

Mrs. Hagen handed the caseworker my bags. "Check and see if you left anything in your room or around the pool."

I found one of my doll's shoes under the bed. I would have been frantic if I had left it behind. Some of the older kids were getting ready to swim, and I wished I could join them. It was not even ten in the morning and the temperature was over ninety degrees. I hoped the new family also had a pool.

Mr. Ferris carried the bags to his trunk. "You got a lot of stuff for a little girl."

"I have a bike, too!"

"I don't have room for a bike," he said.

"How will I get to school?" I asked.

"You'll be riding the bus," Mr. Ferris replied. "Okay, let's get this show on the road."

We drove out of the suburban neighborhood to a rural area outside Plant City where there were no traffic lights, just infrequent stop signs. As the road narrowed, the branches of immense oaks arched across it. Tendrils of Spanish moss draped on the trees like gossamer green ghosts. The pavement was dappled with shimmering light. I imagined I was entering a fairy-tale kingdom inhabited by tree spirits.

The car slowed in front of a rusty metal fence. A rickety gate drooped inward. Mr. Ferris turned down a rutted dirt road, made even bumpier by the roots that crisscrossed it like the veins on an old man's hands. We pulled up to a trailer that was even more decrepit than my portable classroom at Seffner Elementary. There were no children in sight. Maybe we were stopping here for another reason. I leaned back and closed my eyes as I waited to arrive at a more suitable final destination—preferably, a castle with turrets. The car's engine sputtered off.

"You sleeping?" I stirred at this. "Rise and shine and meet your new foster mom," Mr. Ferris said.

A screen door squeaked. "Well, hello, Miles," called a syrupy voice. "And who is this young lady?"

He opened the car door. "She's had a nice nap, haven't you, Ashley?"

I slid out of the car. "I guess," I said, then quickly added, "sir."

He nodded at the woman. "This is Ashley Rhodes. She is one of the best-behaved children we have, and one of the smartest. She gets straight A's."

The woman seemed doubtful. "Isn't that nice?" she said between clenched teeth. "Most of my kids have to attend summer school, but I guess you'll have the whole summer to play, Miss Smarty." She looked me up and down. I sensed she was trying to calculate whether good grades made me low maintenance or more trouble. By now I knew that foster parents were paid for taking care of me and that they could trade troublesome kids with a single call to their worker.

Mr. Ferris started unloading my garbage bags. "Ashley, this is Marjorie Moss. She'll introduce you around because I have to get downtown for a meeting."

"Oh, don't worry about us, Miles, we'll be just fine. Won't we, Ashley?"

"Yes, ma'am!" I smiled hard enough to make my dimples show.

"Isn't she a breath of sunshine?" Mrs. Moss beamed at Miles. The minute she said "sunshine," my stomach

61

flipped and that morning's breakfast rose in my throat. "And who can resist those red curls?" She reached over to muss them. I squirmed away, so she only got a quick feel.

The trailer's front door burst open. "Sissy! Sissy!" I managed to get to the steps before Luke flew into my arms, almost knocking me to the ground.

"Luke!" called Mrs. Moss. "You were told to stay in your room."

"It's Sissy!" He leaped up and locked his legs around my waist.

"Young man, get back to your room right this minute!"

"I'll take him, ma'am," I offered.

Her spine relaxed. "Luke can have a time-out while we get you settled."

I steered my brother up the stairs. "Show me your room, Luke."

"Girls aren't allowed in the boys' room," he replied.

"I won't go inside," I said because Mrs. Moss was following ten steps behind.

"I want to be with you!" he wailed.

"I'm going to be living here now, so we can play later. I need to unpack."

"You staying for real?"

"Yes, for real. Promise."

When we got to the boys' bedroom door, his bottom lip began to quiver. He looked up at Mrs. Moss to see if he would get a reprieve.

"Luke!" She began to count: "One, two—" He bolted in the room so fast that I wondered what would happen if she got to three.

Mrs. Moss showed me the girls' bedroom, which had two

sets of bunk beds, a crib, and a cot. It smelled like diapers. I gagged. "What's wrong?" Her voice was harsher than when the caseworker had been there.

"I'm hot," I said, which was true, since there was no air-conditioning in the trailer.

"You can have something to drink later." We went outside again. A girl about my age approached warily. "Mandy, come and meet Ashley."

"You have a lot of stuff," Mandy said, eyeing my garbage sacks.

"You'll have to sort out the dirty and clean clothes," the foster mother said.

"Everything is clean," I said, "and my dressy dresses are on hangers."

"Where are the dresses?"

I touched the bag where the hoopskirt begged for release. Mrs. Moss grabbed a padlock on a storage shed and inserted a key. She lifted it off the hasp and opened a creaking door. Inside, clothes hung on two poles, and underneath were boxes.

I reached for the sack with my best clothes. "Want me to help you hang them?"

"No need for fancy things here. I'll put them away in another shed." Mrs. Moss peered into the sack that contained my sleeping bag and dolls.

"I'll take those to my room," I said.

"We don't keep personal possessions in the house," Mrs. Moss said. She unlocked another shed and tossed the sack containing my dolls on top of a pile of unmarked boxes and then added the bag with the fancy dresses.

"What about my play clothes?"

She pointed to the first shed. "They'll stay here. Every day two of the kids pick the clothes for everyone else."

"How will they know which are mine?"

Mrs. Moss locked both sheds. I noticed she wore a flashy ring on each finger. "You'll see how it works around here," she said. I had nothing to take in the house.

When we opened the front door, I heard Luke whimpering. "If you keep that up, you're not going to get lunch." Mrs. Moss watched for my reaction. "Your brother was spoiled before he came here. And the language he uses! I hope you aren't like that."

"No, ma'am." I picked a corner of the ceiling where a spider had spun a web as my focal point.

She smiled. "I heard you might be a good influence on him. That's why I took you in; but if you start trouble, I'll call Miles in a heartbeat."

All I wanted to do was get back to the Hagens' and go swimming with the other girls. My mother or somebody else had better come for me soon because I did not think this was a very nice place.

I felt as if Miles Ferris had stranded me on a remote island. Charles and Marjorie Moss lived on a little more than ten acres of land with three fenced areas. The only neighbors were family members living in other trailers. Their home was a double-wide with three bedrooms and two bathrooms. At one point there were as many as fourteen children in there, plus the parents, even though their legal capacity was for only seven. We were all outcasts with convoluted lineages. Luke and I had different last names and fathers, as did Heather and Gordon as well as Mandy and Toby. The baby sisters, Lucy and Clare, looked like twins, but they were a little more than a year apart. It was comforting to know that the other kids' lives were as accidental and chaotic as ours were.

The Moss menagerie also included a mule, goats, cows, and various smaller animals. During the day we were restricted to the fenced areas like livestock, with the sexes separated. Inside, the girls' room was as cramped as a submarine. Beds used up all the floor space. There was no place for any belongings except under the bed and one dresser where we kept our panties, which we could not wear to sleep. Mandy and I shared one bunk bed while Heather was on the top of the other. Clare had the crib, and her younger sister, Lucy, slept in the master bedroom.

When I tried to fall asleep that first night, I ached for something familiar to hug. I had not slept without my dolls in years. Even the Paces had given me a stuffed bunny. My thin pillow was lumpy and had an ammonia scent that burned my nose. A lattice crisscrossed the window and made me feel as if I were imprisoned. No light from the moon, stars, or cars along the distant road pierced the inky blackness. I recalled one very dark night the year before when Mrs. Potts had warned me not to sit on the porch by saying, "If there are no stars out, something bad is about to happen."

"Did you know that when there are no stars, bad things happen?" I whispered.

"That's stupid," Heather retorted.

"Shut up!" Mandy warned.

"Oh, fuck you," Heather, the only teen in the house, said.

We heard footsteps. I was facing the wall, so when the door opened, I saw only a sword-shaped sliver of light.

Mrs. Moss stepped into the room. "Who's talking?"

"The new girl is scared of the dark," Mandy replied in a tremulous voice.

"If I hear another word, ya'll have something to be scared about."

In the morning Clare's crying awakened me. "It's your turn for the shitty diapers," Heather called to Mandy.

Mandy made a gagging sound. "They make me sick."

"Let's get the new girl to do it," Heather chortled.

Heather showed me how to swab Clare's bottom with baby wipes and how to tape a diaper. Mandy carried the baby into the kitchen, lifted her into a high chair, and put some dry cereal on the tray. Heather made toast in batches and handed me one of the first pieces, which I gobbled dry. Then I reached for a second slice.

"You can't eat in the house." Mandy shooed me outside.

"When's breakfast?" I asked.

"You ate it," Heather answered.

"Can I have some milk?"

"Only the babies get milk."

"I'm thirsty," I whined.

She pointed to the garden hose. "That's what we use."

An hour later I went back to the house. I could hear the television through the locked door. I knocked. Mrs. Moss glared down at me. "This is outside time."

Mrs. Moss expected us to remain outdoors for most of the day. Tall oaks shaded much of the Mosses' property, but when the temperature and humidity were both high, we were miserable. Although the house was not much cooler, there were at least fans in there, and Mrs. Moss parked the babies in front of the TV during the hottest part of the afternoon.

Many of the older children were in summer school until around noon, making the mornings especially boring. For some unexplained reason, the girls and the boys could not share the same play area. The boys' side had a wooden swing set, but the girls' side had only a table and chairs. We could play with some old dolls and broken toys, although we mostly made up our own games and caught dragonflies. If I grabbed one's wings, I could get its jaws to clamp on my fingers. With a deft maneuver, I then transferred the dragonfly to my earlobe and wore it like an earring.

By lunchtime I was always starving. Peanut butter sandwiches—sometimes with, sometimes without jelly—were typical; cheese sandwiches were a treat. Mrs. Moss reserved Kool-Aid for caseworkers' visits. I could always tell when someone was having a visitor because the smell of vanilla or chocolate meant Mrs. Moss was baking. Unless it was your worker's day, you were unlikely to taste the special treat. She distributed the extra goodies to the other family members who lived around the property. We were often hungry.

Years later, when I saw the film *Oliver*, I wondered if anyone knew that, like those British boys in the orphanage, American children beg for food in some foster homes. At the Mosses', several of the older boys were so hungry that they stole snacks at night. When Mrs. Moss discovered their crime, she locked the boys in their bedroom, which had a sliding glass door that opened into the indoor dining room.

"Wave your sandwiches at them," Mrs. Moss coaxed us to tease them.

For the next several meals they had to watch us eat. Eventually, she locked them in their room at night with an alarm that sounded if anyone tried to escape, and they were given a bucket to use as a toilet.

I hated mystery casseroles. When Mrs. Moss spooned out a fishy mixture, I pleaded as cutely as possible, "May I pretty please have a bowl of cereal instead?"

"Well, okay," Mrs. Moss said with a sly grin. She poured a meager portion of Lucky Charms into a plastic bowl, and then she rummaged in the refrigerator for a gallon of milk. It poured thickly, with some chunks plopping into the bowl, and I carried it outside to the little plastic table where we kids usually ate our meals. It sloshed on the table as I set it down.

Luke said longingly, "I wish I had some."

The first swallow made me gag. I ran to the hose and rinsed out my mouth. When I came back to the table, Luke was shoveling the cereal in his mouth as fast as he could. "Luke! That's disgusting!"

"It's yummy in my tummy!"

Nausea overwhelmed me. I rushed toward the house. As usual, the door was bolted. I banged on it. Mr. Moss came to the door holding his napkin.

"Gotta go!" I blurted. As I rushed toward the bathroom, my stomach lurched. A flume of vomit arched onto the floor.

"You've ruined the carpet!" Mrs. Moss screeched. She gripped my hair and pushed my face into my puke. I don't know what was worse: the taste of the curdled milk, watching Luke eat the sickening concoction, vomiting, being humiliated, smelling my mess up close, or having to clean it up, which I couldn't do to her satisfaction. Later, as the sour smell lingered, Mrs. Moss reminded everyone that it had been my fault and made me stand in the corner.

The Mosses punished us for anything they could think of. Mrs. Moss kept a bottle of Crystal hot sauce on a turntable with other condiments. If she did not like what someone said, she would announce, "My mother would have made us eat soap—be thankful this is real food." Then she would make the troublemaker swallow spoonfuls of the hot sauce. If you moaned or spit it out, she would force more down.

I decided I would do whatever was necessary to stay on this woman's good side. Unfortunately, my brother had neither the good sense nor the self-control to do the same. Luke was so hungry, he would eat almost anything. If Mrs. Moss caught him biting off hunks of soap, eating big globs of toothpaste, or drinking from the shampoo bottle, he would get the hot-sauce punishment. He hated it; but he never learned to avoid it.

"We're going to have a picnic with some other foster families at the beach!" Mrs. Moss announced one day, sounding unusually jolly. She liberated buckets, shovels, and other sand toys from one of the sheds. "Everyone hurry up and get into your swimsuits."

As soon as we were ready, we lined up for photos, posing first individually in front of some palms and then as a group—"one big happy family." Even though I had lived most of my life in and around Tampa, which is only a short drive from many Gulf of Mexico beaches, I had not been to the shore since the trip with Aunt Leanne in South Carolina.

At the beach Mrs. Moss gave Toby and Mitchell, another of the foster boys, an inflatable shark. Almost immediately, Mitchell pulled it out from under Toby and a fight ensued. Mrs. Moss made the boys sit on their towels. I had a turn with the shark, but when everyone quarreled over who was next, Mrs. Moss stowed it away.

Mandy and I headed for the wet sand closer to the water. I began filling a bucket and packing it, then turning it over to make towers of a castle. I showed her how to take a thin stream of sand and make squiggles to decorate the turrets. Just as I was scooping out the moat, Luke rushed past, kicking clouds of sand in his wake. I knew him well enough to anticipate what he was about to do. "Don't you dare!" I shouted. With one long jump, my brother flattened our castle.

A swell of anger rose from a black, dark space inside me. Luke was the problem all along! If it had not been for him, I would be with my mother! I clenched his arms tightly and shook him. "Don't you ever touch anything of mine again!"

One of the other foster parents broke us apart. "You're with Marjorie Moss, right?" The woman marched us back to face her wrath.

Instead of reprimanding us, Mrs. Moss acted concerned. "Look at you two! Why, your faces are red as beets. Let's get you some cold drinks." She handed us sodas from her cooler.

"I don't know where you get your patience," the other parent said.

"They've been separated and . . ." As she gestured, all her rings glinted in the sun. Then she whispered, "Grandfather . . . shot . . ."

The other woman glanced at us as if we were interesting specimens. "I don't know how you do it."

"All they need is love and attention," Mrs. Moss said, "and I have plenty of both to go around."

My mother's face followed me like a shadow. I mentally cataloged all the injustices in the Moss household—the vomiting episode, going hungry, the hot-sauce treatments—so I could inform her on my next visit. At the end of June, Mrs. Moss handed Luke and me two of our best outfits from the shed and told us that we were going downtown. I suspected that we would see our mother but that we weren't being told in case she did not show. As we entered Miles Ferris's office, Mrs. Moss promised, "If you're good, we'll get ice cream afterward."

During the meeting Luke kept kicking a desk, but I mouthed, *Ice cream.*

"Can you bring them for a visit on July fifth?" Mr. Ferris asked. "Or do you need someone to transport?"

"It's no trouble for me," Mrs. Moss said deferentially. "And don't you think it would be wise if I stayed with them?"

"That would be helpful," the caseworker replied. "How are they adjusting?"

"We've had our struggles, but they are settling down." She lowered her voice. "I just hope this visit from M-O-M doesn't rile them up."

"Your concern is a big plus for these children and the department," he replied.

Mom! Did Mrs. Moss really think I didn't know such a simple word? I was disappointed that I wouldn't be seeing Mama that day, but at least she *was* coming. I even forgot about the ice cream, which Mrs. Moss had only offered in front of the worker to make it seem like she was a good foster parent.

There is one awful day with the Mosses that is most vivid in my mind. That afternoon Mr. and Mrs. Moss took several children to an appointment, leaving the rest of us with Melissa, who was either the wife or girlfriend of Ricky, one of Mrs. Moss's sons. They lived in one of the trailers on the property. Melissa made us sandwiches. After lunch Mandy and I played one of my favorite games—tea party princesses—on the patio.

"Would you care for an icing cake?" I handed Mandy the top of a Tupperware container laden with little stones and leaves as props for my imaginary delicacies.

She took a leaf, then let it flutter away without pretending to taste it. I made refined smacking noises with my lips. "Delicious, don't you think?"

The roar of an engine interrupted our game. "Wow!" Mitchell shouted as Ricky drove his dirt bike into the field on the other side of the boys' fence.

"Whoa! Check that out!" shouted Toby. He ran closer to the fence as Ricky splattered through puddles left by a recent thunderstorm. Toby yelped as some of the muddy water splashed him.

Forgetting the gender boundaries, I rushed in position to be splashed next, with Mandy at my heels. As the bike came around, I held up my arms and got drenched. Playing to his audience, the driver angled closer to the fence and did a wheelie during his next pass. We whooped in appreciation.

As I was cheering, someone clutched my arm and jerked me back. "What are you doing on the boys' side of the yard?" Melissa bellowed.

"W-watching the bike," I stammered.

"I'm going to tell Marjorie," she said, "unless you get back on the patio."

Mandy scurried away, but I lingered long enough to catch another trick.

When Mrs. Moss returned, Melissa told her that we had gone over to the boys' side and blurted, "Ashley wouldn't listen to me."

"You know what that means, girls," Mrs. Moss said. "Twenty-five laps."

Mandy and I marched to the front yard and began to run around the long, horseshoe-shaped driveway, across the grassy spot laced with tree roots, then through the spiky weeds that lashed at my bare legs. Melissa had betrayed us! I was so furious that my eyes blurred. After three laps I stumbled; on the fourth, I tripped over a root. When I tried to stand, I couldn't. "Get up, Ashley!" Mrs. Moss shrieked.

"I can't! I hurt myself."

She gripped a chunk of my hair and jerked me toward her. I yelped like a puppy whose paw had been stepped on.

"Uh-oh!" Mandy gasped. "Ashley's gonna get it now."

Inside the trailer Mrs. Moss drummed her fingers on the counter as she contemplated my punishment. I was hoping to get sent to a corner, where I could fantasize about a grand

Cinderella wedding with Jonathan Rodriquez as my groom. Almost as if she were reading my thoughts, Mrs. Moss said, "Standing in the corner hasn't taught you any lessons. Let's see if squatting gets better results." She pressed me under the kitchen counter. I knew from watching Mrs. Moss punish Heather that I had to hunker down without letting my head touch the top of the counter ledge or my butt or heels rest on the floor. My hands had to be straight at my sides, but I couldn't put my fingertips on the floor to help me balance. "Ten—no, twenty minutes," she announced.

My left foot throbbed from the fall, so I leaned my weight on the right. Concentrating on a splash of light on the floor, I bit the inside of my cheek. I had a strong will and tough leg muscles, but in less than five minutes I needed my fingertips to steady myself.

"I saw that!" Mrs. Moss crowed. She pulled a slotted spoon from a crockery pot on the counter and began pummeling my butt. I tried to escape her by crawling farther under the shelf and trying to reassume the position. I bit down even harder on my cheek and felt a rusty taste in my mouth. She kicked me several times to get me out from under the counter and then struck me even harder.

Blood dribbled down my chin. "Please stop!" I pleaded.

She glanced to where Mr. Moss was watching television. "Go to your room. I don't want to see you until tomorrow," she hissed.

I lay on my bunk and moaned. My mouth was bleeding. My ankle throbbed. My legs were scraped from falling on the roots, and my bottom burned. That night, when I was getting ready to take my bath, I noticed the spoon had made a curious imprint: My skin was red where the spoon had smacked flesh, white where there had been holes.

Only a few more days, I reminded myself. My mother was coming soon to take me home with her and everything would be all right.

This particular visit with my mother is encased in my mind like a scene in a snow dome. The door opened, and I saw her silhouetted in the window light. I ran into her arms, claimed her lap, and forgot about Mrs. Moss, who hovered in the corner. A raw sunburn blotched my shoulders. She examined the red dots that mottled my limbs. Since we spent so much of the day outside, we were covered in bug bites. My sensitive skin reacted to every nibble. My mother fretted over each blemish, sending accusatory glances in my foster mother's direction.

Luke sidled up to her and showed off his bruised arm. "Ashley did this to me at the beach."

Our mother did not seem concerned. "She didn't mean it, did you, Ashley?"

"No," I mumbled.

My mother's latest boyfriend distracted Luke while she gave me a bracelet, a package of crayons, and a coloring book. I started coloring while Mr. Ferris discussed some papers that his predecessor, Clayton Hooper, had sent my mother in May.

"I'm working on everything he asked me to do," my mother said with a self-righteous attitude.

"Are you in rehab?" Mrs. Moss probed.

"I've been clean for a long time," she insisted. "And anyway, I can't afford it."

"What about the parenting class?" Mr. Ferris asked.

"Yeah, sure," she agreed absentmindedly.

"I have referrals for housing and employment." She nodded, but Mr. Ferris became impatient. "If you're serious, you've got to get cracking on these tasks."

My mother turned her attention back to me. "What would you like me to bring you on my next visit?" she asked.

"I am *dying* for an Easy-Bake oven," I said passionately, "and a tea set!"

"What would you like, Luke?" Mr. Ferris asked to make certain he was included.

"A helicopter that really flies!" He zoomed back and forth.

"Well, we'll see," my mother answered. I could not tell what annoyed her more: Luke's buzzing around the room, Mr. Ferris's prompting, or Mrs. Moss's interference.

My mother kissed my neck, and I lavished her with the hugs I reserved only for her. Once more, she promised to be back soon. I held on to her hand and did not want to let go. She uncurled my fingers and stepped back slightly. "Love you, Sunshine," she said as I was tugged away by Mrs. Moss.

❧

The night after my visit, Chelsea—Ricky and Melissa's daughter—cussed, and Mrs. Moss forced her granddaughter to drink hot sauce. "I'm telling!" she screamed, and ran from the house back to her own trailer.

I did not think much of it until two days later, when summer school had resumed after the long holiday weekend.

Two men arrived shortly after the school bus had brought the older kids home. One wore ordinary clothes; the other was in uniform. I waited outside while they called Chelsea in the trailer first. She came out looking defiant and said, "I told them that Grandma hit you with a spoon and that she made me taste hot sauce when I didn't want to." She grinned. "I also said how we're only supposed to tell the good things that happen when people visit."

She looked so pleased with herself that I was not too worried when it was my turn to be questioned inside. The man named Mr. Kull asked me to sit at the table in the kitchen area. "Whatever you say will be confidential," he told me softly. "We're here to protect you and the other children."

I dared not glance over to where Mrs. Moss and Melissa were sitting in the living room, but I knew they were close enough to overhear every word.

"Do you know the difference between a truth and a lie?" the officer asked. I nodded. "Can you tell me what happened?"

After I answered his questions, he asked, "Does anything hurt?" I pointed to the sore inside my right cheek.

"You can go now," the officer said.

Mrs. Moss waved for me to sit by her. She brought me some iced Kool-Aid and pretended to be worried about my wound. "You should have shown me that."

Next, Mr. Kull talked to Heather. She admitted being disciplined by standing in the corner, squatting, and running laps. She said Mrs. Moss had not paddled her, although she had put hot sauce in her mouth. Her brother, Gordon, revealed that he had lived with the Mosses for eighteen months now and liked this home better than the others.

"Are you punished much?" Mr. Kull asked. Gordon shook his head. "Not ever?"

He admitted he sometimes had to run laps and squat. When pressed further, he confessed that he had been forced to swallow hot sauce and pepper.

"Why do you get those punishments?"

"Because I say a lot of bad words."

I was so close to Mrs. Moss, I could hear her teeth grinding.

When it was Toby's turn, his lips formed a rubber-band grin. "I like it here!" he said loud enough for anyone within ten feet of the trailer to hear.

"Do you get punished when you are naughty?" Mr. Kull asked.

The smile remained pasted in place. "Sometimes I stand in the corner."

"Anything else?" Mr. Kull prompted.

"I run laps with the other kids . . . or squat."

"For how long?

"Five or ten minutes?" came out more as a question than an answer.

"Have you ever been paddled?" Toby shook his head. "Given hot sauce?"

"Maybe one little mouthful if I cuss."

"Who gives it to you?"

"Mrs. Moss," he mumbled.

"When was the last time you got hot sauce?"

"The day before yesterday."

"What kind is it?" Toby pointed to the Crystal bottle on the table.

Mitchell claimed the Mosses' home was better than some

of his previous foster placements, yet he confirmed that he had to squat and run laps. He denied that the Mosses ever spanked him and claimed they never gave him hot sauce, only black pepper.

Mandy whispered that she had only run laps twice and that they had never forced her to squat.

"What about hot sauce?" She shook her head. "Did anyone else get hot sauce?"

"I—I'm not sure," she stammered.

Luke kept bobbing his head and shouted "Nope!" to every question he was asked.

"Were you forced to drink hot sauce or swallow pepper?"

"Nope. I ate it on my own!" He glanced over for my approval.

Mr. Kull asked Mrs. Moss if Clare could speak. "Sure, she's smart for her age." The investigator asked the toddler if she liked it there, and she said, "Yeth."

Her endearing lisp tore into me like a dull saw. Unexpectedly, I burst into tears.

Mr. Kull asked, "What's wrong?"

Mrs. Moss elbowed me. I looked up. Her glacial eyes made me shiver. "Ashley has something to say to you." At first I did not understand her scheme, so she prompted me. "You wanted to tell him that you exaggerated, right?"

"I guess," I said slowly as I tried to puzzle out what would happen if I stuck with the truth. If the men did not take me away that afternoon, I would get an even worse punishment than I had before.

"It's okay," the deputy urged. "Just tell us what happened."

"It didn't h-happen the way I said it d-did."

"You weren't hit?" the deputy asked. I shook my head. Tears flew in every direction—not because I was sad, but because I was outraged that nobody was ever going to see through the woman's manipulations. "Then what did happen?" the deputy asked sternly.

"I j-just fell," I said between sobs. "It w-was an accident."

"This one tells stories," Mrs. Moss said between pursed lips. "Been through a lot of trauma . . . saw her grandfather shot . . ." I was furious that she was twisting my story to save her skin, but now she had caught me in her trap.

Mr. Kull checked the inside of my cheek again. "This needs medical attention," he said to Mrs. Moss. "Shall I transport her to the doctor now or will you?"

"I'd be happy to," she replied.

We left for the doctor as soon as the investigator was finished. Even though Mrs. Moss had outsmarted me at her house, I was confident that a doctor would detect the truth. When I went in the examining room, Mrs. Moss trailed behind. She fussed like a concerned mother. "She fell down the stairs and bit the inside of her mouth. I think it got infected!"

I thought: *This doctor is smart. There is no way that he will fall for that old line.* He peered in my ears, waved a light in front of my eyes, and then examined my mouth. "You're not brushing very well, young lady, and that can lead to sores and infections."

I was stunned that he was not more suspicious. The doctor wrote on his pad: *Fell down and bit the right side inside mouth.* Next, he gave Mrs. Moss instructions about gargling with warm salt water. And that was it!

That evening Mrs. Moss prepared her infamous sour broccoli soup, which she made from half-rotten vegetables that she got from a man who delivered crates of supermarket discards. I asked to skip dinner because my mouth hurt.

"You still have to gargle," Mrs. Moss reminded me. She fixed a glass of hot salt water. "Chelsea, take her into the bathroom and make sure she does it properly."

The minute I took a swig of the mixture, my mouth burned even worse than it had with the hot sauce. "Ow!" I spit it out, spraying the mirror.

"Grandma, Ashley's making a mess in here," Chelsea called. I emptied half the glass in the sink. "And she's pouring it down the sink."

Mrs. Moss rushed into the room, pushing Chelsea aside. She clutched the glass in one hand and held my head back with the other. "Doctor's orders," she said, and dumped some water down my throat. I coughed and sputtered, and then she made me swish what was left in the glass. Again, I choked, and this time I sprayed her leg. Her face puffed and her talonlike fingernails gripped my shoulders. The sharp edges of several rings grazed my flesh. Mrs. Moss steered me into the kitchen, grabbed the hot-sauce bottle, and dribbled some into my mouth. She held my cheeks together, pressing the tender spot with her thumb.

"Bet salt water is looking better and better," she said. When she released me, I ran into the bathroom and rinsed and rinsed and rinsed, but the pain only became worse and worse and worse.

6

Nobody listens

At that point I had been in that hateful house for only six weeks. I am sure I would have been safer with my mother— or almost anyone else. In the meantime, I was determined not to be the center of Marjorie Moss's sadistic attention, although I could never tell what might spark her rage. A door slam or a sentence that did not end in "ma'am" could make her furious. There were times when so many children were in so many corners that I would have to hunt for a space for my own punishment. The worst offenders had to wear smelly trash cans over their heads.

Several of the kids had bed-wetting problems, but I had been dry for years until I woke one morning to Heather making gagging sounds. "What stinks?" She sniffed our bunks for the new smell. "Ashley, you pissed your bed!"

"There's no way—," I started to protest, but shut up as I rolled over on a cold, damp spot.

Mrs. Moss caught me stripping my linens. "What's going on here?"

"Ashley peed her bed," Mandy volunteered.

"You know we don't change the sheets but once a month. You'll have to sleep in that bed as your punishment."

A few days later I realized that I had done it again. "I've never wet before," I insisted when Mrs. Moss found out.

Mrs. Moss made me put on one of Clare's diapers. "Now go outside and tell everyone: 'I am a disgusting pig and I pissed myself.'"

"I'm not supposed to say that word."

"You say exactly what I told you. Then maybe you'll stop acting like a pissing baby." Frozen, I stood on the trailer's stoop. Mrs. Moss yelled at me through the door. "Go to the boys first, then back to the girls' side and do what I said." I was barefoot and the patio was hot, so I hurried to where the boys were swatting a beach ball with some branches. "I'm a disgusting pig and p-p-pissed myself."

Toby stopped in mid-swing and gaped. Mitchell started to laugh, but one look from Toby shut him up.

I proceeded to the girls' side. Heather giggled. "Ah, you look so cute!"

Mandy said, "Go back inside." Her voice wobbled as if she was about to cry. One minute the kids would turn on one another; other times we would rally because each knew what it felt like to be the victim of the day.

Unfortunately, Luke never learned to lie low. A favorite trick of his was putting the time-out trash can on his head, then blindly knocking into walls. If he had to stand in the corner, he would jump up and down making farting noises or keep turning around until the time increased. He was trapped in a cycle of acting out and punishment.

We got so dirty playing outside all day that we bathed nightly. After filling the tub with no more than six inches of water, Mandy and I bathed the babies; then it progressed until the oldest was finished, with everyone sharing the same water. I didn't mind washing a little boy named Brandon because he never fussed. One night I removed his diaper while he held the tub's rim. As I lifted him into the water, something warm slipped down my leg. When I realized what had happened, I giggled.

"What's going on?" Mrs. Moss called from the living room.

"Brandon peed all over me!"

Mrs. Moss began to laugh. It was our first humorous interaction. For that brief second I thought she was starting to like me.

Warm water often caused Clare to have a bowel movement, yet no matter how gross the water, Mandy and I would still have to get in it later. If the stools were firm, I could usually fish them out with a cup and flush them down the toilet, but I never knew if the babies peed. If the meager layer of bathwater was filthy, I would try to get away with a quick rinse; but if Mrs. Moss did not think I had washed myself thoroughly, she dragged me back into the bath and scrubbed me so hard with a bristle brush that it sometimes scraped off my skin.

Luke hated baths. When he refused to get in the tub, Mrs. Moss would wash him roughly with a cloth, pour shampoo on his head, and then dunk him to rinse it off. The more he sputtered, the longer she held him under. I could not see what was happening, but I heard him screaming in terror.

At the end of July, Miles Ferris visited Luke and me at the Moss home. We wore our best clothes, and Mrs. Moss shooed the others outside. Mr. Ferris gave us gifts from our mother, including candy, school clothing and supplies, plus backpacks.

"I've enrolled Luke in Head Start," Mrs. Moss said, sounding like the most responsible parent ever. "He could use the extra attention." Mr. Ferris gestured toward me. "She's my big helper."

He raised his eyebrows so high, he looked startled. "Any issues?"

"All children have their moments . . ."

I was relieved that she did not mention that I now wet my bed nightly.

They talked over our heads as though we could not comprehend their shorthand, but I heard enough to figure out that my mother had not fulfilled the requirements to get us back yet. Adele had called to tell Mr. Ferris that my mother was "on the street." Mrs. Moss sighed in a way that made me worry that my mother did not have a place to live.

"She still wants the girl," he said.

Mrs. Moss pretended to be concerned about our future. "What about the boy?"

"Those relatives of his expect me to start the paperwork all over!"

"They're full of demands, aren't they?" Mrs. Moss shook her head as though she sympathized with all the trouble he went through that nobody appreciated.

But I was hung up on the idea that our relatives still

wanted us. I thought of Adele wistfully. She had loved me almost as much as my mother had. I would jump at the chance to live with her so I could leave this hellhole.

Mr. Ferris groaned. "I have to follow up on the request, although I've always believed this one is going to termination."

At the time the word was meaningless to me, but termination of parental rights—usually abbreviated as TPR in the system—is a huge transition in a child's life. Of course, I did not know what that entailed, only that the hushed voices and sideways glances meant that this was a big deal—and I had a stomach-churning sensation that "termination" was not something I would like.

Finally, the broiling, terrifying summer was coming to an end. School was my safe haven, and I was eager to start second grade. Any teacher, even a strict one, would be a welcome change from Mrs. Moss. I volunteered to pick the clothes for the first day of school so I could wear one of the outfits my mother had sent.

"Real breakfast!" Toby reminded everyone. Foster kids, along with others who qualified, received two meals a day at school. I loved the breakfasts with pancakes, scrambled eggs, little bottles of juice, and sausage links. When they served grilled cheese or chicken sandwiches for lunch, I would cadge extras from the children who hardly ever cleaned their plates. Knowing that we ate at school, Mrs. Moss scrimped even more at home, often serving only thin sandwiches for supper.

The second-grade classrooms were set up pod-style,

with a central space where our class built a teepee. If you finished your work, you could go inside to read or draw. I spent a good portion of my day there reading. When we studied the seasons, Mrs. Brush assigned us an essay describing a winter holiday with our family and said the best one would be printed in the school newsletter.

At lunch I asked some friends what they were going to write about. One chose getting a Christmas tree with his dad; another had decided on baking holiday treats with her mom; several were going to focus on vacations with relatives who lived up north.

When I returned to the classroom, tears pricked my eyes as I stared down at my blank paper. Mrs. Brush waved for me to come to her desk. "Did something happen at lunch?" the teacher probed. I shook my head. "Do you need to see the nurse?" I hung my head but did not answer. "Then what's the matter, dear?" she asked softly.

"I don't want to do the winter story."

"That doesn't sound like my eager beaver." Mrs. Brush called me that when I handed in my assignments first or wildly waved my hand to answer a question. "And why is that?"

"I can't t-think of anything I've d-done with my f-family," I stuttered to cover the sob that rose in my throat.

"Oh, dear," she said as she realized my humiliation. "You don't have to put any *people* in your story. What do you like about winter?"

"Snow. I once saw it, but there wasn't enough to build a snowman."

"Then why don't you write about an imaginary snowman?" The teacher beamed.

The words came quickly, and I still remember them: *My snowman is white, my snowman is out of sight. He wears his boots tight as he goes roaming about.* The poem went on to describe how the sun melted him away and how he was hiding in an ice chest until the next winter, when it would be safe for him to come back out and play with me again. I drew pictures around the poem and won the contest. Mrs. Brush sent me into the teepee to recopy the poem neatly for the printer. I memorized the whole poem because I figured that nobody would keep it safely for me. And, of course, nobody did.

My mother was supposed to see us every month, yet four long months passed without any word. Finally, at the end of October, she returned. Mrs. Moss had us wear outfits my mother had sent. Her cleverness about details amazed me. At the visitation office she again sat in the room, listening to every word.

"How's my Sunshine?" my mother asked when I ran into her arms.

"I'm still getting all A's," I bragged.

"I'm in Head Start!" Luke chimed in.

I noticed a big box in a shopping bag. "Is that for me?" My mother handed over the Easy-Bake oven.

While I busied myself opening it, she gave Luke his heli-copter. "It's remote control," my mother told him, "but you have to use it outside."

The Easy-Bake oven kit had everything needed to use it, including pans and powdered cake mix. My mother got water from the restroom, and we made our first cake together. Luke kept interrupting the cooking process, so Mr. Ferris helped him unpack the helicopter.

The cake smelled lemony as it baked. My mother handed her parenting class completion certificate to Mr. Ferris. "There's only a few more tasks on my list before you can come home with me," she said to me.

Mr. Ferris cleared his throat as a warning. "Why don't we sit over here?" He pointed to another table. I followed, gripping my mother's slacks. "You are almost in compliance." He shuffled through some files. "What about substance abuse aftercare?" My mother handed him another paper. "Very good, Mrs. Grover." He looked at his watch. "I'm afraid I have another appointment."

"But I drove more than eight hours to get here!"

He stood as a sign that her time was almost up. "You can schedule monthly visits."

"What else will it take before I can get my children back?" she moaned.

"Just keep up with your case plan. You are making excellent progress."

She quickly cut the tiny cake into five bite-size pieces, and we each ate them.

"Mama!" I said as Mrs. Moss stood to take charge.

"I'll be back next month, Sunshine." As she hugged me, Luke used his head to butt into the embrace.

"I want my mommy!" Luke wailed in the elevator. A few of the other riders looked at him with sympathy.

"She'll be back next month," Mrs. Moss said in her fake soothing voice. "Until then, you have that nice helicopter, right?"

As soon as we returned from the visit with my mother,

Luke begged to try his helicopter. Since I had used my oven, Mrs. Moss allowed it.

"I'll show you how," Mitchell said.

Mitchell got it to fly on the second try, and Luke was thrilled. But soon I heard Luke screaming. "You broke it! You broke my helicopter!"

Mrs. Moss, her wiry hair looking like a Brillo pad, peered out the door of the trailer. "What did you do to him?" she asked Mitchell accusingly.

Mitchell smirked. "He said 'hell.'"

"I said 'helicopter'!" Luke insisted. "You broke it."

"Did not!" Mitchell replied.

"Hell, hell, hell!" Luke screamed.

Mrs. Moss swooped down and gripped my brother's shirt. "I should never have let you play with it."

"It wasn't his fault!" I screamed. Mrs. Moss elbowed me aside and dragged Luke inside.

Mr. Moss stood by a shed pretending nothing was happening. Through the sliding glass door, I saw Mrs. Moss cram Luke into a high chair. He flailed his arms, but she pinned them under the tray. Tears made wavy tracks down his smudged face.

"Luke's gonna get it now," Mitchell said before hightailing it to the boys' yard.

I trembled as I watched Mrs. Moss press Luke's clenched cheek with her thumb and forefinger, making him look like a fish. With her other hand, she forced a bottle of hot sauce between his pursed lips. As he gasped for air, the hot sauce splattered his face and ran down his shirt. The more he spit out, the more Mrs. Moss poured in. His turn had come. It was almost as if Mrs. Moss rolled dice to decide whom she would torment next. We kids felt relieved when she directed her cruelty at someone else because it meant we were safe—at least for a while. That is why we snitched on one another. Better to be the one not chosen in this particular game of chance. But as much as I feared being punished, it was worse watching Luke suffer and not being able to help him.

Early one morning I heard Lucy crying in the master bedroom. I went to get her and walked her into the living room. I patted her back and began singing "You Are My Sunshine" very softly. It seemed to soothe her.

Mrs. Moss came up behind me and took the baby from me. "Do you know there's more to that song?" She sang the next verse in a whisper and then said, "When Toby's up, pick out your best school clothes."

"But there's no school today."

"We're having guests, so I want you to teach the girls all the verses to 'You Are My Sunshine.'"

"Must be somebody's worker," I said to Mandy.

"Yep, she's baking brownies," Mandy agreed.

We were not surprised when a man and a woman arrived for a visit before lunch. They were not any of our regular workers, so they must have been supervisors or licensing inspectors. I kicked a stone across the flagstone patio while Mrs. Moss served coffee and brownies inside. "I'm *not* going to sing that stupid song!"

Mandy was taken aback. "What's your problem?"

"If it wasn't for you, we'd be with our parents."

Mandy clenched her fingers. "What did I do?"

"You didn't tell the truth about what happens here."

She started to cry. "Nobody else wants us, and if we leave, they'll split me and Toby up."

What could I say? Luke and I had been apart more than we had been together, but at least we saw our mother. Mandy did not have anyone to visit.

Mrs. Moss called us inside. "We've been learning a new song." Mrs. Moss acted as if we sang together daily. She waved her arms like a conductor.

"You are my sunshine . . . ," we began in unison.

The words stuck like a chicken bone in my throat. This was *my* song, *our* song. My knees started to wobble. I would have given anything to fall back into my mother's arms and be told that she was there now and everything would be all right. I blinked away slippery tears and tried to force my spine rigid, but that made me tremble even more. At the time I believed Mrs. Moss had picked this song because she knew it meant something to me and this was another one of her cruelties. I began to chew a hangnail to suppress my fury, but I stopped when I realized it wouldn't look like I was singing. Surely Mrs. Moss would punish me if she thought I was ruining her little show, so I forced myself to mouth the words, using the rest of my energy to hold back angry sobs.

Bundles of Christmas gifts prepared by foster parents' associations began arriving in early December. A few packages had the telltale shapes of Caboodles cosmetic cases. Someone tore open a corner to check. When Mrs. Moss saw the rip, she called the girls into the kitchen.

"Who did this?" She gave each one of us her death-ray

stare. "If nobody confesses, I am going to burn everyone's presents in a big fire!" Silence. Mrs. Moss began to toss the gifts into a green trash bag.

"I did it." The words sounded hollow inside my head. I hoped she could tell that this time I really was lying.

"I thought it was you!" She grabbed the ripped package. "You were going to get one of these, but now I'll find somebody who deserves it." She looked at the pile. "And this and this . . . and this."

The guilty party was standing there watching Mrs. Moss remove my gifts, and she did not make a peep. It was probably Mandy, but she was so afraid of her own shadow, she would have let everything burn. On Christmas morning Mandy received her Caboodles kit and a lot more gifts than I did. There were some new clothes and we both got Barbie dolls that Mrs. Moss allowed us to keep in the house, but we had to let the little girls play with them too. By New Year's, Clare had ripped the head off Mandy's doll, so Mandy confiscated mine.

"Do you like living with the Mosses?" my teacher asked after Christmas vacation.

"I guess so."

She nodded. "Would you please go to the guidance office? They need some help with your brother."

When I got there, Luke was crying. He was filthier than usual, with dirt encrusted on his face and ringing his scalp. He also smelled like poop.

The counselor said, "He had a little accident."

"Don't tell on me!" Luke wailed.

"I won't," I promised.

"He said he's afraid he'll have to drink hot sauce again," the counselor said. "Is that possible?"

I looked her straight in the eyes. "Oh, yes. He gets it all the time."

That night as we were getting ready for bed, Mrs. Moss was making pudding. The kitchen smelled like bananas and cream. I figured a caseworker would be coming in the morning and was surprised when Simon Parker, a child protection investigator, came to the door a little while later, along with a deputy sheriff.

By then Heather had moved out, but there were still fourteen of us foster children there.

"What happened to Luke today?" Mr. Parker asked Mrs. Moss.

"Oh, that boy forgets to go to the bathroom sometimes." She clucked as if it was no big deal. "They called me from school to take him home."

"Where is he?"

She looked at the clock. It was almost ten. "In bed. Where else?" She chuckled pleasantly. "Well, he had better be in bed at this hour." She went to his room and brought him out in his jammies. His hair was still wet. We all had bathed that evening, and Mrs. Moss had inspected us carefully. Now I knew why.

Mr. Parker walked Luke back to his bedroom. "It's quite warm back there," he said when he returned to the kitchen. "And the air circulation is poor." He glanced at the full ash-tray on the table. "The smoking doesn't help."

Mr. Moss, who rarely said anything, spoke up. "I'm fixin' to put in some circulating fans."

"Other than the musty air and it being a bit overcrowded, I don't see any problems here," Mr. Parker said.

"We have a few new sibling groups here on a temporary basis. It's a shame to separate them, so we do what we can until they can find someone else to take them as a unit." Mrs. Moss smiled. "Would you like some of my fresh banana pudding?"

Mr. Parker and the deputy declined.

"Well, we do our best with what little we've got," Mrs. Moss continued. She pointed to a shelf of children's videos. "You may find newer homes but not happier ones."

Two days later a female investigator interviewed each of us at school. At first I told her everything was fine.

"We're all alone, hon," she said in a corner of the guidance office. "Nothing bad will happen if you tell the truth, do you understand?" I nodded, but I still doubted her. "Do you take a bath every night?"

"Uh-huh." A crack in a wall steadied my eyes and prevented me from feeling as though I were falling.

"Do you help anyone else take a bath?"

I explained how Mandy and I bathed the younger girls and ourselves in the same water and helped with the smaller boys.

"Did Mrs. Moss threaten to burn your Christmas gifts?" she asked.

I was surprised she knew about this. "I always take the blame for the other children," I replied.

"Anything else you'd like to tell me?"

I seized on this opportunity to complain about my dolls being locked in the shed, and she said she would see what she could do.

On the bus ride home I asked Luke, "What did you tell the lady who came today?"

"I said how Mrs. Moss threw a doll at me 'cause I couldn't keep my arms raised up during a time-out." He looked worried. "Was that okay?"

Mitchell, who was sitting behind us, said, "I told her it was because you called her a bitch."

Luke spun around and made a fist at Mitchell. "And I also told her that I hit you until your eyes popped out and your head split open."

"What else did you tell the lady?" I asked Mitchell.

"About how Mrs. Moss shoved food down Candace's mouth till she almost barfed." He looked out the window. "Anyway, nothin' I tell will matter because Mrs. Moss told me she has a special paper saying she can keep us in the corner as long as she wants." He shrugged. "I guess I'm gonna get it when we get home."

"We all told stuff," I said to comfort him. "I bet our workers will be there to take us away the minute we get back."

"No, they'll say it's my fault. Nobody wants me because of my temper. That is why we're all there. The Mosses take the ones nobody else wants."

"My mother wants me!" I retorted.

"And me, too!" chimed Luke, even though I knew by that time that Mama wanted only me and that he was going back to Dusty.

"Anyway," Mitchell added, "I stuck up for you."

"Did you tell her about the Caboodles?" I asked.

"Yeah. I said you took the blame even though you didn't do it."

This time I really did expect Mr. Ferris to be waiting for Luke and me after school with our belongings in plastic bags. Finally, my dolls and dresses would be freed from the shed and we would go to a safer home. However, just like before, nothing happened.

Miles Ferris did not visit us again until the end of January. I overheard Mrs. Moss telling him, "Ashley likes to go to school and tell stories about my home and family." Mr. Ferris arched his eyebrows reprovingly. She apparently took this as a sign that he was on her side and grumbled, "I don't know how much more I can take from that girl."

I was surprised when he showed up again the next week because he usually came only every few months. The visit was brief. On the way out the door he bent close to my ear. "You be good now and don't make any waves."

Two weeks later we celebrated Valentine's Day at school. A few mothers brought cupcakes and passed out heart-shaped candies with sayings printed on them. I had saved my biggest valentine—the one we were supposed to take home to our mothers—and gave it to my teacher, Mrs. Brush. She pinned it to the bulletin board. I had no idea that was to be my last week in her class.

When I returned from school on Friday, I found Miles Ferris waiting for me. This time my belongings were stuffed into a plastic sack.

"Here, I'll take that." Mr. Ferris lifted my backpack.

I started for the bedroom, but Mrs. Moss stopped me. "I packed everything. You've got your toothbrush, underwear, shoes, and all your clothes."

"What about the outfits my mother sent?" I asked tentatively.

"Of course," she claimed.

"What about my dress with the hoop?"

"It don't fit you no more."

I appealed to Mr. Ferris. "Did you get my Precious Moments sleeping bag?"

"She gave me everything." He pushed me toward the car.

I watched as he put my backpack and one meager garbage sack in the trunk. He did not have anything from the shed.

"What about my dolls and my Easy-Bake oven?" I started to panic.

Mr. Ferris rolled his eyes toward Mrs. Moss.

"She has a big imagination," Mrs. Moss stated.

"You saw the oven when my mother visited me!" I said vehemently. He was more interested in getting me into the car than dealing with my protests. "Where's Luke?"

"You'll have visits," Mr. Ferris said in a flat voice. He buckled me in.

"Please, I need my dolls, my stuff in the shed," I begged.

"I'll get them later," he said to mollify me, then slammed the door.

As we pulled out of the driveway, I heard a shattering sound inside my head as if a glass had broken between my ears. My school . . . Mrs. Brush . . . my friends . . . Mandy and Toby . . . little Clare . . . Lilly and Katie . . . and—Luke! I was escaping, but he was left behind. He needed me to warn him, to protect him, to comfort him. And yet . . . I felt as worthless as the junk in my trash bag. Once again, I was the one being tossed out and thrown away.

7

Orphan by decree

"Are you taking me to my mother?" I asked Miles Ferris as he drove. He kept his eyes on the road and did not reply. "Why isn't Luke coming with us?" Still no answer. "Why don't you ever say anything?" I snapped.

"And why don't you ever tell the truth, young lady?" he spit back. "The Mosses run one of our finest foster homes, and you were trying to ruin it for everyone."

My head exploded with a kaleidoscope of colors. For a second my mother's face radiated sunshine yellow, then it flared into orange and then bright, burning red—the color of fire, the color of hate, the color of my hair. I was a fire child, a furious child, my gut clamped over a molten core radiating my hostility. Mrs. Moss might have gotten away with it this time, but not forever. To quell my feelings of hopelessness and anger, I chewed on the side of my thumb until it was raw. Someday my mother and I would show up and demand the release of Luke and our possessions—and then that witch would be sorry!

As we drove on, I slumped into my seat. Slowly, the red receded, and blurry blues surrounded me. By the time Mr. Ferris dumped me at the Lake Magdalene Children's shelter, my mood had faded toward gray. The residential campus, which took kids who had no place else to go, had small houses clustered around dismal, sun-parched lawns. I moved into Shelter Three.

A counselor unpacked my plastic bag. "That's all you have?"

"Oh, no, but they didn't let me take everything," I said, because I still hoped there would be a way to get my precious possessions from the sheds.

"We have a clothes room where you can pick out whatever you like."

"Do I have to share my outfits?" I asked.

She gave me a funny look. "That's not allowed here."

I smiled for the first time that day.

Then she noticed my hands. "My word, girl, what's wrong with your thumb?" My biting had left it looking like raw hamburger. "You wash that with soap; otherwise, it will get infected," she said in a voice more maternal than angry.

Dinner in the shelter was even better than lunch at school because I could have as much as I wanted. Best of all, the beds had clean sheets with a fresh, floral smell and the air was deliciously cool.

The girls in my shelter were all older. My roommate, Ella, was fourteen and had a baby who lived with off-campus foster parents. Some of the most difficult kids lived in a dormitory, which also contained a padded restraining room. Fortunately, the staff hardly ever reprimanded me. When a caseworker visited, my counselor told her, "She's not a girl, she's a little lady."

I remember watching Sir Mix-a-Lot's "Baby Got Back" video on MTV. The older girls would mimic the backup dancers' routine. "C'mon, Ashley," Ella urged, "you gotta shake your booty, girl. Shake it!"

The girls snickered when they heard me sing along with the lyrics. "You don't know what that's about," Latoya, one of the toughest girls, teased.

"Do too."

"Okay then, what's an anaconda?"

A staff member called out, "You're all going to be late for school!"

"What's an anaconda?" I asked the counselor when they were gone.

"A big snake, why?"

I attended the Dorothy Thomas Center, the on-campus school. Since most of the students were transient and many had behavior problems, the curriculum was designed more to keep us out of trouble than on grade level. My best friend in class was Tyler. He wore box-frame glasses and had unruly brown hair. One afternoon he asked if I wanted to join the softball game that was about to start.

Someone called out, "But she's a girl!"

"Maybe she could be in the outfield," Tyler yelled back.

"I'm a really good pitcher," I bragged.

"Oh yeah? Prove it!" A lanky boy turned, spit in the sand, and then tossed me a ball.

After a few hard throws and catches they decided I knew

what I was doing, but I did not have a glove. When it was my turn to pitch, Tyler, who was on the other team, came up to bat. I threw the ball a little softer so he was sure to get a good hit. Wham! The ball flew straight back to me. I caught it bare-handed, then dropped it like a hot potato. I jumped up and down holding my hand. My left pinky angled to one side.

"I'm sorry," Tyler said. "I didn't mean it!"

The nurse told me to ice it and it would be fine. It hurt for several weeks. It still sticks out at an unnatural angle and has a bump on the bone. It probably had been broken and should have been set.

Tyler and I wrote notes to each other, and I kept his replies under my pillow. One night I dreamed that I came to school and found his chair empty. The teacher told me he had left, and I could not believe he had not said good-bye. I woke in tears. That morning he saw me heading for the cafeteria and caught up with me. "Hey, guess what?" he blurted. "I'm being released today."

"Released to what?" I asked.

"I'm going home."

My bad dream had come true! After that, I tried to force myself to dream that I was being released to my mother.

Once I was out of the clutches of Mrs. and Mr. Moss, I complained about them to anyone who would listen, and there were plenty of sympathetic ears at Lake Magdalene. Even though I do not remember instigating the investigations, the Mosses later claimed that I had called in nine "false" abuse reports using the hotline number. I have no recollection of ever making a single call, although I did answer questions from teachers and guidance counselors, and they may have called. The one time I was most injured, Chelsea, not me, made the complaint.

The day I was moved to the shelter, Luke went to live with Stan and Lola Merritt. Mr. Merritt was a pastor with the Seventh-day Adventist Church, and his wife was a nurse. Luke was distraught and kept asking for me, but luckily, Lake Mag was less than two miles from where they lived, and the staff allowed me to visit him at the Merritts' home.

On one of the first trips Mrs. Merritt asked me how I liked the shelter. "It's okay," I said.

"Better than the last foster home?" she asked.

"Anything is better than that dump!"

"Why is that?" she queried in her ladylike voice.

"Because of what they did to us."

"What do you mean?" she probed. I ran down the list, from the hot sauce to the squatting to the beatings. "One time Mrs. Moss pulled me off my top bunk by the hair, and a bunch of it was yanked out by the roots! Then she kicked me while I was on the floor."

"Why would she do that?"

I covered my face with my hands because I did not want to mention my bed-wetting, which had stopped immediately after I left the Moss home.

Mrs. Merritt did not press me. "Did they hurt Luke, too?"

"He got it worse because he didn't follow the rules."

Luke had told her similar stories, but she had not known whether to believe him.

A few nights later the counselor on duty at the shelter

woke me. "Somebody wants to talk to you," she said softly.

The silhouette of a uniformed police officer loomed in the doorway. My mind raced over the last few days. What had I done that was illegal? I had borrowed a pen from my teacher, although I was certain I had returned it. Was someone else blaming me to save his or her own skin?

"Hi," the officer said. "What's your name?"

I was too sleepy to find a distant focal point. Yawning, I answered his questions about my date of birth and grade in school.

"How long have you been at Lake Mag?"

"A few weeks," I said, still trying to prod my sleepy brain.

"Where did you live before this?"

"With Marjorie and Charles Moss."

"Is that a foster home?" he asked.

"Yes."

"What do you think of Mr. and Mrs. Merritt?" he asked.

"They're nice. Did you know they are vegetarians because Seventh-day Adventists don't eat meat and they worship on Saturdays?"

He laughed at how chatty I had become now that I was more alert. "What about the Mosses? Were they nice?"

I froze. For a moment I felt as if Mrs. Moss might be listening outside the door. Then I heard one of the older girls laughing at a TV show in the distance. Mrs. Moss was nowhere around, and Luke was safe too. "They were the most horrible, disgusting people!" I said. "They hurt my brother. They poured hot sauce down his throat and almost drowned him in the bathtub. You should ask him about it."

"I just came from there," he said. "What about you? Did they hurt you, too?"

I went through the list of horrors so fast that I had to catch my breath. I saw the counselor hovering in the doorway sipping a soda. "You okay?" she asked. I nodded.

"Did they ever take you to a doctor for your injuries?" the officer continued.

"Yes!" I told him about my cheek. "But the stupid doctor believed what Mrs. Moss said about me falling and didn't check further." The officer wrote down everything I said. "Tell that doctor to ask better questions."

"Okay," the officer said. "Anything else?"

"Yes. Don't let them hurt more kids."

"I'll try." He closed his notebook. "You go back to sleep and don't worry about a thing. You're safe here."

According to Florida law, dependency cases are supposed to be brought before the court every six months. For some reason, the lawyers had overlooked our case for more than two years. By then the judge had changed our goal from reunification to termination of Lorraine's and Dusty's parental rights.

I didn't know what was happening, only that I was getting another visit with my mother. And since I never left Lake Mag except for visits with my mother or Luke, I was bursting with excitement when I was told I would see them both. Mama brought us Easter baskets, stuffed animals, and new clothes. Luke played by himself with a small basketball set while I showed off backbends. There was the usual chitchat with the supervising worker, a woman I had not seen before, although this time it had an edgy tone.

"Have you started counseling yet?" the new worker asked.

"I told the judge I would," my mother snapped.

"Don't forget the testing and psychological report."

"You're just hassling me because you don't approve of my lifestyle."

"When are you going to tell him?" The worker nodded toward Luke.

"I said I would!" my mother hissed under her breath.

I did not realize that she had voluntarily signed away her rights to my brother. Before we left, our mother took Luke aside. She crouched to his height.

"Luke, I want you to pay attention, okay?"

He nodded solemnly and tried to press himself against her. She held him off a bit. "I—" She wiped her tears with the back of her free hand. "I won't be seeing you for a very long time." She stared up at the caseworker, who nodded encouragement. "Maybe never." She coughed. "See, you belong to Dusty, not me."

I exhaled, because even if my mother did not want Luke anymore, I knew she would always come back for me. In any case, that was the last time my then five-year-old brother ever saw our mother.

Clueless as to the importance of what had just happened, I returned to Lake Mag and displayed my new wardrobe to Ella. "Which should I wear tomorrow?" I asked.

"Who gives a shit?" she replied.

I laid out the yellow shorts and the striped shirt at the bottom of my bed. In the morning I picked up the shirt. All the buttons were scattered on the floor. I stormed into the common area. "Who ripped off the buttons to my new shirt?" I screeched.

"You shouldn't take out your anger by destroying things," a counselor said.

My face burned like a griddle. "I wouldn't destroy something from my mother!"

"You can sew them back on yourself." The woman handed me a needle and thread. "Then maybe you'll find better ways to seek attention."

I cried in outrage. Why had they assumed I had done it? I had no idea how to sew. With shaking hands, I threaded the needle and figured out how to stab it through the buttonhole, but it came right out the other side. After a few more tries I tied the thread around the button. The result was slightly uneven, although once I buttoned the blouse, it was presentable. I hated the girl who did it. This was another confirmation that nobody—besides my mother—cared for my feelings or for me.

A few days after saying farewell to Luke, my mother asked to see only me. I remember sitting on her lap in Mr. Ferris's office. She combed her fingers through my hair. "Guess what, Sunshine? I have a good job and a nice house. I'm living with a lady named Babette, and she has a son whose name is Drew."

"How old is Drew?"

"He's six."

"When can I live there with you, Mama?"

"As soon as—"

Mr. Ferris cleared his throat to warn my mother not to cross an invisible line. "The judge will decide where you will live," Mr. Ferris said in the mushy voice I had come to despise. He turned to my mother. "Mrs. Grover, please remember the rules about discussing these matters in front of your child."

"But I am supposed to tell her about Luke, right?" she asked in a more deferential manner. He waved his hand like a king giving dispensation. "Sunshine, remember when I told you that you are mine and Luke is Dusty's?"

I held my breath. The shell around that once-perfect egg that held my childish faith was more fragile than ever, and I feared she was going to say something hurtful. "Well, Dusty isn't always a nice man when he doesn't get his way. He might even harm me if I tried to keep Luke. So I moved back to Florida to stay away from him and get you back." She paused. "Do you understand what I am saying?"

"I'm going to live with you and Drew and his mother, but Luke isn't."

"I hope so." She glanced at the caseworker for approval. "Soon as I get permission from the judge."

"And Luke will go to live with Dusty?"

"Maybe, but I don't know about that."

I pressed my face into my mother's blouse. She smelled like a smoky chicken nugget. Mr. Ferris showed her some papers, and she signed them while holding me.

I shuddered. She patted my back. "Soon, Sunshine, soon."

A worker transported me to Dr. Howard Black for some tests. I was happy to get away from Lake Mag, although I protested. "Why do I need to see a doctor? I'm not sick."

"He's not that kind of doctor," the woman said.

Dr. Black had a serious face that seemed to be hiding a smile. "How old are you?" he asked.

"I'll be eight and a half next week." I crossed my legs and straightened my back.

"Why are you living at Lake Mag?" he asked.

"Because they blamed me for causing trouble."

"What sort of trouble was that?"

The seal on his diploma, which was precisely aligned on the wall with his right ear, made for the perfect place to concentrate my attention. "Telling about how the Mosses punished us."

"How did they punish you, Ashley?"

I went through the list and he made notes, but I could not tell whether he believed me or not. "You told other people, right?"

"Oh, yes—my teacher and the policeman and Mrs. Merritt."

He nodded. "Do you like Lake Mag?"

"I'd rather live with my mother."

"What was it like when you were with her?"

"It was okay, except when Dusty was around—he's Luke's father. See, Mama is afraid of Dusty, so she had to give Luke to him."

"Do you want to be with your brother?"

I stared down for the first time. "Oh, yes!" I covered my lapse by yawning, so the doctor gave me some drawing games.

The best part of the session was looking at pictures and making up stories, like I had when Adele took me to the therapist in South Carolina. There were many sad pictures about other children who had mean parents or who could not live with the one they wanted or who had lost toys.

"Ashley, do you know the difference between a truth and a lie?"

I returned my attention to the diploma seal and then nodded.

"When you told me the story just now about the lost child, was that the truth?"

I found his question insulting. "I made it up after looking at that picture."

"Was that a lie?"

"No, it was a *story*."

"What's your favorite story?"

"The one about Alice in Wonderland and also the Little Princess."

"Was what you told me about how you were punished in foster care a story too?"

"No, that really happened." I stared him down, and he blinked first.

When our time was up, he shook my hand and wished me luck.

A different worker drove me back to the shelter. She asked me if I was happy at Lake Mag. "I can live there until my mom gets things together," I replied. "You see, her girlfriend—her name is Babette—is becoming a foster parent, so this time it's all going to work out."

The Merritts arranged frequent visits for me and Luke at their home, which was a tidy, five-bedroom house not far from Lake Magdalene. Their two daughters, Leah and Betsy, were away at college. They also had an adopted son,

Matthew, who was about twelve; Luke; and a foster baby named Keisha.

One afternoon as Mrs. Merritt drove me back to Lake Mag, I started singing.

"Where did you hear that song?" Mrs. Merritt asked.

"MTV."

"What else do you like to watch on television?" she probed.

"Movies, especially scary ones!" I bragged. "We saw *Children of the Corn* last weekend. The whole field started moving like this"—my hand made a wavy motion—"and a guy came out with a huge curved knife and—"

She cut me off. "That's enough."

The Merritts asked to become my foster parents. On Memorial Day weekend, I moved in with them. I shared Keisha's room with her, while Matthew and Luke each had their own. Mrs. Merritt worked as a pediatric nurse some nights, so we had to be quiet during the day if she was sleeping. After the cruelty at the Mosses' and the boisterousness of the shelter, I relished the serene environment.

The first morning at the Merritts', I heard Keisha stirring and went to tend her. Mrs. Merritt came in tying her robe. "What are you doing?"

"She's wet," I said.

"You can't change her diaper," Mrs. Merritt responded.

"I did it all the time at the Mosses'."

"In this house I am the mother and you are the child," she said so adamantly that I stiffened and fluttered my gaze to a corner before she could attack.

"If you think Keisha needs something, call me or Dad." She noticed my lower lip quivering. "You aren't in any trouble. Keisha has a medical problem called diabetes. That means her body doesn't process sugar normally, and so we sometimes have to give her a quick dose of medicine or something sweet like ice cream."

Needing ice cream quickly hardly sounded serious. Whenever Keisha showed worrisome symptoms, the Merritts acted as if it was a life-threatening emergency, which made me feel left out. On the other hand, Luke was so happy to be with me again, he shadowed me. When I wanted privacy in the bathroom, I had to kick his shoe out from the door. "Luke," I wailed, "stop pestering me!"

At mealtimes he sometimes pinched me under the table. I would jump and he would laugh, annoying the Merritts. He was worst at bedtime.

"Brush your teeth right now or you'll get a time-out," I warned. He made a raspberry, spitting toothpaste all over the mirror. I tried to wipe it with toilet paper, but I only smeared it more.

Mrs. Merritt took me aside. "Luke is your brother, not your child." She used a teacher's voice. "Do you understand?" I shrugged. "It means that I will tell him when he has to do things and what the consequences for not doing them are."

"But he only listens to me!"

"Was he listening to you in the bathroom?" Mrs. Merritt studied my face to see if I had accepted her point. She tilted her head from side to side as if she knew about my force field and was trying to find a way to penetrate it.

"Obviously not," I said to appease her, but she was wrong. If this did not work out, they could move us someplace worse and probably separate us again. *My* job was to see that that did not happen. *She* was the one who could pick up the phone at any moment and ask that either one of us be taken away. I crossed my arms and stared back.

"Now do you understand?"

"Yes, ma'am," I said to get her off my back.

"Okay, now you can have your bath."

I grinned. Ever since the disgusting baths at the Mosses' and the quick showers at Lake Mag, my idea of heaven was soaking in a tub of fresh, bubbly water. Mrs. Merritt shook her head. "I've never seen a child who liked a bath as much as you do."

A week after I moved in with the Merritts, we traveled to Michigan to attend Leah's college graduation from Andrews University. I admired the long expanses of lawns mown in precise lines and the huge, graceful trees. Leah, Betsy, and their friends looked like models in shampoo commercials. Best of all, we were treated as if we belonged in their family.

Still, I knew I did not fit into their world, which was governed by ritual and prayer. If we were good on their Sabbath, we were rewarded with an ice-cream or a Disney video.

"What are you doing?" Luke asked after church.

I was trying to do my required reading and ignored him. He reached for the cover. As I held the book behind my head so he could not get it, something boiled up inside me and I grabbed the back of his head and yanked his hair. He ran sobbing into Mrs. Merritt's arms.

"Why did you do that?" she asked me.

"He was being a jerk!"

"We don't talk like that in this house," Mrs. Merritt said.

"Why don't you just get rid of me?" I blurted. "I hate it here anyway!" It would be easier if they threw me out before I really wanted to stay. Why had I allowed myself to relax? My nails had even grown out, and Mrs. Merritt had complimented me on them. I deliberately bit them off one by one.

By now I was accustomed to all sorts of workers coming to visit us in our various foster homes. I resented Lena Jamison because she had taken me away from Adele, and it still irked me that Miles Ferris had robbed me of my possessions. After all, he was the one who transferred me to the Moss home in the first place, so he knew how many clothes and toys I came with, plus he had seen my mother give me the Easy-Bake oven and yet pretended it didn't exist. Although I sulked about my toys, my darkest moods erupted when I realized that Miles Ferris should have taken me away from the Mosses when the investigators found out that some of us were being abused. He should have known that Mrs. Moss made me say that I was lying. And if he didn't want to believe me, he should have trusted the teachers who called the hotline so many times. I could not understand how anyone could take me away from my loving relatives and make me live with strangers who were mostly indifferent and sometimes brutal.

I no longer had faith in any of the caseworkers. So when Mary Miller stopped by to check on Keisha when I was visiting Luke at the Merritts' shortly before I moved in, I assumed she was just another one and ignored her. She was dressed in tailored slacks and a crisp blouse. Her blond hair was precision cut, and her jewelry was subdued yet elegant. She looked more like a Ralph Lauren model than a child welfare worker. She was polite to me, and I liked her serene smile.

"We've wondered why Keisha has a guardian, while these kids"—Mrs. Merritt indicated Luke and me—"who've already been in foster care for five years, don't."

"There aren't enough of us to go around," Mary Miller explained. "Babies, especially those who are medically needy, are at the top of the list."

"Ashley shouldn't have been mingling with those tough teens at Lake Mag," Mrs. Merritt grumbled, "and this boy needs services he isn't getting."

"I'll talk with my coordinator and see if she will appoint me to their case."

The next time I saw Mary Miller, I'd been living with Luke at the Merritts' for a couple of weeks. She crouched next to me and said, "I'm your Guardian ad Litem."

"Is that like a guardian angel?" I asked.

Luke looked up from his toy cars on the carpet. "Do you have wings?"

"Sorry, no," she said with a throaty laugh. Noticing my cynical look, she added quickly, "I'm also not a caseworker. I will represent your best interests in court."

I diverted my stare to the wall and made no pretense that I was paying attention to her. "What can I do for you?" she inquired. Until then, *nobody* had ever asked me that question.

"Nothing." I shrugged.

"Let me know if you think of something later." Mary Miller straightened her back.

"Wait! Can you get my Easy-Bake oven and my Barbie radio?"

"I can't buy you things."

"My mother gave them to me."

"Ashley arrived with almost nothing," Mrs. Merritt explained. "Her brother didn't come with any toys either, although he claims he had a helicopter."

"I can try to retrieve those for you. Anything else?"

"I've been in foster care my whole life!" I sighed. "If I could only be with my mother, everything would be wonderful." I gave her my most winsome smile.

"You want to be with your mother," Mary repeated to be certain she had it right.

"Yes, but she doesn't always come to visit when she says she will. I don't think anyone helps her. Could you?"

I was always hungry for anyone to give me one-on-one attention, so I was pleased when Mrs. Merritt took me aside one day. "You're going to visit your mother today, but Luke will stay home." She closed her eyes for a moment. "Can you be a big girl and not mention it to him so he doesn't feel left out?"

"I know that he doesn't belong to her anymore." I tried to make myself sound mature, but there was a tinge of bragging in my voice because my mother wanted me and not him.

I was dressed and waiting for Miles Ferris at the appointed time, but he was late. When the phone rang, I heard Mrs. Merritt say, "Yes, Miles. I understand." My heart thudded with every syllable. "I'll tell her." Obviously, my mother was canceling again.

Mrs. Merritt came into the living room shaking her head. "Can you imagine? Your mother and Mary Miller are waiting on you, but Miles forgot to pick you up. He's on his way now."

When I arrived at the visit, I flew into my mother's arms. "I thought you forgot about me!" I was on the verge of tears.

"That man didn't arrange for someone to bring you here." My mother stared accusingly at Mr. Ferris.

I pouted. "You *said* you would be back soon, and it's been weeks and weeks."

"I had to go to South Carolina for a bit," she cooed. "There are a lot of arrangements to be made, Sunshine, but you'll be living with us soon."

My mother introduced me to Deputy Sheriff Babette Burke and her son, Drew. "This is my roommate."

I noticed Mary Miller in the background. Her expression was not as composed as when she visited us at the Merritt home; in fact, she seemed aggravated by something—probably the fact that I'd arrived late, although it had not been my fault.

"I brought you a present." My mother handed me a jewelry box inlaid with flowers and a little clock. "It's a music box." She wound the key.

I opened the lid expecting to hear "You Are My Sunshine." Some other tune tinkled out. "What's that song?"

"It's by some famous composer," she said lamely. "I wanted to get 'You Are My Sunshine,' but they didn't have it."

I stroked the polished lid. "That's okay." I slipped into my mother's lap. She caressed my arm as the music box played each tinny note increasingly slower. My eyes began to sting. I pressed my face against my mother's chest and sobbed. The final plink of the tune was suspended in the air expectantly, waiting for the next note that would never come. Something else had ended midsong. Nobody in that room knew what I sensed: that I would never see my mother again.

In the early days I thought that Mary Miller was just a well-mannered woman who checked on our progress. Behind the scenes, though, she became our champion, and it would be years before I realized everything she had accomplished on Luke's and my behalf. It would be years, too, before I understood that she had always kept my best interests in mind, even if I wouldn't have agreed with her decisions at the time.

Mary reviewed our legal, criminal, medical, and psychological records. She was aghast that we had been in legal limbo for so long and thought that five years should have been plenty of time for my mother to get her act together. Mary was suspicious of my mother because Lorraine claimed she had held a job for more than a month, but Mary learned that it had lasted for one day. My mother also claimed to be sober, yet she had tested positive for cocaine right after my last visit with her.

I would have been horrified if I had known that two days after I received the music box, Mary Miller wrote Mr. Ferris requesting that parental contact be stopped altogether. She also asked the Florida Department of Children and Families' lawyers to begin termination proceedings for Dusty Grover's rights to Luke and my mother's rights to me.

Dealing with my mother was a legal chore, but Mary met her match in Marjorie Moss. Like an ambassador to a hostile foreign country, my Guardian ad Litem was educated, elegant, and intimidating; however, Mrs. Moss ruled her fiefdom with an iron fist. So far, no brat or bureaucrat had ever been able to outsmart her. At first Mary had not been sure whom to believe about the goings-on in the Moss household. Mrs. Merritt was convinced that the Mosses had been abusive, but the foster care supervisor said the Mosses were model foster parents who even taught the training classes for other foster parents. The caseworker blamed my problems on my mother, claiming that I did not start my "false accusations" until after she had renewed her visitations.

When Mary stopped by the department's office, someone pointed out Mrs. Moss. Mary marched right up to her and asked for my possessions. Mary offered to drive out to Plant City to pick them up that afternoon. Mrs. Moss said she was busy that day but agreed to give them to Miles Ferris.

"When can I visit my mom?" I pestered Mr. Ferris when I saw him at the Merritts'.

"That's not a good idea right now," he responded.

"Why?" I demanded. "Aren't you supposed to take me for monthly visits?"

"Actually, the judge is going to decide that," Mr. Ferris said, and went to play with Luke, who did not ask tough questions.

The Merritts took me to see Dr. Flanders, another

doctor who asked me how I was feeling. I shrugged. "Are you happy? Sad? Angry?"

"I'm fine."

"Tell me about your father."

"I don't have one, except Dusty, who is really only Luke's father."

"What's he like?"

"He steals and he tried to murder my mother twice."

"What about your mother?"

"I love her more than anything in the world. And I don't see why I can't be with her. She has a house now and she's waiting for me."

"Does waiting make you angry?" he asked.

I stared him down. "It makes me tired."

School kept my mind off my worries most of the time. The Merritts enrolled us at the Seventh-day Adventist Academy. I liked this private school with its small classes, where I received a lot of attention from Ms. Holback. Because Luke had been so disruptive, he had to repeat kindergarten, and he continued to bother me whenever he felt the need to quell his anxieties.

Why didn't anyone realize that Luke was the problem? I would ask myself. If it were not for him, I would be with my mother. I believed it was my responsibility to stick with him no matter what, yet I resented the fact that I had to give up what was dearest to me because I was all that he had. Whenever the authorities separated us, I would be slightly relieved, but then the worry over how he was doing would only add to my anxieties. I was better off knowing he was okay rather than imagining that another Mrs. Moss might be abusing him. All my life—even today—I've wondered how to balance my responsibilities to him with my need to look out for myself.

The Merritts led an orderly life that I found comforting. We prayed before meals and attended Saturday services at the Tampa First Seventh-day Adventist Church. Saturday nights we had popcorn and movies. Television was restricted, but they had a large collection of approved videos.

"Are you going to get a pumpkin for Halloween?" I asked Mrs. Merritt when I saw some at an outdoor stand.

"We don't believe in doing that," she replied.

"Do you celebrate birthdays?" I asked anxiously, since mine was approaching.

"Of course," Mrs. Merritt promised.

When we were getting ready for bed, I became annoyed because Luke kept running into my room. The third time I punched him. He ran sobbing to Mrs. Merritt. A few days later she took me to a nurse-practitioner, who listened to my yearnings for my mother.

"Some medication for depression might help her," the nurse suggested.

"I have to ask her caseworker to sign the medical forms," Mrs. Merritt replied.

I overheard some angry phone calls. "Either I get them some help or I can't keep them both," Mrs. Merritt told Mr. Ferris.

I also overheard her conversation with Mary Miller. "Yes, Mary, I agree. Lake Mag would be bad even on a temporary basis. . . ." I tensed like violin strings tuned to the highest note. "No, not an emergency . . . of course she needs to say good-bye this time."

"Ashley, today will be your last day at school," Mrs. Merritt warned me before dropping me off. I did not need any further explanation.

Ms. Holback had arranged a little farewell party and gave me a card saying, *It has been a joy to have you in my class. Although I will miss you, I'm so excited about you getting ready for adoption. We will keep you in our prayers. We love you.* Each of my classmates had added a smiley-face sticker and signed it.

When I arrived home, I found that Mrs. Merritt had packed everything I owned. "I don't want to be adopted!" I snapped. "I want to go back to my mother."

"That may not be God's plan for you."

"Is L-Luke coming too?"

"No. He's making progress here."

"I can make progress," I choked.

Later that afternoon Mr. Merritt drove me to Violet Chavez's home in Riverview, about thirty miles southeast of Tampa. After leaving the highway, we crossed the Alafia River, passed some strawberry fields, then turned into a shaded lane where a long driveway led to a yellow house surrounded by towering trees. Mr. Merritt carried in my trash bags and left them piled in the hallway. After a few awkward minutes he left.

"Welcome, my dear!" called Violet Chavez.

Ethnic masks lined the walls and artificial floral arrangements filled the shadows. My gaze fell on a pumpkin decoration. "Do you celebrate Halloween?" I asked.

"Of course," Violet Chavez replied. "Do you have a costume?"

"No. The Merritts don't believe in Halloween."

Madeline, Mrs. Chavez's teenage daughter, gestured with her hands. "Look at that red hair! Don't you think she'd be the perfect Annie?"

"We'll have the dress made," Mrs. Chavez said. "And we'll curl her hair."

"Or get a wig," Madeline suggested. "Would you like that?"

Annie! Wow! *I think I'm going to like it here,* I said to myself, and started dragging my plastic bags down the hallway to my new bedroom.

"Come, help me make dinner," Mrs. Chavez called in a musical accent.

I sat on a stool and asked, "Where are you from?"

"Many places," she replied. "Like you, I have had several families."

She browned some onions, then rubbed a big nut on a grater. "What's that?"

"Nutmeg. It grows on Grenada, the island where I was born." The fragrant steam was more exotic than anything from the Merritts' kitchen. "How old are you?" she asked as she added chicken pieces.

"Almost nine. My birthday's next month."

"When I was your age, my mother went to another island."

"Did you miss her?"

"Yes, very much." Mrs. Chavez poured some dry rice into a pot and added water.

When it was ready, she called the others to the table.

Two of Mrs. Chavez's children—Madeline, eighteen, and Mario, sixteen—were still at home. Her eldest daughter, Mercedes, was away at college. Everyone seemed to talk loudly and at once.

"Is everything okay?" Madeline asked when she saw me pushing my food around.

"Yes," I said meekly. "I was just wondering what the rules are here."

"We respect each other," Mrs. Chavez said. "We don't go outside without permission; we keep our room and belongings tidied up."

"What about food?"

"Nobody goes hungry in my house."

When Mrs. Chavez started to clear the table, I carried my plate into the kitchen.

"Thank you, Ashley," she said. "I appreciate your help."

"Oh, it will be great around here for the first few weeks. I'll be very polite and sweet. After that, everything will go downhill and you will send me away."

"Why is that?" Mrs. Chavez asked.

"Because that's how it always happens."

Violet Chavez tilted her head. "We'll see."

She enrolled me in third grade at Boyette Springs Elementary School. Because I was excellent at jump rope, the "in" sport at the time, I made friends quickly. My teacher, Mrs. Lovelace, sent me to take some tests in the guidance office. Eventually, a letter arrived saying that I had been accepted to a magnet school for gifted children.

When I found out that Mrs. Chavez had accidentally left the letter at the salon where she worked as a manicurist, I was livid. "You go find that letter right away!" I ordered.

"Don't disrespect me!" Mrs. Chavez replied sternly.

"But I *have* to go to that school or my life will be *ruined*!"

"That's for your caseworker to decide."

Violet Chavez went all out for my ninth birthday. She baked a Barbie cake with a skirt of pink and blue icing and wrote *Happy Birthday Ashley* in loopy script. This was the first birthday party I had ever had.

After the meal there were organized games. Madeline filled water balloons to toss and handed out raw eggs, which we kids were going to pass under our chins. One of the girls, a blonde named Amelia, was wearing a plaid dress. When it came time for the outside games, Amelia complained, "I can't get my dress dirty."

"You can borrow something of Ashley's." Mrs. Chavez loaned her the striped shirt that had had the buttons torn off at Lake Mag.

"You can't wear that," I snarled. "My mother gave it to me."

"Don't be a party pooper." Madeline tossed me a water balloon.

I knew the Chavezes were trying to make me feel welcome, yet I also knew the day would come when their hospitality would end suddenly and I would find my stuff in garbage bags again.

I had been living at the Chavez home for only a few days when Mary Miller called to check on me. Mario answered the phone and told her that his mother was running errands.

"Hi, Ashley. How are you?" Mary asked when he put me on the phone.

"Good. I like it here."

"When's Mrs. Chavez coming back?" Her voice was tense.

"Oh, soon." I answered her questions as quickly as I could because one of my favorite television shows, *Full House*, was on. Later I learned she complained that a teenage boy was supervising me, which was against regulations.

After school I attended day care at L'il Ranchers. I didn't like it because I did not know anyone and there was no point in trying to make new friends when I moved so often.

I was sitting motionless on a swing when I looked up and saw Mary Miller coming my way with long, purposeful strides. She took the empty seat beside me. "How high can you go?" she asked.

I kept my eyes on the clouds as I pumped back and forth so I could avoid anything I did not want to see or hear. I gave one-word answers to her inquiries about school.

When she paused, I asked the only question that mattered: "When am I going to live with my mother again?"

"You aren't going to." Her voice was both tender and firm.

"Why?" The word felt like a pebble lodged in my throat.

"Because she can't take care of you."

"Ever?" came out in a frog's croak.

"No, Ashley, not ever."

I kicked the hollow of dirt under the swing without daring to look down. "Then, who will?"

"We will find a family who wants to care for you forever."

I twisted in my seat. "What about Luke?"

"We will find a family who wants both of you."

"When is that going to happen?"

"I don't know," Mary replied. "But it *will* happen." I pushed harder with my foot, kicking up dust. "What sort of family would you like?" Mary asked.

Until that moment, I had never allowed myself any dream other than going home with my mother. The breeze caught my hair as I pumped the swing higher. After a few long arcs, I braked hard with both feet. I thought for a moment, then swiveled my seat to face Mary. "I want a big house with two stories, lion statues to guard the front door, and a bedroom that I don't have to share with anyone. I want a canopy bed and a hammock for lots of stuffed animals. I want all my dolls back and even more and lots of clothes for them and for me. And dogs, including a female who has puppies, so I can have one of my own."

"What about Luke?"

"Oh, he can come too, but he has to live in the doghouse."

"What sort of parents do you want?"

"I don't care, as long as they are not like the Mosses."

A worker took me to see Dr. Wolfe, a psychiatrist, who asked the same questions the other doctors had. Once again, the diploma seal over the doctor's left shoulder made for a good visual target. I did not care if he knew I was not looking at him, because even if I said I knew the difference between truth and lies, he would not believe me. When he asked whether I had ever been abused, I said I had not, since I knew he wasn't going to do anything even if I told him about the Mosses.

"What do you do when you feel sad?" he asked.

"I read my Bible." I thought the Merritts would have liked that answer.

"When was your saddest time?" he asked.

"When they told me I couldn't see my mother anymore."

"What do you want to do now?" he queried.

"I want to wear high heels!" I said to change the subject.

"What do you want to be when you grow up?"

"A nurse, an artist, and a poet."

"And if you had three wishes, what might they be?"

"To be with my mother, to live in a decent home, and to have plenty to eat."

That seemed to satisfy him, because I never had to see him again.

The rituals I had learned in the prim Seventh-day Adventist service were completely different from the way people worshipped at Mass at the Resurrection Catholic Church, which had a red neon sign and crucifix out front. As soon as we entered the church, we dipped our fingers in holy water and made the sign of the cross. I kept mixing up which shoulder to touch first. When we got to the pew, Madeline reminded me: "Forehead, heart, left shoulder, right shoulder, hands together."

There was a lot of standing, then kneeling on the padded rail. I soon learned the Hail Mary. Mostly, I was bored and my mind wandered. I focused on the Virgin Mary statue's stone-eyed stare and wondered what secret message she might be trying to send me. Both my mother and the Holy Virgin had been teen mothers, so that meant my mother was not all bad. Mary was also the name of my Guardian ad Litem. Maybe Mary Miller *was* an angel and God did have a plan for me, like Mrs. Merritt had said.

I asked Madeline's friend Kyle why some people prayed on Saturday and others on Sunday. "They're both celebrating the Sabbath, they just interpret which day it is differently," he responded.

"Wouldn't people like each other better if everyone went to the same church?"

Kyle laughed. "You're going to grow up to become either the president or a bomb-maker."

Mercedes came home for Christmas, and other relatives gathered at the Chavez house. My pile of presents was the largest it had been since being with Adele and Grandpa, although there was nothing from my mother. I received the Polly Pocket pizzeria I had wanted, but I could not enjoy the commotion. The family often spoke in Spanish—sometimes purposefully when they didn't want me to know what was going on. They referred to various saint's days that had significance to members of the family, but none related to me. They didn't seem concerned about spending hours lying in the sun, because their olive skin only burnished and became more radiant, while mine either freckled or fried. They hugged one another at each hello or good-bye, but since they knew I didn't like to be touched, they avoided me. I was an outsider by race, religion, culture—and blood.

Even so, Madeline often went out of her way to be kind. She knew I hated after-school day care. If her community-college classes were finished early, she would pick me up before her mother got home from the nail salon in Tampa. During strawberry season Madeline would stop at a farm stand and buy me my own pint of juicy berries.

I was sitting on the kitchen stool eating some fresh berries when the phone rang. "Oh, hello," Mrs. Chavez said in the higher-octave voice she reserved for her nail clients. She turned to me. "Ashley, one of your foster mothers wants you to spend the weekend. Would you like to go?"

I thought it was Mrs. Merritt. "I guess," I said, because I had not seen Luke since Christmas vacation.

"She'd love to come, Mrs. Moss," Violet Chavez replied. I shook my head vehemently and mouthed *No!* but she ignored me. "Okay, I'll have her ready for Miles in the morning."

"That's the horrible lady who was mean to us!"

"She sounds very nice, and she said her daughter is anxious to see you again."

"I won't go!"

"I think your brother is there."

"Luke is with the Merritts."

"He left their home right after Christmas."

"Mary Miller would never have allowed him to go back to the Mosses!"

Madeline came in the kitchen. "What's up, Mom?"

"Ashley has been invited to visit one of her old foster families." Mrs. Chavez smiled slyly. "Maybe we'll go to Disney for the weekend while she's gone."

I ran to my room and slammed the door. So, this was their way of getting rid of me! I did not mind leaving—what else was new?—but how could they send me back to that witch, who, in my nightmares, baked her for-show cookies out of foster children.

In the morning Mrs. Chavez handed me Mario's gym duffel. "This should be all you need for one night."

One night! I felt reprieved. I tossed my oldest clothes in the bag, just in case the Mosses decided to keep any of my outfits.

Mr. Ferris tried to be friendly, but I scowled the whole way there. I had one bright thought: I might be able to get back my dolls, radio, and Easy-Bake oven. As I started spotting recognizable landmarks, I felt as though I were watching an all-too-familiar horror movie, but the creepy scenes still made me jump. The Mosses' mailbox was overgrown with an even heavier layer of bottle green lichen than before. The trees draped in Spanish moss were even spookier, the brambly bushes thicker, the hairy vines more twisted. The trailer was seedier than I remembered, and the babies' play area was a mucky mess. The smell of wet cow and pig manure permeated my pores. I had returned to hell.

"See you Sunday," Mr. Ferris said heartily. As soon as I shut the car door, he sped off. If I had not kept my bag on my lap for the ride, he would have left with it.

I took a deep breath, walked up the cement steps, and knocked on the off-kilter screen door. Mrs. Moss peered over my head. "Did Miles leave already?" she asked in the silvery tone she used to charm caseworkers.

"Yes, ma'am," I responded with a quavering voice.

"Too bad. I baked a treat for him." She stepped outside. "Ashley, I want to ask you one question." She was still talking in the phony cadence, but her gaze was steely.

"Remember all those nasty things you said about us? They weren't true, *right*?"

I squirmed and tried to find a point to steady my gaze, but my eyes blurred. My pulse pounded. I had not been so fearful since the last time I had been there. Was an investigator in the house waiting for me to change my story again? Even if one was not, Mrs. Moss could do whatever she wanted to me for the next two days. I would not give her the satisfaction of falsely apologizing aloud, so I stared at the doorsill and shook my head.

"Good, I didn't think so. Come on in and get settled. It'll be just like old times."

Nothing much had changed in more than a year, although the rooms seemed smaller and more cluttered. The air still smelled of wet cigarettes and ammonia. As if they were a part of the décor, punished children faced each corner. Mr. Moss was planted in his recliner, smoking and staring at the television screen.

Mandy came around the corner shyly. "Hi," she said. Her face was thinner and her hair was wispy.

"Would you girls like some milk and cookies?" Mrs. Moss asked.

I was caught off guard. Maybe she was going to treat me like a guest so I would report that everything was fine. Mandy, who was even more skittish than I remembered, was reluctant to sit at the table, but in a few minutes we were enjoying the snack.

I looked around. Mandy's brother, Toby, was still there, as were Lucy and Clare, who occupied two of the corners.

"Where's Luke?" I asked.

"Oh, that *guardian* of yours didn't like him staying here,

so they took him to some *shelter*." Mrs. Moss's raspy tone had returned in full force.

"Lake Mag?" I worried that Luke would get picked on in that rough-and-tumble place.

"They don't tell me those things." Mrs. Moss went to watch television.

I passed Mandy my last cookie, and she smiled in gratitude. "We don't have time-outs where I live now," I boasted.

"You're lucky," Mandy murmured.

Mrs. Moss jumped out of her seat as if she had sat on a hot coil. She grabbed Mandy's arm and pinched it hard. "Remember, Mandy, you're mine now, and I can beat the shit out of you anytime I want."

"Yes, ma'am," Mandy said. Panic creased her face, and she looked more like a frightened old lady than a girl of ten.

"Take Ashley to the new girls' room," Mrs. Moss ordered. "I need to keep my eyes on these bad children." She flicked her multi-ringed fingers on the shoulder of the kid in the closest corner. He twitched, then resumed his position.

Trembling slightly, I slung Mario's gym bag over my shoulder and started down the hall to the girls' room. Mandy indicated the other direction. We walked out the sliding glass door and into the shed where we used to pick out clothes. It had been converted into another bedroom. The Little Mermaid sheets were the same, and I wondered when they had last been washed. Mandy said that I could have the top bunk next to hers. "They took the safety rails off," she pointed out. "The rules are different because we're adopted now."

"I hope they don't want to adopt me!" I blurted.

After a better-than-average meal of spaghetti and fruit salad, I changed into my pajamas. I thought I had put my toothbrush in one of the gym bag's side pockets. When I fumbled for it, I pulled out a small foil square that had a transparent back. Inside was a hard rubber ring with a slippery center. "Look what I found." I showed it to Mandy.

"Open it," she prodded with a giggle.

I ripped the package. "Ick! Why is it so gooey?"

"It's for boys!" Mandy said. "You shouldn't have opened it."

"You told me to!"

"You'd better hide it," Mandy warned.

"You never get in trouble for telling the truth," I said, parroting Mrs. Merritt.

Mandy lurked in the shadows as I approached the house. "Ma'am," I said to Mrs. Moss as I interrupted the television show. "I found something that didn't belong to me and opened it by mistake." I handed her the flaccid tube.

Mrs. Moss's eyes almost exploded. "Where did you get a condom?"

So, this was a condom! The Lake Mag girls had mentioned them, yet I had never seen one. I made sure to stare directly in her eye so she would believe me. "I found it in my bag and wanted to see what it was."

"If it wasn't yours, why did you open it?" She saw Mandy slinking in the doorway. "Mandy, did you have anything to do with this?"

"Ashley just showed it to me," Mandy's voice wavered.

"You haven't changed a bit, Ashley Rhodes." Mrs. Moss shook her head as if writing me off. "Throw that in the trash and go to bed. If I hear another word, I'm separating you two."

I was happy to comply. The sooner I fell asleep, the sooner Sunday would come and I could leave. I was not really even angry with Mandy, who had urged me to open it and then lied to save her skin. She had to do what was necessary to survive.

When Mr. Ferris arrived the next day, the condom was in a plastic bag. Mrs. Moss waved it at him as evidence. "She brought it on purpose!" Mrs. Moss said with disgust. "She showed everyone how it's used—even the little ones!" Her tone changed to phony concern. "That child needs help. You know the first thing she told me when she arrived? She said, 'I'm sorry I caused you so much trouble by telling those lies about you.' Then she comes into my home and throws this in my face!"

Mr. Ferris was gruff with me. "Get your stuff and get in the car."

I ducked under Mr. Ferris's arm and into his musty-smelling car. As he started the motor, I looked at the shed where I knew my toys were stored, but I did not dare ask about them.

Neither of us spoke until we were almost at Mrs. Chavez's. "Ashley," Mr. Ferris said sternly, "the most important part of someone's character is being honest. Nobody likes a liar. You keep getting in trouble with these behaviors."

"Where's Luke?" I asked.

"He's at Joshua House."

"Is that a foster home?"

"No, a shelter."

"When can I see him?"

"I'll try to arrange a visit with him next week."

Poor Lukie, I thought. But this time, at least, he had Mary Miller watching out for him.

When I returned from my overnight at the Mosses', I asked Madeline if she brought me anything from Disney World.

"We never went," Madeline said. "We were only teasing you."

That spring Vivian, a foster child who was slightly younger than me, moved in and slept on a cot in Mrs. Chavez's room. Mrs. Chavez mentioned that Vivian was "free for adoption," which sounded like she was a kitten being given away at the flea market. Mary Miller had said something about me being adopted, yet adoption had trapped Mandy in the Moss family, where she could be punished as much as they wanted without anyone checking. I did not want that to happen to me. Still, when I overheard Mrs. Chavez say that Vivian would fit in with their family, I was jealous. Vivian was African American, and I was the only white person in the house. Even if I wanted to stay, they would not keep me. No matter how hard I tried, I would never be chosen by them—or anyone.

Until Mary Miller took our case, the legal issues concerning Luke and me had been neglected for years and were in violation of all the laws that were supposed to either return children to their parents or come up with another permanent family. First, she finished clearing Luke for adoption, then she started working on getting me relinquished as well. She took the necessary steps to deal with my unknown father's rights, but my mother refused to give me up. Because Mary suspected that my mother was still using drugs, she had convinced the judge to halt our visits, but if my mother tested clean, reunification was still possible.

At a crucial court hearing my mother brought proof that she had completed rehab. Still, Mary Miller was suspicious. She asked the judge to order one final screening. Maybe my mother had celebrated her rehab graduation prematurely and knew what the result of another test would be. In any case, she refused to take the drug test and signed a paper for the termination of her parental rights to me instead. Judge Giglio wrote in his order that it was "manifestly in the best interest of said child for the mother's parental rights to be terminated" and that the state was to receive permanent commitment of said child and "place said child in an adoptive home."

Mrs. Chavez always looked the other way when I talked about my mother, and none of my caseworkers answered any questions about when my next visit would be. Although Mary Miller tried to explain that I would never live with my mother again, she had avoided telling me that I would never see her either. I suppose she realized that I couldn't handle everything at once—and she was right. Still, I knew something was different. I sensed that something had changed. Until the court papers were finalized, there had been a chance that the tides would reverse, the world would stop spinning, and I would be my mother's Sunshine again. Until the judge signed the documents, everything else had been temporary. Once the judge ruled, I was an orphan. I had no parents, and no possibilities were in sight.

8

Campus for crazy kids

My transfer to The Children's Home of Tampa was my thirteenth move in the seven years I had been in foster care. Mary Miller told me I would be able to live with Luke again and promised I could finish third grade at Boyette Springs, which made me feel slightly better, but I still didn't want to leave the Chavezes' because I was afraid the home might be far worse.

My new caseworker, Dixie Elmer, talked up the new place as though it were a magical kingdom, but it sounded more like Lake Mag than Disney World. During the entrance tests, they gave me some sentences to complete. After *I am afraid . . .* , I wrote: *I will never see my mother again;* and after *My mother . . .* , I added: *is on drugs.* After *My father . . .* , I answered: *I really don't know my father.* Finally, beside *I need my parents . . .* , I finished with: *when I'm alone, feeling blue, and need someone.*

"And what if you had three wishes?" the intake worker asked.

I scanned the room and settled on a stuffed tiger to stare at. "I would like to be with my mother, be very well educated, and have enough money to support my family, if I ever have one."

I must have passed, because I moved to The Children's Home in June. I carried a blue box. Its lid was stamped TIFFANY & CO. At Christmas, Mrs. Chavez had been thrilled to receive a vase that was bought from that store. When I knew I was leaving, I asked for the box to hold my precious possessions, and Mrs. Chavez had given it grudgingly. Ms. Elmer lugged the garbage bags stuffed with my clothes into the administration building. A grandmotherly woman with a sweet smile spoke into the phone at the front desk. "Ashley has arrived," she announced.

I heard the click of high heels approaching. A formidable woman dressed in a long skirt held out her hand. "My name is Beth Reese. I'm the director of treatment services," she said to the caseworker, then nodded to me. "You can call me 'Ms. Beth.'"

She turned to someone who had come up more quietly in sneakers. "This is Ms. Sandnes. She'll be your primary." The other woman, who looked like a college student, wore an inside-out sweatshirt, and she had combed her blond hair into a taut ponytail.

"Hi, Sandra," said Ms. Elmer, mistaking my primary's name.

"It's spelled S-A-N-D-N-E-S. The 'd' is silent, so it's pronounced 'San-ness.'" She wrinkled her nose toward me. "I know, it's weird."

"Let me show you around," Ms. Sandnes said. She reached for my box, and I reluctantly let her have it. "Don't worry, Ms. Margy will watch over your stuff."

Ms. Sandnes led the way down the hallway and poked her head in an open door. A man waved. "Welcome, Ashley." At the far end of his office three boys were tossing a foam ball into the hoop above the window.

The tallest boy called out, "Where's she going to live?"

"Lykes Cottage," Ms. Sandnes replied, "with your brothers."

"How long have they lived here?" I asked as we continued down the hall.

"Three, maybe four years."

"How long will I be here?"

"Probably a year—maybe more, maybe less. Most of our children either go home to their families or are adopted."

"Could I go home to my mother?"

Ms. Sandnes bit her lip as she decided what to say. "In your case, no." She checked her watch. "I want to get you settled in before dinner."

When it was time to return to the reception area, I hurried back. Ms. Margy was locking the door to her office. "Nobody touched your stuff." Her eyes twinkled like the fairy godmother's in *Cinderella*.

As we walked across the quad, Ms. Sandnes pointed out the six coed cottages, each housing twelve children, which were spaced around a circular drive. She indicated the building next to the playground. "That's Conn Cottage. Your brother will live there with the younger children," Ms. Sandnes said. "You're going to be in Lykes with me. Our cottage has later bedtimes and more privileges."

Children of all ages, sizes, and colors zoomed by on bikes. "I had a bike at the Chavezes', but they told me I couldn't have one here."

"Of course you can. We'll borrow one from storage for you, and then we'll ask your caseworker to retrieve your bike from Mrs. Chavez."

"Oh, caseworkers never get your stuff. Ask Mary Miller, she's my guardian."

When we arrived at Lykes, several children were climbing into a white van. A man helped the smallest one up. Ms. Sandnes beamed at him. "Ashley, this is Mr. Todd; he's one of the staff in our cottage."

"I'm taking a couple of families to the movies tonight." A few more kids clustered around him like chicks to a hen. He winked at Ms. Sandnes and me. "See you later, Ashley-gator."

"Is he cool?" I asked her.

"Oh, very. Ours is the coolest cottage on campus."

I followed Ms. Sandnes inside. On one end of the entrance hall there was a *Lion King* poster. Well-worn couches and comfy chairs filled the room on the right, where some kids were watching television. There was also an empty aquarium.

"Why aren't there any fish?"

"Someone poured juice in the tank and it killed them," she explained.

A man, who was taking notes, glanced up. "Hey! I'm Mr. Irvin," he said. "Welcome!" A few kids were eating at the kitchen table. "Are you hungry?" he asked. "We're having a pack-out dinner tonight, so you can eat whenever you want."

Pack-out? Primary? Families? What language were they speaking?

"We'll get her settled first," Ms. Sandnes answered for me.

She led me to my bedroom. "Are you nervous?" She did not wait for a response. "Well, I am. I'll let you in on a secret. I've never been a primary before."

On top of my bed was a new bed-in-a-bag, with Pocahontas sheets, pillowcase, and coverlet. "What do you mean by 'family' and 'primary'?" I asked.

While we made the bed, she explained that "primary" was short for "primary caregiver." Every primary had several children in his or her "family." Families engaged in at least one fun event a week, like going to a movie or bowling.

"Do you live here?"

"No, I have a shift, but I'm usually here from two in the afternoon until bedtime."

I showed her the music box my mother gave me. Ms. Sandnes said, "This is very precious, isn't it?" I nodded. "Let's put it on the tip-top shelf in your closet."

It did not take long to organize my meager possessions. "Are you ready to eat?" Ms. Sandnes asked.

"Pack-out" did not sound very appetizing. "I don't think so."

"Well, I am," she said. "Let's see what they brought over from the caf."

I followed her into the kitchen. She lifted the foil on some pans. "There's fried chicken, baked beans, coleslaw, and peaches. Want me to make you a plate?"

"I'm kind of picky."

"Me too."

"I don't like chicken on the bone."

"I can cut it off."

"I don't want anything touching."

"You can have separate plates."

Was she always this nice, or was this just how they treated a new kid? I wondered. She and I sat at one end of the long table. The food was not hot, but it was tasty.

"Would you like to take your shower early?" she asked. "It takes a long time for all the showers."

"Why?"

"We have a lot of rules here, but they are for your privacy and safety."

She handed me a neon pink bucket containing a fresh tube of toothpaste, a new toothbrush, and a small bottle of shampoo. With a marker, she wrote ASHLEY on the bucket, with fat dots on the ends of the letters. After my shower Ms. Sandnes introduced me to my roommate, Sabrina, who was a year younger than I was.

"Sorry you couldn't go see *Casper* with us," Sabrina said. At first I thought she was rubbing it in, but her wide eyes like black olives made her seem sincere.

Crossing campus the next morning, I heard a familiar voice. Luke, who had just arrived at The Children's Home, ran full speed toward me and flung his arms around my waist. "Mr. Tom!" he called to his new primary from Conn Cottage, "this is my sister!"

"Ouch!" I tried to pry his arms from around me. "Not so tight!"

"Luke!" Mr. Tom called. "Catch!" He tossed a tennis ball and Luke caught it.

"Ever play tennis?" Mr. Tom asked Luke.

"Nope." Luke shook his head.

"We can play after you unpack," Mr. Tom said.

Luke threw the ball in the air, then scampered off with Mr. Tom.

Relieved that I didn't have to worry about him, I followed Sabrina and Daphne, another girl from Lykes Cottage who was a year older than I was and who seemed savvier than Sabrina. We waited by the administration building until Sabrina's therapist came for her. "Therapy sucks," Daphne said.

"Well, I'm not going," I announced as we headed back to the cottage.

"Oh yes you are," she retorted. "It's required."

My therapist was Mary Fernandez, and I found her probing irritating. I planted myself in a seat in her office, crossed my arms, lined my eyes up with a crack in the wall, and braced for the inquisition.

"How are you?" she asked pleasantly.

"Fine."

"How's the cottage?"

"Fine."

"When did you last see your mother?" she asked to stimulate a conversation.

"I don't know."

"You look sad about it." I bit my lip. "Are you angry?" She pointed to a chart that listed feelings. "How about any of those?"

"I don't feel *anything* about it."

"Why?"

"There's nothing I can do anyway, is there?" My voice may have vacillated too much.

"It's normal to miss your mother."

"Maybe I'm not normal." I instantly regretted admitting something was wrong.

"In what other ways do you feel different, Ashley?"

We sat in silence while my session dribbled to an end.

Part of the therapy routine was playing what's called the "Talking, Feeling, and Doing Game." When I landed on blue, for sad, the card might read: *When do you feel sad?*

This was ridiculous. A red space did not mean I was angry or a yellow one that I was happy. The therapist's tricks might work on a dumber kid, but not me. Why should I discuss my mother with anybody when nobody had even given us a chance to say good-bye?

Besides having to endure sessions with Ms. Fernandez, I had family therapy with Luke. Luke was willing to play the games, although he would not follow the rules. The more he fooled around, the more aggravated I became.

When the Merritts heard we were going to The Children's Home, they said they wanted to stay involved in our lives in an honorary "aunt" and "uncle" role. At the end of July, Mr. Bruce, the family therapist, invited the Merritts to Luke's birthday party in the therapy conference room.

At one point Mr. Bruce noticed me sulking. "When's your birthday?"

"November twenty-second."

"We'll have a celebration for you, too," he said.

I groaned. "I've been promised birthdays before that haven't worked out."

To outsiders, the campus seemed like a prep school where adorable children lived in cute cottages and had excellent recreational facilities. Yet each resident had hidden terrors that lurked like sea monsters in the murky bottom of an unfathomable lagoon. Several residents had been raped by family members. Two siblings had had their hands superglued to the wall and then were abandoned by their parents. Another's brother had been starved to death in a closet. Most of the time our personal monsters stayed submerged, even though the constantly undulating water kept us on edge. Every once in a while a creature's tail, fin, or snout would surface as some peculiar behavior.

At night Sabrina screamed out, "Get off me!"

Sometimes I would awaken sobbing, saying that someone had been shot and that blood was everywhere.

Others dealt with their demons differently. Sam would haul off and punch anyone who annoyed him. Leroy's trademark was scratching. Keri was full of surprises. One minute she would be cute as a button, the next she would transform into a raging fiend. She plugged the sinks, turned on the taps full force, and flooded three bathrooms simultaneously. She climbed on dressers, unscrewed lightbulbs, and shoved hangers into the sockets until sparks flew out. Some days she might only stand on a chair and spit on everyone who got in range. Even though Keri was small for her age, she was strong and daring. Trying to flee Mr. Irvin, she jumped on the Ping-Pong table in the rec room. When he tried to grab her, she dove headfirst and split her chin on the table's edge. A few days later she tore off her bandages and plucked out her stitches. When the blood began to flow, she giggled maniacally as she ran around trying to drip blood on as many kids as possible. Keri's weird laugh was a warning. Next, her head would bob a bit and her eyes would take on the intensity of a wild predator. She was as flexible as Gumby, so restraining her was difficult. Once, she twisted around and bit Ms. Sandnes's hand so severely, Ms. Sandnes needed to take antibiotics.

I was excited when a beautician volunteered to give the girls in our cottage manicures. Because I had watched Mrs. Chavez at work, I knew all the procedures. As the manicurist unpacked her tools, I pointed to a tube that looked like an accordion. "That's cuticle remover." I indicated a stone. "And that's a pterygium stone."

"Well, you know a lot!" she said. "Would you like to go first?"

"Why does Ashley get everything first?" Keri screeched.

Keri grabbed a bottle of clear liquid. Before anyone could react, she uncapped it and threw it in my face. The beautician screamed, "That's acetone!"

My eyes felt as if they were on fire. "Help me!"

Ms. Lisa, who worked in the cottage, steered me into the staff bathroom and poured water over my face to flush out the chemical. "Are your eyes okay?"

"I think so." I blinked. "But they're still burning a little."

Ms. Lisa was shaking. "You could have been blinded."

After that, my survival strategy was to mind my own business and stay out of trouble.

As I was having lunch with Sabrina in the dining hall, she nudged me to look in the direction of one of the staff tables. "You know who they are?" I noticed a man and a woman chatting with Mary Fernandez and some Lopez Cottage primaries.

"New staff?" I guessed.

"Shoppers!" Sabrina said under her breath.

"What are they going to buy here?"

"Us." She rolled her eyes. "They're a family looking for a kid. They are pretending they aren't watching us, but see if you can totally tell who they're checking out."

"Nadine?" Sabrina nodded. I asked her, "Have you ever seen anyone who seemed interested in you?"

"Not yet, but I'll know when it happens."

"Me too," I replied with confidence.

I began to pay attention to the mating dance of adoption. The staff told prospective parents something about a child, then permitted them to observe her or him during meals, campus events, sports, or talent shows. Which of the bystanders would I want as parents? My ideal mother would look like Ms. Sandnes, and I would not have minded Mr. Todd or Mr. Irvin for a father. And I wouldn't care if my parents were Caucasian or African American either. I liked the women who wore tailored slacks or shorts, pastel tops, trendy loafers, and quality earrings, like Mary Miller's. The men who dressed in golf shirts with the horse logo seemed the most well-to-do.

If a family picked you, they gave you their album.

Some contained a few snapshots of their house and family members. Others were elaborate scrapbooks depicting trips to Disney or the Grand Canyon and included formal portraits of relatives. I liked the ones that showed every room in their house. After a day or so, you would meet your family and your official period of visitation began. The chosen ones returned from restaurant meals and overnights hand in hand with their new "mom" and "dad." Eventually, they drove off into the sunset with their "forever families"—or so they thought. Many came back. Sometimes it was weeks after placement, sometimes years after the adoption finali-zation had taken place. Workers called this a "disruption," as if it were temporary, though few children ever returned to the same adoptive family.

I remember when Ms. Beth sent for Daphne after school. Her brother and sister, who lived in other cottages, went as well. When she returned, she was carrying an album. My chest felt like it was filled with lead. Why her? There were three of them and only two of us. Her sister was just as problematic as Luke was, and I was not only younger than Daphne, but I had better grades. It was not fair!

Then Scott starting visiting with a family, leaving his two brothers behind, including Ryan, who was my favorite guy on campus.

"That's terrible," I said to commiserate with him.

"I want Scott to have a chance."

"Maybe if they like him, they'll take you, too," I suggested.

"Not many people want three teenage boys."

I worried that someone would want Luke and not me. I always assumed I would be the one rejected because that is what had happened before in foster homes. But for the first time, I realized a separation could be permanent.

After Will and Leroy joined Ms. Sandnes's family, I had to share her time with two troubled boys.

"I have to get some poster board for my science project," I told Ms. Sandnes one day while she was restraining Leroy.

"Can't you see I'm busy now!" she snapped.

I went to my room and lost control. I started pulling out hunks of my hair. Finally, Ms. Sandnes checked on me. "Ashley, let's talk about what's bothering you." Ms. Sandnes rubbed my back. How could I tell her that I wanted her all to myself?

Mary Fernandez started a photo album for me containing the pathetically few pictures I had managed to accumulate over the past nine years. She pointed to one of Grandpa feeding the chickens. "Tell me about him," she urged.

"I don't remember him very well."

"What happened the last time you saw him?"

I tried to find a place to concentrate my vision, but my eyes ached. "I'm tired." I slumped in my chair and then blurted, "He was shot." Tears welled up faster than I could corral them.

During family work Mr. Bruce showed us the photos the Mosses had taken the day we went to the beach. Luke erupted like a volcano. "I hate those people!"

Mr. Bruce asked him, "What do you think should happen to them?"

Luke had been running around the room slapping the walls as he passed. He leaped on the couch. "Marjorie Moss should go to the electric chair!" He continued jumping on and off the couch as though it were a piece of gym equipment until the session was over.

Many of the residents, including Luke, attended Parkhill School on campus, which was designed for children with behavioral or emotional problems. Others, like me, attended public schools. I was in the gifted program at Dickenson Elementary School. In October the other pupils elected me Student Council representative for the fourth grade. Ms. Sandnes was thrilled. "Next year you could run for president!" she said.

"Do you think I'll be here next year?" I asked. Since I had never completed a full year at one school, this was good news—except it also meant that maybe the administration did not think anyone would adopt me.

Although I rode the bus with several other Children's Home residents, I sat as far away from them as I could. One afternoon while standing in the bus line, I noticed two girls staring at me. Both were fifth graders. The blonde had French braids; the other had short brown pigtails. They both had on floral-print dresses with lacy socks folded down over shiny Mary Janes and looked like child models in doll commercials. The blonde approached me hesitantly. "Are you really from that orphan place?"

"Yeah, so what?"

"You brush your hair, and your clothes even match," the other girl replied.

The blonde asked, "What's it like living in an orphanage?"

"There's always someone to play with," I replied. "And we have a big gym, a pool, and lots of field trips."

The next day they sought me out on the playground and brought others to hear about my life in foster care. I had a stockpile of Moss horror stories that kept them entertained for weeks. Soon others chimed in with their own woeful tales. One of the girls said that her mom had run off with the mailman. A boy admitted that when his father got drunk, he beat him with a belt. Several divulged that their fathers slapped their mothers. After someone disclosed that his father was in jail for possession of marijuana, I bragged, "My uncle is in prison for murder."

To keep my audience enthralled, I developed a comedic routine featuring "funny" lines about my life. "Every time my mother came around, she was with a different man." I paused for effect. "The last time she brought a woman!"

I really got them interested when I told stories about living with my grandfather. I went into detail about driving fast and playing chicken in the beat-up car with no doors and seat belts. "I thought I was going to *die*!" I said theatrically. "But I only busted my lip."

When I had earned my place as the center of attention, I launched into the tale of Grandpa's gunfight. I made popping sounds with my mouth, then staggered around. Falling to the ground in slow motion, I got shrieks of appreciation.

I had just read a book about Egypt and was determined to be Cleopatra for Halloween. I made a list of all the accessories I would require, including a black wig and a golden armband shaped like a snake. Ms. Sandnes found hand-me-downs for the other kids and spent most of her budget on me since she knew I wanted the costume so badly. Because of security concerns, we could not trick-or-treat in regular neighborhoods, so the staff drove us to dorms at the University of South Florida, where student volunteers decorated their doors and stocked treats as a community service program. Just like kids all over the country, we ran around collecting as much candy as we could, but we had to do so in this phony situation. Then we were herded back to the cottages, where the staff locked away our loot and doled it out later.

In November the Merritts showed up for my tenth birthday. Mrs. Merritt had crocheted a vest for me and made a pillow from one of the latch-hook projects I had made at her house. Luke, Mary Miller, and our therapists joined us for cake in the conference room. Luke ripped open my presents, tasted the icing before the cake was cut, and as he blew out my candles, he spit all over everything—spoiling every aspect of my party.

At the end Mary Miller said, "I have another surprise for you."

We went out to her car, and she lifted out the bike I had left with Mrs. Chavez. Then she handed me a brown box. "I'm sorry it isn't in better shape." I opened the lid. Inside was my Easy-Bake oven. The original carton was soggy and smelled like the Mosses' moldy shed. The packages containing the cake mix were mildewed.

"What about my dolls and sleeping bag?"

"Mrs. Moss claimed that this was all she could find."

I returned to my cottage fuming about Luke's behavior, my ruined oven, everything else that Mrs. Moss had kept, all my other possessions that had been left behind in various foster homes, and even the bike, which had rusted in the rain. I also wondered whether my mother remembered what day it was.

A few days later we had my cottage birthday party. Ms. Sandnes picked out gifts from among the donated clothes and toys in the storage unit. She bought me another cake studded with icing flowers and adorned with my name in green letters. Everyone gathered to gobble the cake and ice cream. It was the same party we had every few weeks for one or another of the cottage kids, so I did not feel particularly special.

For months, though, the excitement built around Christmas. In October the staff had given us forms and told us to list anything we wanted.

"What's the limit?" I wondered.

"There is none," Sabrina told me.

"What are you asking for?"

"Lots of clothes, a music box like yours, a bike—"

"You already have a bike."

"You can get one every year," she said, as if explaining something to a toddler. "The lists are given to our sponsors—really rich people, even companies—and they go out and buy us everything."

For the next few days we would watch television with our lists on our laps. Every time a commercial would come on, we would scribble the toy on the form. I asked for

Barbie dolls, children's beauty and nail supplies, stuffed animals, a new bike, and Rollerblades. The staff doled out money for us to buy gifts for a few special people. I purchased something for my teacher, my brother, and Ms. Sandnes. On campus the big event was the Christmas Cantata, a musical program put on by the residents, followed by fancy food served in the cottages. We all wore our dressiest clothes and were on our best behavior because sponsors and outsiders—who might be prospective parents—visited.

Christmas morning was a feeding frenzy. We all dove into the huge stack of packages, grabbing anything with our names on it. Sabrina had been right. We each received most of the items on our lists—and more. Foster parent groups provided some of the basics, and our sponsors bought the big-ticket items. Everything was from "Santa," so we did not know who had contributed what. Kids ripped open their boxes, checked the contents, tossed them behind their chair, then attacked another. Paper, cardboard, and Styrofoam piled up in drifts around us. As we reached the bottom, the other kids' faces registered an is-that-all-there-is? expression. By the end of the day half the toys were missing parts, broken, or trampled. Even though I tried to take more care with mine, some of my gifts disappeared into the tangle of wrappings.

"Where's my French Barbie?" I shouted into the living room.

"Sabrina has it," Daphne said.

"I wrote down French Barbie too!" Sabrina claimed.

"Did not!" I screeched. I gathered up as much as I

could and took it to my room, but by the time I got back, Will and Leroy were playing catch with my softball and had already smudged it. I was disgusted and wondered why I couldn't live with a regular family and have a nice, quiet Christmas like everyone I saw in holiday specials on television.

Living in an institution with a myriad of regulations, it was impossible to lead a normal life. When my school had a fund-raiser, I was determined to sell enough to win one of the prizes. Ms. Sandnes squashed my plans to go door-to-door in the neighborhood. "Sorry, it's against the rules."

That afternoon I grumbled in therapy. "You could show the brochure around campus," Mary Fernandez suggested.

I started with Mr. Bruce, who placed an order. He offered to accompany me on my rounds. By the time I returned to Lykes Cottage, I had made one hundred fifty dollars in sales, enough for one of the better prizes. I gave the envelope filled with checks and cash to Ms. Sandnes for safekeeping before I went to change into play clothes.

When I returned, Ms. Sandnes looked ill. "Ashley, did you take the envelope back to your room?"

"No, you put it on your desk." My pulse quickened. "Is it missing?"

"I'm afraid so. I was gone just a minute or two."

Nobody found the envelope and the deadline to turn in the order forms passed. I was more upset about accepting everyone's money and not having anything to show for it than not winning the prize. A week later someone noticed that Daphne, who had not moved in with her adoptive family yet, had used a twenty-dollar bill when they went to a store. Eventually, she admitted to taking the money and made a halfhearted apology to me.

I held in my fury for a few days. On the way back from the gym after a soccer game, Daphne kept trying to trip me. My seething started in my gut and exploded through my fists. I punched her above her eye. I expected I would be punished, but I did not care. To my surprise, no one ever said anything about the incident.

Isabel, the other redhead in my fourth-grade class, was my best friend. She invited me to her home often, though I was never permitted to go—not even for her birthday party. Because campus residents could be unpredictable, they always had to be accompanied by staff. I pestered Ms. Sandnes for a visit so many times that she finally agreed to take me on a playdate.

Isabel's mother was tense because I had come from "that place" and needed supervision. The four of us sat in the living room staring at one another until Isabel asked, "Want to see my birds and guinea pigs?"

The room smelled like cedar chips, and animal cages and tanks lined the walls. Isabel handed me a fuzzy guinea pig, which I petted until I noticed the raisin-like poops on its fur, then hurriedly gave him back. Because Ms. Sandnes had to be on duty at the cottage, we had to leave after only an hour. That was the first—and last—time I visited with a friend until I went to my adoptive family.

I had come to The Children's Home expecting to be gone in a few months, but a year passed without anyone adopting us. I saw a few kids leave . . . and some returned because it had not worked out. I figured that I probably would be there until I was eighteen, but at least I was not at the Mosses' or with some of the other creepy parents I heard about. I decided to take it day by day and forget about everything—and everybody—else.

9

Let's make a deal

In August, I started fifth grade at Dickenson Elementary.
For the first time in my life, I was no longer the new girl.
The school selected me as a safety patrol, and Mrs. Trojello,
my teacher in the gifted program, encouraged me to run
for Student Council president. This required speaking
in the auditorium to all the students at each grade level.
I asked Mr. Irvin for a hunk of accordion-style computer
paper. When it came time for the candidates' speeches, I
stood behind the lectern and let the paper cascade off the
stage onto the floor. "Dear Santa," I began. "I would like a
new bike, some Barbie dolls, a radio, and—whoops." I let
a few more feet of paper tumble forward so it looked like a
massive document. "Unless our principal has turned into a
jolly old man, I have the wrong speech!" The first graders
burst out laughing, and I hoped the gag would be as suc-
cessful with all the classes.

The results were announced over the intercom. "And

your new Student Council president is Ashley Rhodes!"

Ms. Sandnes glowed when I told her the news. By dinnertime the whole campus knew I had won, and I received congratulations from every member of the staff I encountered.

Neither Sabrina nor Daphne said a word to me.

"Here comes the brownnoser," Leroy said, rubbing the tip of his nose.

Although his words stung, it was more important to me to get recognition at school than from the campus kids because I did not respect their opinions.

Still, I was hungry for attention. I was in my gifted class when I started hiccuping, which made the others laugh. I forced more air into my throat so the hiccups would become more obnoxious.

"Go get a drink of water and come back when you have those under control," Mrs. Trojello said, and then asked me to stay after class.

"Ashley, I know where you live, so I can guess you've had some tough times," she began. I thought she was going to lecture me about my past not being an excuse for poor behavior. Instead, she went on to tell me that she had come from a rough background herself and knew what it was like to struggle without support at home. Mrs. Trojello handed me a book. "You have a lot in common with Anne of Green Gables."

Reading the book, I began to see what she meant. Lucy Maud Montgomery could have been describing me. It also reminded me of Annie, the most famous girl orphan. I remember thinking that all three of us had red hair, sunny smiles, plucky dispositions, and names that begin with *A*. But perhaps Mrs. Trojello also wanted me to see that some stories—like her own—had happy endings.

At least twice a year we attended adoption picnics. Even though there were carnival games and hot dogs and burgers on the grill, the real purpose was to display the merchandise: the children nobody else wanted. Some of the "shoppers" were discreet and stood at a distance; others were chatty—even pushy. One prospective parent even poked me! A chubby lady ran her fingers through Luke's hair and said to her husband, "Isn't he cute as a button!" Then she turned to Luke. "We'd love to adopt you!"

"I'm going to be adopted!" Luke bragged on the way home.

Luke and I were selected to be on the Christian Television Network. A bubbly blonde reporter interviewed us in the arts-and-crafts room on campus. "What sort of family do you want?" she asked me.

"Oh, I'm not too picky," I replied. "I just want someone to take care of us, to treat us nice—just . . . a family." I hoped I had hit the right note, but Luke made silly faces and purposely yawned, stealing my moment.

"What about you, Luke?"

"I want frogs and a baseball glove and a mom."

"In that order?" The reporter laughed. "I'm praying that people will call in if the Lord has touched their hearts, because these children are praying for a family."

When nobody responded, I felt hopeless. I also had few expectations for my eleventh birthday later that month. It would be the same old cottage party; I would get a few generic gifts and then meet the Merritts in the therapy conference room. Whoopee.

"Happy Birthday!" Mary Fernandez said when she came to take me to the therapy wing after my cottage cake.

I did not look up from some beads I was stringing for a Thanksgiving program. "What's so happy about it?"

"Several kids threw cake," Ms. Sandnes said to explain my rudeness.

My therapist had more bad news. "I'm sorry you had a difficult day, and I'm sorry the Merritts can't make it either."

"I don't care."

"Ashley," Mary Fernandez said gently, "Matthew Merritt was hit by a car."

I dropped my beads with a clatter. "Is he okay?"

"Yes, it isn't life threatening. They want to have your party in his hospital room."

Bruce Weslowski, our family therapist, drove Luke and me to Tampa General Hospital.

"Happy birthday!" Mrs. Merritt sang out.

"Hey," Mathew said, "thanks for bringing your party to me."

Mary Miller handed out my gifts. The Merritts gave me a silver vanity set complete with brush, comb, and rotating mirror, which was the sort of elegant gift I preferred over toys. But I remember thinking that the disinfectant smell of the hospital ruined the cake's taste.

I should have known not to anticipate a great birthday because I had always been disappointed before. Even when Mrs. Chavez hosted my ninth birthday party, it was spoiled by Amelia wearing the outfit my mother had given me. At my tenth Luke hogged my candles and messed up my cake. Now even my eleventh was a letdown. This time, at least, Luke was more interested in Matthew's leg cast than in harassing me, but it was hardly the birthday party of my dreams.

After a while the staff felt Luke was mature enough to move into Lykes Cottage—but they were wrong. Although he was almost nine, he followed at my heels like a pesky puppy. If I ignored a request, he pulled my arm, tugged my hair, or did something so annoying that I pushed him away. I loved him; but I did not want him hanging on me all the time, so I went out of my way to avoid him.

What I could not avoid was an irrational throbbing for my mother that came in waves. As long as I kept busy, I managed to skip over most of my feelings by reminding myself that this was another bad habit, like biting my nails. But during quiet moments I could be overwhelmed by thoughts about where she was and why she had never come for me. Worst of all were the times when I couldn't fall asleep quickly because Sabrina cried out during the nightmares caused by her abuse. Mary Miller had told me that my mother's parental rights were gone, yet I did not think that any official pronouncement would make the slightest difference to her because she had always returned in the past—even when the caseworkers had tried to limit her visits.

I believed that she yearned for me as much as I did for her. There were times when this longing dissolved all my defenses until all that was left were tears that couldn't be contained. If someone found me crying, I'd refuse to answer their probing questions because I did not want to have to explain my feelings to Ms. Sandnes, Mary Fernandez, and Mr. Bruce over and over, as if words alone would bring my mother back.

In many ways The Children's Home was more pleasant than any of my foster homes, and I was not worried about them sending me away without warning because they had promised I could stay as long as I liked. I decided it would be better to remain with Ms. Sandnes, Mr. Todd, Mr. Irvin, and my friends than risk some snooty parents kicking me out the minute they tired of me. Besides, the only parent I wanted was my mother, and if I could not have her, then having nobody was better than somebody else.

The cottage staff told all the TPRed kids—the obnoxious acronym had somehow become an adjective—that we were going to have our photos taken by a professional photographer for an adoption catalog.

Mr. Irvin was surprised I was not ready. "Hey, Ashfoot"—he had given me that nickname because my feet were growing so fast—"what's wrong?"

I lay on my bed facing the wall. "I don't want my picture in a stupid book."

"How will a family find you if they don't see those cute freckles?"

"I hate my freckles and don't care if I am ever adopted."

"Too bad, because I know how much you like contests." My ears perked up. I had recently won third place in a poster contest for a race-car show.

"What contest?"

"At the photography studio. The best drawing will be on the cover of the book."

"I guess I'll go," I said.

"That's my Ashfoot." He grinned. "Just don't let them take a picture of your feet or you might break their equipment!"

While I waited for my turn to have my photo taken with Luke, I drew a picture of two couples. On the left was a man in a suit and a woman wearing a long dress and pearls standing next to a three-story house. Beside a ranch house on the right was a man in a T-shirt and shorts and a woman dressed in a blouse and short skirt. Underneath the picture I wrote:

> *I'd love a family rich or mid as long*
> *as they want a loving kid. If they love*
> *me and care for me, that's all I*
> *want in a family.*

I was very pleased with it, but nobody told me whether I had won or not.

On Easter Sunday the Lykes staff took us to one of our sponsor's homes—an elegant waterfront mansion—for an egg hunt. There was a five-dollar bill in every plastic egg! Within a few minutes, some of us had more money than we had been able to accumulate in a year of cottage allowances. As we drove away from the upscale neighborhood, I stuck my head out of the van's window and shouted, "Hey! Anyone want a kid?" It seemed as useful a recruiting strategy as anything else.

There were several events on campus to which alumni and their families were invited. We suspected some shoppers were sprinkled in as well. One of these was the opening of the summer Murphey Awards, the campus's mini-Olympics. As everyone gathered by the flagpole for the Pledge of Allegiance and some patriotic songs, I scanned the crowd to see if there was anyone who seemed to be paying attention to me. I heard some laughter from the audience and realized that Luke had wriggled to the front and was miming the words to the song.

"Isn't he darling?" a slim woman in tight slacks gushed to her husband.

"We have an annual essay contest, and the winner gets to deliver it," the announcer said. "This year the honor goes to the pride of the Lykes Lions, Ashley Rhodes."

I stepped to the lectern and began delivering the speech I had written in verse.

Again, I heard inappropriate laughter. Luke was making faces. I wanted to strangle him, but I plowed on and the audience rewarded me with resounding applause. Afterward some Children's Home staff members praised me, but most of the strangers fawned over my towheaded brother, which infuriated me further.

At my first adoption picnic, Luke climbed a tree and refused to come down. I pretended I did not know him and went home with the first vanload of kids. When they announced the July picnic, I told Ms. Sandnes I did not want to go.

"Why not, Ash?" she asked.

"They're like slave auctions!" She waited. "I thought the parents were going to bid on us after we left."

The morning of the picnic Ms. Sandnes came into my room and pulled out my favorite outfit. "I love you in this color," she said.

I turned my back on her. "I am not going!"

She handed me the turquoise shirt and white shorts without saying anything more. I put them on, then went through all my jewelry, slowly putting on every necklace and bracelet I owned. She herded me to the van.

The midday July sun beat down on Rowlett Park. I felt dizzy in the heat and headed to the shadier pavilion. A little girl's pink balloon floated by my face, and I pushed it away rudely. Parents strolled the perimeter gawking at us as if we were freaks.

"Hey, look at me!" Luke called. He was dribbling his snow cone in the dirt to make a pattern, but most of it stained his shirt. I suspected that nobody wanted me because Luke was part of the package.

"Hi there." A woman came up beside me. "May we get you a cold drink?" I looked up at a couple wearing matching khaki shorts and Polo shirts with the collars at preppy salute. Their name tags read JESS and LES. Somehow I found myself in line for sodas with Jess while Luke's worker steered him into the line.

Jess pulled out some waterless hand cleaner while her husband went to get the four of us hot dogs. "Ashley, we use this before we eat."

Another lady, whose name tag read GAY, turned around. "I like your necklaces," she said.

I gave her a polite half smile. Jess quickly redirected my

attention and guided me to where we would be sitting.

After lunch another worker said there was someone else she wanted us to meet, but Luke took the opportunity to bolt toward the baseball diamond. Somebody chased him as another woman asked me the usual dumb questions about what grade I was in and what my favorite color was.

"We're taking Luke back," Mr. Todd said. "Do you want to go with us?"

"Sure," I said, because I was sick of potential parents who chatted for a few seconds, then went in search of cuter, younger specimens.

"Look at all the stuff I won!" I showed Mr. Todd my bulging goody bag. Luke tried to grab it and it ripped. Favors started to fall out.

"May I help you?" a kind-eyed man asked.

"I won so much stuff that I can't hold it all!" I crowed.

"Wait a sec." The man found a larger bag that had contained brochures and helped consolidate my trinkets.

"That should do it," said the man with PHIL written on his name tag. He carried the bag to the van for me. I figured he was one of the workers from another agency and forgot about him the minute we left the adoption fair.

I was anxious about several upcoming changes in my life. I had to have an egg-size cyst removed from my back, which was a relief because Will had started calling me "Humpback." I was also about to start middle school, where I would be a lowly sixth grader. None of that would have been so daunting if the worst thing in the world was not about to happen: Ms. Sandnes was leaving to get her master's degree in social work! Well, I told myself, she wasn't my family, so it didn't really matter. I started thinking about ways to find out where my mother might be and how I might contact her. While the authorities had kept my whereabouts a secret from her, she might be living nearby, hoping I would find her.

Added to that, I was being awakened by frightening dreams that involved shouts in the dark, men with bloody hands, and women screaming. Before I could fall back to sleep, I would go sit with the night security guard and sip a glass of water. Nothing was private at the cottage. Logbooks of our behaviors were kept. So after I answered one sympathetic guard's questions, Mary Fernandez brought the subject up at therapy. I hated rehashing everything—and I was a little bit afraid she would want to link my bad dreams to my feelings about my mother—so I vowed to keep any future nightmares to myself.

Just before school started, the whole campus—including cottage staff and therapists—moved to the camp that we had attended the year before. There was a cool lake for tubing, waterskiing, and fishing; a swimming pool; crafts; even archery and BB gun ranges.

One afternoon a man was filming the kids in the pool. "Mr. Cameraman, watch this!" I said before I attempted my first dive. When I popped up, I looked in his direction. "Did you get it?"

"Sure did," the familiar-looking man responded.

"What are you filming?" one of the other kids called out.

"A movie about camp," he called back.

Nothing special registered in my brain. I was looking

forward to that evening's capture-the-flag contest, because I often led the pack. Later, as we sat around the bonfire singing folk songs and roasting marshmallows, I thought: *This is what regular kids do.* Okay, maybe we had more than our share of emergency room visits, like the time one of the boys had to get BBs sucked out of his ears, but in the beautiful forest by the lake, the insanity seemed less intense. Best of all, I was too busy most of the time to worry about losing my mother—and now Ms. Sandnes.

After camp I had my cyst removed. The doctor did not give me sufficient anesthetic, so it wore off in the middle of the surgery. Then he removed the stitches too early and the wound ruptured. The resulting scar was uglier than the cyst. Will changed my nickname from "Humpback" to "Scar." I did not care about it as much as the fact that Ms. Sandnes was leaving in only a few days. The idea of not having her any longer made me ache like there was something wrong with my bones.

The day of her departure we handed her farewell cards. Sabrina started clinging to her, and then Sam and Will latched on as well. I watched from a distance as Ms. Sandnes tried to disengage them. "I've got to go now." She gave me a half smile. "I'll be around for my internship, so it's not like I'm going to China."

An overwhelming sensation crushed my chest so that I could barely breathe. I felt as though I were having a heart attack.

"We won't let her leave!" Sam shouted.

Leroy ran outside and jumped on the hood of her car. Ms. Sandnes looked over her shoulder and back at me. She did not know which way to turn. Sam and Will had joined Leroy. Ms. Sandnes peeled Sabrina off. Then Sabrina also rushed out to the car.

Ms. Sandnes's eyes were teary as she came toward me. "Ash, I'll miss you." I fell into her arms and, for the very first time, hugged her as if I would never let go. "Ash . . ." I heard the catch in her throat. "Everything good is going to happen for you. I *know* it."

"*You're* the only g-good thing—" I jerked away and rushed out the door. Sam, Will, and Sabrina were lying under the wheels of the car. Leroy sat on the hood. I threw myself against the driver's door. "Don't leave me!" I sobbed.

Another staff member helped peel us off the car while Ms. Sandnes climbed into the driver's seat. She checked to make sure she was not backing up on any of us and then drove off without waving.

I did not know what Ms. Sandnes knew: I had a family.

Mr. Todd interrupted my dinner and asked me to step out into the lobby. "What did I do?" I asked in response to his stern look.

"It's okay," he said. "Ms. Beth just wants to ask you something." He led me to her office. Instead of returning to the cafeteria, he slouched against the door.

"Ashley," Ms. Beth began in her gentlest tone. "How would you feel if you and Luke were both adopted—but by different families who live near each other?"

"Whatever you think's best." I gulped for air. "D-do I have a family?"

"We just wanted your opinion so we could check out some options."

There was something odd about her expression that made me think this wasn't theoretical, but I was too timid to ask anything else.

When I returned to the cafeteria, Mr. Irvin handed me my plate, but I waved it away. "You done?" he asked.

My stomach felt as if it would reject anything I ate, so I said, "I guess."

"I understand," he said with a wink that could have meant that he knew something or merely that it was okay to skip the meal.

The next day a staff member told me that I had a dental appointment. Ms. Sharon Williamson, my new primary, came into my room. "You ready?"

"I have to brush my teeth first."

"Why?"

"Aren't I going to the dentist?"

"Oh." She looked uncomfortable. "You have to see Ms. Beth . . . first."

"Hi, Ashley," Ms. Beth said. She handed me a blue book with gilt-edged pages.

"You can open it!" Ms. Sharon's voice sounded like she was more excited to see it than I was.

I looked down. *Album* was written in gold script. I turned the page to see the exterior of a two-story house. I flipped to the next page. It read: *A recent photo of the Courter Family*.

"Do you remember seeing these people at the last adoption picnic?" Ms. Sharon asked.

"No."

"They've been around the campus and also filmed at camp."

The cameraman wanted to adopt me? Did that happen after he saw me dive or before . . . or . . . ? I stared at the first family portrait. One son was in a cap and gown; the other son and the father were wearing shirts and ties, while the mother had on a striped suit and a floppy hat. They looked stiff and their smiles were goofy. Nobody looked familiar. The images blurred. "May I take it back to the cottage?"

"Of course, Ashley, it's yours," Ms. Beth said.

Ms. Sharon and I crossed the quad. The dentist was forgotten. I called to the kids watching television, "I've got a family," and tossed my album on the table.

Will grabbed it. "Wow!" he said. "Look at that boat and the dock!"

Sam joined in. "And get a load of that gigantic Christmas tree."

"Why would they show you a table full of food?" Sabrina wrinkled her nose.

I snatched the album back and thumbed through it again. At the end there was a letter written to me: *We are the Courters. Phil and Gay met when we were working for the same company in New York City in 1968. At that time, we were making films for children. We fell in love almost from the minute we met and were married within that year. We have been together ever since and have a very happy marriage and home. . . . We still make movies and videos, often about children and families. Sometimes we have to travel for business, but we often take our children with us. . . .*

As a few more kids trickled in, Will announced, "Ashley's got a family!"

"Me too!" cried Luke. He rushed into the room waving another album.

I checked out the Hudsons, who were younger and more like what I had in mind. The Hudsons also had dogs, which I preferred to the Courters' five cats; but it was the Courters' home that won me over. Although it did not have lion statues guarding the front door, it was close to my dream castle.

I went to my room so I could continue reading the letter from the Courters in private. They had two sons. Blake was twenty-three and had just graduated from college; Josh was twenty and still in college. Gay was a writer who was just finishing her eighth book, and Philip made films. The letter mentioned that they flew airplanes. I could not imagine what this family was like or why they would want me.

The letter went on to describe their five cats—one had only three legs, and they all had peculiar names. Then it continued: *Outside our house is the Crystal River. In the winter, the manatees are all around us and sometimes dolphins swim up to the dock. There are many types of birds, fish in the water, and sometimes a whole family of otters. At night, there are alligators that we can see if we take flashlights. There are also raccoons, possums, and armadillos hanging around. Now and then, you can even spot a wild pig in the road! And there are all sorts of frogs, toads, and bugs too!* This sounded more like a place that Luke would enjoy. He liked cats and bugs and would be thrilled to see a gator. None of that interested me.

I went back to the photos and studied the paisley bed-spread in the room that would be mine, the tiles edging the swimming pool, the curvy sofa in the living room, the size of the boat tied at the dock, and the pots hanging over the kitchen sink. I tried to imagine walking from room to room, sleeping in the large bed without an annoying room-mate, or strolling along the seawall to see the manatees. I wondered if they would let me invite friends over for a pool party or even sleepovers.

I continued reading the letter. *We have a very happy, fun family. We always try to help each other out and make sure that everyone is feeling okay. Phil and Gay take turns with chores and taking care of our children. If there is a big job, we all pitch in together to get it done, and then we can be free to have fun sooner. We have a lot of love to give to more children and we believe that if everyone cares about each other, everyone can be happy.*

That sounded like something they thought they should write, because on closer inspection, their expressions in the photographs did not look as happy-go-lucky as their words claimed, but I figured they would be able to offer me opportunities. I couldn't decide if they seemed more like one of those quirky sitcom families or a bunch of weirdos who make a good first impression but flip out behind closed doors. But I realized that it would be stupid to pass up this opportunity—with or without Luke. It looked like a good deal; I'd get a lot of attention, a lot of stuff, and it couldn't be worse than most of the places I had been. If I really hated it, I could always come back to The Children's Home. Lots of others had—even after they had been adopted.

"They're coming! They're coming!" Luke called out. He had been on lookout since dawn.

I watched both families get out of a van. All four were wearing T-shirts, shorts, and sandals. After brief introductions the Hudson family steered Luke to a picnic bench near the parking lot. The staff picked the farthest table for themselves so they could be inconspicuous.

Gay and Phil positioned themselves on a bench with me in the middle. I managed to squirm enough so I did not have to touch them. Nobody spoke. I gazed up at the trees where a deflated red balloon was caught in some branches.

Phil broke the silence. "Do you have any questions for us?"

"Where did you get that necklace?" I asked Gay without looking directly at her.

"At a craft shop in Maine." Gay lifted it over her head and handed it to me. All the beads were made from blown glass.

"What will my bedtime be?" I said as I fingered the smooth leaves interspersed with bird and fish shapes on her necklace.

"That depends on what time school starts," Phil said.

"How much allowance will I get?"

"Our sons got five dollars a week in middle school," he replied.

Gay changed the subject. "Want a snack?"

Phil fetched the cooler, which they had filled with sodas, juices, various kinds of cheese, several boxes of crackers, and jars of peanut butter and jelly.

I slipped Gay's necklace over my neck. "How did you know I love cheese?"

Gay grinned. "A little mouse clued us in."

I thought this was her lame attempt to be funny. I glanced over to the table where Ms. Sandnes was sitting. She had come back for the day to be supportive. "Ms. Sandnes?"

"Actually, it was your guardian," Gay admitted.

The cracker tasted like paste and the juice was too sweet. "Want to see my room?" I led the way to the cottage.

"Why don't you adopt me?" Will shouted as we walked past the living room.

"My room's back here," I said, "but men aren't allowed."

"It's okay," said Ms. Sandnes, who had been trailing us.

"Can you reach that?" I pointed to the Tiffany & Co. box on my top shelf. When Phil handed it down, I opened it. "My mother gave me this music box."

"It's beautiful," Gay said. "Your mother really cared about you."

I twisted her beads so hard I thought they might snap.

Ms. Sandnes coughed. "I guess we need to be going," Phil said, "but we can come back on Monday, if that's okay with you?"

"Sure," I said.

Outside, Luke hugged the Hudsons and said, "Bye, Mom. Bye, Dad."

The Courters stood stiffly. I kept my distance as we walked to the parking area. Phil opened the car door for Gay. She hesitated and waved.

"Wait!" I called. "Don't forget your necklace."

"Do you want to borrow it?" she asked.

"What if something happens to it?"

"We care about people, not things."

When they arrived for dinner on Monday, I could barely face Gay.

"What's wrong?" she asked.

I gulped. "I accidentally broke your necklace." I explained that I had worn it to school. "When a girl grabbed for it, I decided to put it in my book bag, but it got squashed on the school bus and one of the glass leaves split in half."

"It's my fault," Gay responded. "I should have realized it was too fragile."

"You're not mad at me?"

"Of course not!" she said, although I was not sure she meant it.

We had pizza, but I barely ate anything. "How long have you known about me?"

"We first heard about you six months ago," Phil said.

"Have you seen me before?"

"Many times," Phil said with a laugh.

When the Courters rattled off how often they had been at The Children's Home, I was shocked. I could not believe they heard my welcoming speech at the Murphey Awards and saw me dance at an event several months earlier. I knew that Phil had filmed me at the camp pool but not that Gay had watched my Lucille Ball skit at the talent show. How could I have been oblivious to the family that had been shopping for me?

The next step was a visit to my family's home. Beth Lord and Sharon Ambrose drove Luke and me to Citrus County. First, we dropped Luke and Ms. Sharon at the Hudsons' home in a wooded glen, and then Ms. Beth took me about ten miles farther to Crystal River.

"Hi!" Phil said as he opened the glass front door. I passed by him, ignored Gay, and walked down the hall to a door with a sign that read ASHLEY'S ROOM. I surveyed the room briefly, then returned to the car, retrieved my Tiffany box, and placed it on a shelf in the bedroom. Next, I carried in a garbage bag containing my stuffed animals.

"Are you moving in?" Phil chuckled tensely.

"Just putting my stuff where it will be safe."

"Okay . . ." Gay glanced first at Phil, then at Beth Lord.

"Are you hungry?" Gay asked. My stomach was doing cartwheels, so I only shrugged. "Do you like pasta?"

"I guess."

Phil led the way into the kitchen. "Have you ever made noodles from scratch?" I shook my head. "Do you want thinner spaghetti or fatter fettuccini?"

"Fettuccini." It sounded more sophisticated, although I was not sure what the difference was. I helped Phil pour the eggs, water, and flour into a machine, then hang the strands on a rotating stand he had built.

Gay chopped onions and peeled tomatoes. "I can make any kind of sauce. Would you prefer white or red?" I did not react. "Some people prefer it plain with butter. . . ."

"Just Ragú."

"Let me check the pantry."

For a minute I thought she had said "panty" and was confused. She came out of a little room holding a jar. "We use it for pizza," she said apologetically to Beth Lord. She started to pour it in a pot.

"I prefer it cold."

Gay grimaced but allowed me to dump the sauce directly on the pasta from the jar. I stirred it around, took a few bites. The noodles were too chewy. When Phil noticed I had not touched most of my food, I apologized. "I'm a picky eater."

"We'll figure out what you like, and you might learn to try new foods." He grinned. "Like sushi."

"What's that?"

"Raw fish."

He was kidding, right? There was a pause. I forced a laugh. They laughed. What had I gotten myself into?

A few days later Gay arrived to take me clothes shopping. She wanted to buy me a fancy dress because we were going to see *Phantom of the Opera* for her birthday.

Gay held up a purple dress with a lace collar and puffy sleeves. "That's dorky," I said, moving toward a rack of silky dresses with spaghetti straps. I picked out a turquoise one with a low-cut neckline. Gay shook her head. "But I look better in blue and I despise purple."

"It's not the color" was all she said.

We found two dresses I didn't hate, and we picked out some other things I really liked: overall shorts, striped shirts in several colors, and a pair of designer jeans.

"Okay, let's try them on," Gay said.

I refused to go into the dressing room. "How will you know if they fit?" she asked.

"Ms. Sandnes bought my clothes for me. If they didn't fit, she returned them."

"I live two hours away, Ashley, so you'll have to try them on now." I could tell she was annoyed. "You can have your privacy; just show me the ones you like."

I stormed out of the store because I did not want to admit that I had never been in a dressing room before.

Gay caught up with me. "How about a snack?"

We shared a large cinnamon pretzel and had lemonade, but the sugar caught in my throat and the drink was too sour.

For the next visit the Courters were permitted to take me to their home without a staff member supervising, but I could not stay overnight. I half expected they would change their minds, yet Phil was right on time to pick me up. We went out on their boat and swam in their pool. I especially liked the way Phil made grilled cheese sandwiches.

I checked out the pictures of the family on the walls. Several featured Phil piloting a small plane. Maybe I would go flying with him someday.

When Gay drove me home that evening, she prattled on about some girls my age in the neighborhood. "You'll like them; they're really nice."

Yeah, nice, I thought. *This person does not have a clue about me.* "When I was in foster care, some of the people weren't very nice," I began tentatively.

She nodded. "Did you know that I'm a Guardian ad Litem like Mary Miller? I've visited some pretty ghastly foster homes."

"Not as bad as this one."

"Tell me about it."

Instead of freaking when I described the most gruesome of the Mosses' punishments, she spoke calmly. "That sounds like it would have made you angry."

"It did!" I began telling her about the hot sauce, and by

181

the time we reached the cottage, I had revealed more to her in two hours than I had to Mary Fernandez in two years.

After several daytime visits I was allowed to stay with the Courters overnight. Ms. Sandnes, who was now doing her master's internship at the home's therapy department, dropped me off. When we pulled into the circular driveway, I asked, "Couldn't I just stay a little while and then go back with you?"

"Ashley, you'll be fine," Ms. Sandnes insisted. "Here." She reached behind her and pulled her college sweatshirt from the backseat. "You can borrow this."

I put it on inside out and wore it the whole time I was there. Twenty-four hours later I was eager to return to the campus, although after fifteen minutes of the usual cottage commotion, I wanted to be back with the Courters.

For Gay's birthday I wore a black velvet dress with white stripes down the sides that Ms. Sandnes had picked out. Gay also had chosen a black-and-white outfit, so we matched. At the restaurant at the Tampa Bay Performing Arts Center, the mingling smells of buffet food made me queasy. I only took a few bites of a dinner roll.

"Would you like butter on that?" Gay asked. I wrinkled my nose.

"How about dessert?" Phil pointed out an array of cakes and pies.

"I don't like many sweets."

We climbed the steps to the performing arts center. I glanced from my left to my right. Were this balding man and this intimidating woman really going to be my parents?

10

Testing, testing

Ever since Ms. Sandnes left, I found everything about The Children's Home irritating. I saw no reason to do well in my new middle school. My first sixth-grade report card was the worst I had ever received.

"When can I move already?" I asked Beth Lord.

"Everyone has to follow the visitation schedule." Her eyes crinkled as she gave a secretive smile. "But I have good news. The judge signed the order giving you permission to go to New England with the Courters next week."

Though I wanted to meet my new brothers, I was worried about being alone with the Courters for so long—and getting enough regular food to eat.

When we arrived at the airport, I was surprised to be at a gate for a large airplane. "I thought you guys had your own plane."

"We don't have one anymore." Phil sighed.

"It's a long story," Gay said slowly.

"Did you crash it or something?"

"Actually, we did," Phil said. "And you should be glad."

It seemed to me that I never knew what the Courters were going to say next, and that made me feel uncomfortable—like I would never belong.

Gay fumbled in her purse and came up with a stack of pictures. She shuffled through recent ones of her sons and lots of me. On the bottom were several photos showing a plane with a broken wing and a smashed propeller in a field.

"The three of us were on our way to Blake's graduation from Princeton," Gay began. "Josh had just completed his first year at Hampshire College and was going to begin his internship with a commercial film-editing house in New York the following week, so we packed the plane with all his stuff and flew north from here. It was a gorgeous day—not a cloud in the sky—and we were so happy and proud."

Her voice faltered and Phil took over. "We had just crossed the Chesapeake Bay and I did not want to have to deal with Philadelphia's busy air traffic controllers, so I descended to stay out of their jurisdiction and headed for Trenton."

Neither of them spoke for a moment. "There was a loud bang." Gay was staring out at a jet that was coming in for a landing with a constricted expression on her face.

"What happened?" I asked.

"Total engine failure." Phil paused. "We used our instruments to find the nearest airport."

"And I picked up the microphone and told the Trenton tower about the emergency," Gay added.

"There should have been a small airport five miles

away," Phil said. "Josh noticed a break between some trees that might have been a grass strip, but we couldn't line up for it without any engine."

"Then Josh spied an L-shaped field, which was the only open space in miles of forest, and told Phil, 'Dad, I think that's the best we're going to do,'" Gay continued.

"Yeah," Phil muttered.

"I looked out my side window and saw the field rushing up. We had landed on grass strips before, but this one was dotted with mounds that looked like waves undulating toward us." Gay made a dipping motion with her hand. "There was a stand of pine trees at the far end of the field. I prayed that we would not smash full force into the woods. To our right was a small red barn. Phil steered away from it, but it was connected to a fence directly in our path."

Gay's eyes locked with Phil's. "I kept talking to the tower. 'We're touching down . . . it's bumpy . . . we're going through a fence . . .'"

"A fence post made from a railroad tie had hit the center of the right wing violently enough to spin the plane sideways," Phil explained. "Brown dust engulfed the plane as we slid down the field that angled out to the right. Both the swift turn and the thick soil slowed the plane, and we came to a jerky stop."

"Were you hurt?" I asked, looking at them differently. They no longer seemed like cardboard parents, but flesh-and-blood people who had almost died before I had even met them.

"No, we were fine." Gay's voice quaked as she relived her shock. "Phil and I rushed out the front door. The rear door had already flown open when the plane made the sharp turn. Josh was almost thrown out, but the seat belt held him inside. We dashed as far away from the plane as possible. 'Back farther!' Phil ordered when he saw fuel dripping from the broken right wing."

"Did it explode?"

Gay pointed to the picture. "No, this is how it ended up. The sandy earth absorbed the volatile fluid."

"We checked each other and we were all okay, except Josh had an abrasion from the seat belt," Phil added.

Gay glanced from me to Phil and back to me. "Then something magical happened." She gave me the most relaxed smile I had seen on her face so far. "Phil hugged me and said, 'I think we survived because we're meant to do something else.'"

Phil nudged me with his elbow. "And that, my dear, would be you."

On the plane Gay asked if I wanted a snack. She had cheese slices and peanut butter crackers in her purse. "I also packed ramen noodles, mac-and-cheese, and a travel hot pot."

I nodded and stared straight ahead as if the phone in the back of the seat in front of me were the most fascinating object I had ever seen. "Do I have to call you 'Dad' and 'Mom'?"

"Of course not," Phil replied.

"Ever?" I directed my words to Gay.

"It's entirely your decision," she said.

From her bottomless carry-on, Gay pulled out magnetic checkers, a mini Yahtzee set, and Go Fish and Old Maid cards, which we played until we landed in Hartford.

As soon as we were on the highway, I gasped at the foliage. It was every color I could remember from a Crayola box and more—orange-red, green-yellow, mahogany, gold.

We passed a pick-it-yourself orchard. "Apples! May I pick one?"

Phil stopped, and I ran up to the first tree, plucked an apple, and took a huge bite. Sticky juice ran down my chin, but I did not care. It was the most scrumptious apple I had ever tasted.

After filling a bag with me, Gay checked her watch. "Josh is probably waiting for us."

We were attending parents' weekend at Hampshire College in Amherst, Massachusetts. This campus had little in common with Andrews University, where the Merritts' daughters had gone. Both had dramatic vistas over rolling lawns and tall trees, but the students here were almost a different species. Hampshire hairstyles ranged from dreadlocks to electric blue Mohawks to shaved heads. Men and women flaunted wicked tattoos and piercings in crazy places, and most wore comfortable rather than trendy clothing.

"You must be Josh's folks," a girl in a long, homespun skirt said as we entered a courtyard. "He'll be back in a few."

The back door to his dorm—called a "mod"—banged open. "Hey, buddy!" Phil exclaimed. He and Josh hugged and patted each other's backs.

Josh walked over to me. His wavy hair was longer than

mine and pulled back in a ponytail. "So, this is my little sister!" he said with a wide grin.

The next day Blake drove in from Boston to join us. He shook my hand like a business client, yet he sounded like a cowboy when he said, "Howdy." The gap between his front teeth made him look friendly.

We crowded into Josh's car, which had more room than our rental, and headed to New Hampshire to have lunch with Phil's mother and his brother's family.

The Courters were so busy catching up and joking with one another that they did not pay much attention to me. I noticed that Blake looked like Phil but seemed to have more of Gay's abrupt personality, whereas Josh resembled Gay yet had Phil's mellow mood. I could not figure out where I would fit into this tight-knit group.

Phil's brother, Dan, was a pastor. He and his wife, Linda, reminded me of the Merritts. As I held their newborn granddaughter, I thought, *They would never consider getting rid of her, but I could be sent back at any time.*

"How about a family reunion shot?" Grandma Courter suggested. I did not think that I would be included, but Gay made sure I was in the front row.

Dan said, "Will you look at this great bunch of Courters—and Ashley fits right in." Linda agreed that I looked like their youngest daughter, who also had red hair.

Instead of finding her observation comforting, I was offended. My hair color had nothing to do with whether these people accepted me or not. I felt as if Phil and Gay were showing off their "good deed" and nobody realized I was overwhelmed and frightened.

The next morning we said good-bye to Josh and headed

to Boston with Blake. "Ash, why don't you ride with me?" he suggested when his parents pulled up in the rental car. The inside of his van looked like a living room. There were no seats in the back, just an Oriental carpet and a stereo the size of a home entertainment center.

"Want to hear my new CD?" I asked. "Play track three."

As the music to "Barbie Girl" started, Blake winced at the high-pitched voices mimicking Ken and Barbie. "Play it again," he said. Soon he was singing the male parts while I did the female. We kept it up for the rest of the trip.

We were going to stay with Gay's cousins, Bob and Shirley Zimmerman, who lived on the top two floors of a Back Bay town house. They greeted us with outstretched arms. I disliked being hugged and had been relieved that the Courters in New Hampshire hadn't been touchy-feely, but when Shirley reached out, I didn't want to seem impolite.

"Hey, Blake," Bob said, "Your hairline is getting to look like your old man's. If you keep it up, it will look like mine." Without warning, Bob whipped off his toupee. I lurched so hard, I almost fell back into their china cabinet.

"Ashley," Blake said, "welcome to our crazy family."

I despised most of the meals Gay cooked.

"I know you're a fussy eater," she said, "but I'm not a mind reader." She asked me to write out a list of the foods I liked.

On my next visit Phil started to grill hamburgers. "I only eat junior bacon cheeseburgers." I announced. "Can we go and buy one?"

"We're also having mashed potatoes, fruit salad, cole-slaw, and carrot and celery sticks. I am sure you'll find something to eat," Gay replied.

"I don't think so." I gave Phil my cutest pout.

"If you're still hungry when I drive you back to Tampa, we'll stop for something," he said.

I picked at some of the mashed potatoes—which were more delicious than I let on—but as soon as we were in the car, I begged Phil to stop at Wendy's.

"Can't send you back hungry," he said.

"Are you going to tell Gay?" I asked.

"Gay and I stick together on everything."

"But *she* didn't want me to have extra food."

"Ashley, both of us want to make you happy. Give Gay a chance, okay?"

I knew Gay was trying to please me, but for some reason, I resisted every attempt she made. She made chicken nuggets in the oven so they'd have a KFC flavor but not as much fat. They were quite good, although I was annoyed by the way she preached to me about eating healthy foods. One of the few veggies I would eat was cauliflower, and Gay smiled whenever I gobbled it down with either buttered bread crumbs or a cheddar cheese sauce. The Courters preferred fancy salads, but Gay would make me a separate one with chunks of plain iceberg. I could not tolerate anything with a sauce or any foods combined, so Gay would separate the meat and vegetables for me.

Gay wanted me to taste the food she'd make before asking for an alternative dinner. Sometimes she would prod me to try a few more bites. Mostly, she would shrug, and then I could leave the table and make ramen noodles, canned soup, SpaghettiOs, macaroni-and-cheese, or grilled cheese.

When Gay reheated some chicken from the night before, I said, "We never have to eat leftovers at The Children's Home."

"Help yourself to an alternative meal if you want," she responded.

I poked around in the pantry and came out cradling a bag of Doritos.

"That's not a nutritious choice," Gay groaned.

I rattled the chip bag, then slowly parted the sides. My mischievous look dared Gay to say something as the bag burst open.

"Put that back!"

"Would you like me to make you a grilled cheese sandwich?" Phil asked.

"Sure. I'm *starving*! I want five."

"Five!" Gay exploded. "You can have two," she sputtered, "then have some salad or fruit. If you are hungry after that, you can have more."

"It's okay. I'll just make her what she'll eat," Phil replied.

"She'll never eat five sandwiches."

"Then she'll learn to self-limit," he said.

I wolfed down three of the sandwiches, belching loudly to punctuate my victory. I plopped myself on the couch to watch television. Gay fumed as she cleaned up the waste.

I overheard her whispering to Phil in the kitchen. "We have to teach her healthy eating habits. And, besides, this was about control."

"Who lost control?" he countered.

"You didn't back me up, so she won."

"She's lost control of her whole life. Isn't it good that she has some now?"

"There's a difference between self-control and manipulation," Gay snarled, and stomped upstairs to her office.

Phil came and sat beside me on the sofa. I plopped my feet in his lap—a signal for a foot rub. It was nice to have him on my side.

After the New England trip I asked to move in with the Courters full-time. "You haven't completed the visitation schedule," Beth Lord reminded me.

"I don't want to waste more time at Roland Park Middle."

"There are technical problems," the adoption worker admitted. "The Department of Children and Families hasn't completed some paperwork."

The next time I saw Gay, I appealed to her. "I want to celebrate my birthday with my new family; and now because they can't get the papers done in time, I can't."

Gay contacted Mary Miller. "We're licensed as foster parents," she told my guardian. "We can take her as a foster child while they work out the details."

Mary Miller agreed to the plan; however, the department didn't have anyone available who could supervise me. Beth Lord, who often visited her mother in Citrus County, offered to do it.

My last day at The Children's Home was Halloween. For Luke's sake, I went trick-or-treating in the university dorms. The next day Phil picked me up. I packed every last possession, said my farewells to Sabrina, the rest of the cottage staff, and the other kids, and headed out the door.

Luke trailed me. "Don't go yet," he whined.

"The Hudsons are picking you up soon," I said. "You're going to visit them." He clutched my arm. "C'mon, Lukie. I gotta go." It was like trying to disengage an octopus. As soon as I unwound one arm, he curled his leg around mine.

When a staff member pulled him off me, Luke turned and kicked the wall. Phil hurried me to the car. In the distance I could hear my brother screaming. "Leave me alone! Leave me alone!"

When I arrived at the Courters', Gay helped me unpack. She held up one of my collared Roland Park shirts. "Since you won't be wearing uniforms, you'll need more school outfits."

"May I get new sneakers, too?"

"Yes," Gay said. "But you still have to try everything on."

I agreed, but I refused to allow Gay in the fitting room.

Phil asked me to model my new outfits. "Which should I wear the first day?"

"What about the overalls?" he suggested.

"That sounds good," I said, and laid them out with a pink tie-dyed shirt.

At bedtime the Courters came to tuck me in. Phil said, "We like to give good-night kisses. Is that all right with you?"

"Yes," I replied, "but I'll never kiss you back."

"That's fine"—he brushed my forehead with his lips—"though you can always change your mind."

After Phil left the room, Gay stroked my hair. "It's okay not to love us." I kept my face buried in my pillow, yet my ears were on full alert. "And I'm not going to say that I love you, because I haven't known you long enough to

193

feel that way. I like you very much and I want you to be my daughter forever, but love is something that grows with shared experiences. I feel the buds of love growing, but it hasn't blossomed yet."

I could not believe she was being so honest. She took a long breath. "There is nothing we can say to make you believe that we'll be here for you. You'll only learn it by living with us year after year after year." She smoothed my hair again and stood up. The bedsprings creaked. I turned enough to see her hovering over me, and for the first time, I saw her as more of a protector than a stranger. "Ashley, one of these days I will tell you that I love you. When you hear those three words from my lips, you will know they come from my heart. Sweet dreams, sweetie," she said, and stepped out in the hall.

On my first day of school Phil handed me a lunch box containing cheese sandwiches and pickles. "I want to be certain you'll have something you like."

"I've never taken my own lunch." I had always been a free-lunch kid.

He handed me two dollars. "Here's money in case you want to buy something else. Later you can choose whether you want to pack lunch or buy it."

Since Phil's office was close to the school, he said he would drive me. "You'd have to get up an hour earlier for the school bus, and some of those kids can be tough."

"No kidding!" I told him about the time one of The Children's Home kids had terrorized a bus and the police had to rescue us.

The guidance counselor knew Phil, and they chatted while he filled out the enrollment forms. Phil noticed that I was quivering. "Cutie-pie, you're going to be fine, but if you need me, I can come back in two seconds."

A girl walked up to me. "I'm Grace Morrow," she said. "I'm here to walk you to Ms. Mac's class." I followed her closely because my eyes were blurring. "We have a bunch of the same classes." The hallway swarmed with so many students that I almost lost sight of my guide. Grace waved me into the science classroom.

"Hi, I'm Ms. MacDonald, but everyone calls me 'Ms. Mac.'" The teacher smiled. "You came on a good day, because we're watching a movie and having popcorn. But don't think it's always this much fun."

A pack of students thundered into the room. My knees felt like jelly. Tears spurted unexpectedly. Ms. Mac steered me into the hall. "Honey, are you okay?"

"I w-want to go h-home!" I wailed.

Ms. Mac asked Grace to take me back to the guidance office. In a few minutes Phil was sitting beside me. "Take me home!" I begged.

"Ash, I'll do that if you want, but you'll still have to come back tomorrow." I soaked Phil's handkerchief. "Okay, cutie-pie? You can do it!"

Grace walked me back to the class, where everyone was now watching the movie. At the bell Ms. Mac said, "Why don't you stay and help me pop the popcorn for the rest of my classes today?"

Gay picked me up at the end of the day. "We're proud of you for sticking it out," she said. "Tomorrow will be easier, and in a few days you'll make a friend."

"I doubt it," I mumbled, although two days later Grace invited me to a slumber party at her house with her friend Tess. I had never been allowed to stay overnight at a friend's house before. "Please can I go?" I begged Gay.

"You're still a foster child."

"So I can't go?"

"I don't want to risk them sending you back on a technicality, even for a few weeks, but there's no reason Grace can't come to our house." She gave a theatrical groan. "And then we have to plan for your birthday the week after that."

"I hardly know anyone here to invite." I sighed.

"The only solution is to have two parties," Gay replied. "We'll have a few of your school friends and family here, and then we'll invite all of your Children's Home friends to a restaurant in Tampa. Is that okay with you?"

"Sure," I said, fully expecting something would go wrong the way it always did.

On Friday, November 21, we had a dinner party at our house to celebrate my twelfth birthday. Guests included two girls in our neighborhood, Tabitha and Jillian; Gay's father, Grampy Weisman; the Hudsons and Luke, who was having an overnight visit with them; and a few other family friends. Gay somehow knew that I had never recovered my dolls from Mrs. Moss and gave me a doll designed to look like me. It came with an overalls outfit and a nightgown along with matching clothes in my size. Even though I really was too old for a doll, I was glad to have it. I had chosen the dinner menu, so I liked everything—especially the ice-cream cake.

Early the next morning the phone rang. Gay came into

the kitchen with a peculiar expression on her face. "There's been a slight change of plans."

I expected that somebody at the cottage had flipped out and ruined the day for everyone. "So is the party off?" I asked.

"Not all news is bad news," Gay said. "That was the director of the Dave Thomas Foundation for Adoption inviting us to Busch Gardens for an event later today. She also said we could bring other adoptive families with us."

Daphne, who was now living with her family full-time, was coming to my party, so I asked if her family could be included.

"I already invited them."

During the long drive I asked the Courters, "How did you hear about me since you live so far from Tampa?"

"We have some friends from there—in fact, you'll meet them at Busch Gardens today," Phil said. "They handed us Hillsborough County's children-in-waiting directory, which had your picture with Luke."

"Phil, remember how it had a clever poem and picture on the cover that was signed by someone named Ashley?"

"And you thought it might be the Ashley whose photo was inside," he continued.

"Were there two couples and two houses in the drawing?" I asked.

"Yes!" Gay said. She turned to Phil. "I told you it was *our* Ashley!"

"Gay fell in love with you then," Phil said, "but she's a sucker for sappy poems."

So I *had* won the contest! And the Courters had seen it! What if Mr. Irvin hadn't talked me into going to the photo shoot that day? Maybe my luck really was turning and this would be my best birthday ever.

All the kids from Lykes, as well as some of my friends from other cottages, met us at a buffet restaurant. Gay had ordered a cake decorated in the autumn colors I had decided were my favorites. I showed off my twin doll and received a giant card signed by all the cottage residents. Next, it was off to Busch Gardens with Daphne's family and the Paines—the people who first had told the Courters about me.

"Did you know that Dave Thomas was adopted?" Phil asked me. "That's why he wants every child to find a home."

At the pavilion Mr. Thomas was about to receive a donation for the foundation in the form of a giant cardboard check. As a photographer positioned everyone for the best angle, the foundation's director pushed me forward. "Go stand next to Dave. You are what this is all about," she said.

I hesitated, but Dave Thomas waved me forward. "It's going to be all right," he said as they snapped the pictures. "You'll see."

The next week was Thanksgiving, and my new brothers were coming home for the first time since I had moved in. My room had once been Blake's. Phil set up a folding cot for him in Josh's room.

"Will he be okay with that?" I asked.

"The boys often shared a room, even when they had their own," Phil said. "Besides, he went to prep school at Groton almost ten years ago and really hasn't lived here since."

I hovered in the background as my brothers carried their

suitcases down the hall. Josh tossed his stuff in his room on the left. Blake headed for mine on the right and then stopped short. "Hey, where am I sleeping?" he asked.

"There's a bed in here for you," Josh called.

Blake glanced into his old room and saw my stuffed animals littering the bed. "I guess I don't live here anymore." He shuffled into Josh's room and closed the door.

A few minutes later Phil knocked on their door. "Hey, guys, we have a new mat for the trampoline." Josh came out. "Why don't you show Ashley some of your tricks?" Soon Josh and I were jumping together, but Blake remained in the house.

Ever since the first night I had slept at the Courters', they had expected me to help in the kitchen. I never had to do dishes at The Children's Home and resented being treated like a servant. When I did not scrub all the crud off a pot, Gay would say "Reject" and hand it back. The more I tried to rush, the more rejects I received. "If you would do it right the first time, it would be easier."

Gay created piles of filthy pots as she cooked the holiday meal. Without anyone asking, Blake or Josh would saunter in, wash a stack, and then go back to playing bluegrass music or working in the shop. I stayed as far from the mess—and the revolting food—as possible. They used a homemade gadget for scraping corn off the cob and added globs of butter, cream, and salt. Everyone raved about this Pennsylvania Dutch specialty, but I thought it tasted gross. One particularly disgusting conglomeration— oyster dressing—looked like baked barf. For me, Gay put out slices of cheddar cheese and added some Wonder bread to the breadbasket.

Blake held up a piece of the bread and asked his mother, "Why are you babying her?"

The meal began with everyone saying what they were thankful for, and predictably, everyone said they were thankful that I had joined the family. Then it was my turn. "I'm grateful for everything everyone else said," I offered grudgingly. I did not want to sound like a perky Annie thanking them for rescuing me from the orphanage.

"Here's the moistest piece of white meat." Phil slipped it on my plate.

"It's better with gravy," Cousin Esther insisted. I pulled my plate away before she could douse it, but the ladle dribbled some on the lace tablecloth.

"Try the wild rice," Josh cajoled. "It's nutty."

"Leave her be," Grampy Weisman said. "She doesn't look like she's starving."

Although Gay did not comment, her silence was almost worse than her nagging.

As soon as I could, I ducked into my room. Blake knocked on my door. "I have one question, Ashley," he barked. I opened it slightly. "Are you a guest or a family member?"

Josh came around the corner. "Hey, Blake, take it easy." He gave me a crooked grin. "Listen, Ash, we want a sister, but it's new for us, too."

"Yeah, sis." Blake snapped me with a dishtowel. "Do you want to wash or dry?"

By early December, I was more comfortable with the Courters' routine. One afternoon I rushed into the house, plopped my backpack in the hallway, and pitched my sweater in the middle of the living room floor.

"Ashley, your backpack and sweater . . ."

I rolled my eyes, retrieved my backpack, and then went to my room, closing my door with a purposeful thud. The phone rang, so I had to come out and walk by Gay to get it in the kitchen.

When I hung up, Gay pointed to the sweater, which lay between us like a thrown gauntlet. "Ashley . . ." She exhaled. "What's the deal with the sweater?"

"What'll happen if I leave it there?"

She wrinkled her brow as she considered the question. "I would prefer your cooperation, but I'll pick up your stuff for fifty cents. I'll give you one warning, then if it isn't put away in a half hour, I'll deduct the money from your allowance."

I calculated quickly. "Not worth it," I mumbled, and removed my sweater.

The phone rang again. It was my new friend, Brooke. She had just moved to our neighborhood from another city. Her gossip was more amusing than a sweater war with Gay. I took the portable phone in the other room and complained about Gay.

"I have ways of getting back at my mom when she annoys me."

"How?" I asked.

"Just do something that will piss her off but that she can't pin on you." She gave me a cunning laugh. "I drop my mom's ironed shirts on the floor and make it look like they fell off the hanger."

I found a lizard that the cats had partially eaten. I plopped it into the toe of one of Gay's favorite shoes. I never heard what happened when she found it, but she probably thought one of the cats put it there. One of my dumber tricks was to pee in her favorite rosebush, which was planted in a pot on the patio outside my bedroom door. Another time I slicked the rim of Gay's travel mug with dish soap. I did not hear any complaints and wondered whether she had guessed what I had done. Maybe she was making a misconduct list so she could justify sending me back.

I hid out in my room as much as possible, although Gay often tried to get me out, if only to do chores. I was on the portable phone with Tess when Gay knocked on the door. When I did not reply, she cracked it open and said, "Dinner will be in about an hour. Sometime before that, would you please empty the dishwasher and set the table?"

I turned my back and thought she had gone. "Gay's such a demanding bitch!"

Gay was still standing in the doorway. She struggled to compose her face. "Do you want broccoli or cauliflower?"

"Cauliflower, I guess." She closed the door with a hard clunk.

When I came out at the last possible minute, Gay had begun to place the napkins herself. "You know I heard what you said on the phone." I crossed my arms and waited for a lecture. "Ash, I am not the mother who abandoned you." Her voice took on a tone I had never heard before. It was deeper and it commanded that I listen. "I am not Mrs. Moss. I am not the ten others who sent you away for one reason or another." I tried to block her voice by humming inside my head, but her words penetrated anyway. "I *am* the mother who will be here for the rest of my life." She started tossing lettuce aggressively. "You can blame me for anything that is my fault, but you can't hate me for what the others did to you."

Phil came into the room whistling. "What smells so good, girls?" he asked. He saw us scowling at each other. "I can see this is going to be another pleasant family meal," he said facetiously. "What's going on?"

"Gay's always on my case!" I yelled.

Phil backed away from both of us. "I'm going to sit in the car until you work it out."

"What about your dinner?" Gay called.

"It's already ruined," he said, and left the house.

I was not sure whether I had won or lost.

Christmas made me nervous for a lot of reasons. In foster homes, holidays always had a way of making me feel like an outsider—and now the stakes were higher. I wondered if Blake would still be upset that I was sleeping in his bed and if the food would be even weirder than at Thanksgiving. The gifts that had been donated to The Children's Home were lavish and expensive, and we had been warned not to expect as much after we were adopted. The Courters hadn't asked me to make a list, and I had no idea what they might give me—or what I was supposed to give them. They carried on with all their holiday traditions, and I didn't know how to join in.

"Come help," Phil coaxed as they decorated the Christmas tree that touched the ceiling in their two-story living room.

I was snuggled under an afghan on the sofa. "I hate decorating trees."

"What did you do at the cottage?" Blake asked.

I tucked the afghan tighter under me. "We stood in line, were given one ornament, placed it on a branch, and then had to go back to the end to wait our next turn."

"That doesn't sound like much fun," Blake agreed. "Here it's a free-for-all."

Josh was standing on a ladder, but he could not reach the tip of the tree. "I have an idea." He brought in an extension ladder. "Ash, we need you to place the angel."

"But the ladder isn't leaning against anything!" Gay warned.

"We'll steady her," Josh replied. "Blake, you should have seen her on the climbing wall at Hampshire. She's a natural."

I jumped off the sofa, gave Gay a dare-me stare, and zipped up to the top without looking down. As I reached for the angel, the fifteen-foot ladder swayed a bit, but I slipped the decoration into place.

"Hang in there!" Blake called. Josh handed up more ornaments with an extended pincer tool, and I snagged them on the branches.

"Isn't she cool?" Josh said admiringly. I scampered down and took a bow.

Gay's family also celebrated Hanukkah. On December 23 we lit the first candle and I received my first Harry Potter book.

Luke had moved in with the Hudsons by now, and our families got together on Christmas Eve. Every few minutes he would call, "Mom, look at this!" or "Dad, watch me!" I was relieved he would not have another holiday at The Children's Home.

On Christmas morning there was a mountain of gifts under the tree. Josh, in a Santa hat, made piles for each person. "Youngest first," he insisted.

I opened a package. It was a nightgown. I tossed it behind me on the floor and opened the next. It contained two CDs. I started for the third.

"Who's that from?" Gay asked.

"I dunno," I replied.

Phil retrieved a tag from the trash that had accumulated at my feet. "This card is from Grandma Courter. Which was her gift?"

"Maybe the nightgown?" Gay suggested. "No, wait, Aunt Robin sent her that." Her voice was exasperated. "Let's mark down what you have received so far."

"Why do you have to ruin everything?" I screeched.

Phil sat on the footrest in front of me. "When you were in foster care, you received presents from donors, so it didn't matter who they were from. But now someone who cares about you selected each one of these gifts. All we want to know is which present came from which person so they can be acknowledged." His voice was warm yet firm. "That's how we do it in this family."

"My turn," Josh said to get me off the hook.

The big family gift was a hot tub. "Let's have a girls-only hot tub," Gay suggested when the boys were out with their friends.

We each found comfortable positions. Gay leaned back and closed her eyes.

"You will always love Josh and Blake more than me, won't you?" I blurted.

It was too dark to see the expression on Gay's face. "Yes," she said in a throaty voice, "that's if length of time equals amount of love. On that basis, I have been with Phil the longest, so I love him the most. Even though I have only known you a few months, I know love is growing in my heart, because—" She waited a long beat. "Well, I almost had a heart attack when you were on that ladder!" She turned off the hot tub jets to make certain I was hearing her. "You are our chosen child, our only daughter. We missed so much of your life, and we cannot erase some of the tragedies." Gay started to climb out of the hot tub. She turned and smiled. "All we can do is help you be the person you want to be from now on."

I had never been able to stay up until midnight, but the Courters allowed me to ring in the New Year. Phil poured champagne for the adults while my friends and I drank fizzy grape juice.

At one o'clock Gay turned to my friends and me. "Girls, time for bed." Blake's and Josh's friends were going to continue their party on the patio. A few hours later voices in the living room awakened Gay. She peered over the balcony and saw Tess and me sitting in the living room with my brothers and their friends.

Later that day I overheard Gay scolding her sons. "It was inappropriate for those sixth-grade girls to be prancing around in their nighties around your friends."

Josh tried to calm her down. "The girls just wanted to hang out."

"Did I get you in trouble?" I asked him when Gay went to stew in her study.

"Let's go for a walk," Josh suggested.

It was windy out, and I hadn't taken a sweater. Blake joined us. When he saw me shivering, he laughed. "Florida girl." Halfway down the street Blake said, "Even though we're a lot older than you, we're not your parents."

Josh added, "But we do want to be your brothers."

"In other words, we are always going to support *you*, not the 'rents," Blake continued.

"If Mom hadn't seen you last night, we never would have said anything," Josh added.

"But now she knows," I said. I was trembling from the cold, as well as from anxiety.

Josh put his arm around me. "Oh, don't mind her. She's like a match. If she rubs up against something, she flares up for a second, but then she fizzles out very quickly."

"And Phil?"

"He's harder to pin down. He'll let something eat away at him without mentioning it, but if you really disappoint him . . ." Josh let the words linger.

"The point is, they are the best parents ever," Blake said. "They have always been there for us and they will always be there for you. And so will we."

11

What do I have to do?

In the back of my mind I kept wondering what I would have to do wrong for the Courters to send me back. Refusing to eat something or having a messy room was not going to annoy them enough. I had found all sorts of ways to incite a quarrel between Phil and Gay, which gave me a perverse satisfaction—until Phil lost his usual cool and stormed out to his workshop. I never wanted to hurt his feelings; but I did love to see Gay crumble.

"Want to go to the mall?" Gay asked on a Saturday morning.

"Not particularly." I was painting my stubby nails.

"Are you sure? There are some great clothing sales."

After lunch Phil wondered if I wanted to go to the mall with him. "Sure," I said.

Gay blew up. "I was going to buy her clothes!"

Phil put his hands up in surrender. "I'm just getting a battery at Sears."

Gay fumed for a while, but the next morning she was cheerful. "Every day is a new day," she said. Then her voice darkened. "But Phil is different. He's very slow to anger, but it takes him a long time to forgive and forget. He'll go the extra ten miles, but if you break faith with him . . ." Her words trailed off ominously.

Over at the Hudsons', Luke was testing limits more and more. I overheard Gay trying to calm down Georgia over the phone: "They love to wave the red flag in the bullring. But you don't have to react." Gay nodded sympathetically. "I know, I know. I lose it too!"

After Luke was cruel to their dog, the Hudsons admitted that he may have not been ready to live with them, and he returned to The Children's Home.

I was furious—not at the Hudsons, who had been so patient and loving, but at Luke, who had blown his big chance.

He was not the only reject. Daphne's sister was sent back for intensive therapy. Will bounced into and out of a family, and Sabrina's adoption disrupted. We were the boomerang kids. No matter how far we were thrown, we ended up back at our place of origin. I was determined to enjoy my freedom while it lasted.

The Courters traveled for their film business and usually took me along, pulling me out of school for a few days. In January of my sixth-grade year, Josh joined us as a second cameraman at a judges' conference in Santa Barbara, California. After a long day of shooting, Phil and Gay went to a meeting while Josh and I rented recumbent bikes on the beach. Alone with Josh, I felt a genuine acceptance that I had not yet sensed with his parents. With the wind in my hair and the surf pounding in my ears, I thought: *This is about as far away from foster care as I can get.* But I still warned myself not to let down my guard.

A few weeks later we were off to film again in Washington, D.C. I tagged along while Phil and Gay interviewed some members of Congress. A group of staffers invited me to explain the problems faced by foster children. They were shocked by how often I had changed schools.

When we had a break, Phil asked what I would like to do.

"How about going to the White House to meet the president?"

He grinned. "Okay, we'll arrange that for next time."

I decided on the Holocaust Memorial Museum. At the entrance I picked up a card with a young woman's picture and followed her story. Her life became worse and worse, and I wondered if she had learned to turn off her feelings the way I had. She was separated from all her family members too. At the end of the tour I learned that she perished at Auschwitz. Afterward I wandered around the lobby in a daze.

"Where were you?" Phil asked in annoyance when they finally found me.

"We're going to have to hustle for our next appointment," Gay said.

As we hurried toward the Metro, I lagged behind. Phil paid our fares just as a train was coming into the station. The Courters leaped on the train. Since I had never seen a subway before this trip, I feared that the doors were going to squash me. Feeling overwhelmed for a moment, the doors closed while I was still standing on the platform. Phil yelled, "Take the next train to Union Station." His eyes were wide and Gay looked frantic.

I took the next train and was relieved to get to Union Station. I climbed the stairs, and went directly to the officer at the information booth and said I was looking for my parents. He called the other station and said my parents were at the other end of the platform.

Phil and Gay came panting toward me. "Where were you?" I asked.

"Where the hell were you?" Phil bellowed.

"I was here the whole time."

"We were covering both ends of the platform. How did you slip away from us?" he shouted, as if I had done it to defy him.

I pushed through the turnstile to get away from them. Phil was right behind me and grabbed the collar of my jacket. "Don't you ever, ever pull a stunt like that again!" His face was mottled with red patches. "We thought we had lost you!"

Gay was shaking. "Why didn't you get on the train with us?"

"The door closed." I shrugged Phil's arm off. "You're hurting me!"

"You hurt *me*, Ashley," he growled. "Anything could have happened to you!"

We trudged up Capitol Hill in silence. We were staying with some business associates of the Courters, so they could not continue to berate me. After dinner I hurried to get ready for bed and turned out the light hoping I could fall asleep and wake up with one of Gay's fresh starts. I heard creaking on the stairs in the old house and feared someone was coming to have a little talk with me.

I heard my door's handle turning slowly. I rolled over to

face the wall, which was illuminated with a plank of light from the hallway.

Gay sat on the end of the bed. "This hasn't been the best day, but it's something we went through together. Now it's woven into the fabric of our family story."

"Threads break," I mumbled.

"Not if you use tough fibers. If you were not made of resilient material, you would not have come this far. Just remember, you aren't alone anymore—we're here to back you up." She started to close the door behind her. The latch clicked closed, but I did not hear her footsteps moving away. The door snapped open again. "Ashley," Gay whispered through the gap, "I love you, sweetie. Night-night."

I pretended I had not heard her.

Even if Gay really thought she loved me, I felt nothing. The Hudsons had said they loved Luke, but that didn't stop them from sending him back. My mother swore that she loved me, and she abandoned me in the end. Adele, Aunt Leanne, even some of my foster moms had used the *L* word, then disappeared. I liked the Courters' large house, my school, and my friends. I just had to figure out how not to blow it.

In April we went to Colorado to film foster children who were placed for adoption with military families and remained a few extra days so I could try skiing. Driving up the mountain, it began to snow. "Please stop!" I called out. Phil parked at an overlook. I jumped from the car and thrust out my tongue. Finally, after more than seven years, I tasted the icy tang of snow again! As it tickled my upturned face, I remembered what Adele had said about taking me to Colorado. Now I was there, but with another family. A few years earlier I might have felt guilty that I was having the experience without Luke or any of my other relatives, but I was beginning to accept that I was meant to go on with my life—even a good life—without them. Still, I wondered whether Adele—or my mother—ever thought about me.

Our next trip was a cruise in the Caribbean. I remembered Mrs. Chavez telling me about her mother moving from one island to another and how she had later come to the United States. I started to count all the places I had lived over the past nine years and ran out of fingers. For the first time, I sensed this might be my last move.

On one island we hiked up a steep hill after swimming under a waterfall. Gay panted, "I think I can, I think I can."

"What are you talking about?" I asked.

"It's what the Little Engine That Could said. Didn't anyone ever read it to you?" I shook my head. "Did you ever hear any bedtime stories?"

"Not that I remember."

After we returned home, Gay started reading me children's books like *Pat the Bunny*, *Goodnight Moon*, and *Where the Wild Things Are* at bedtime. I liked being babied more than I dared to admit. One evening I started babbling in baby talk.

Gay played along. "Baby want her ba-ba?" She handed me an invisible bottle.

"I've always wanted a bottle!" I announced in a regular voice. "My mother took mine away too soon."

The next day she actually bought me a bottle. I filled it with juice, relaxed on the couch, and drank it. "This is great!" I tossed it in the air. "And it doesn't spill."

After Gay read *Horton Hatches the Egg*, we both were quiet as we contemplated how the mother bird left the elephant to sit on her egg.

"Do you still wish your mother would come back for you?" Gay asked.

I said, "No," although I was not certain I meant it.

"If you want, you can still see her," Gay said as she switched off my table lamp. I turned my cheek for the usual kiss. Gay said, "Someday maybe you'll kiss me back."

I sat up and stared just past her. "I told you I would *never* kiss you!" She looked as startled as if I had slapped her. I gazed at my ceiling that twinkled with glow-in-the-dark stars. Somewhere my mother was still out there. I would keep my promise to her even if she had not kept any of hers to me, and I would *never* love anyone else.

A few days later the official adoption papers arrived. We had been expecting them for several months, but my case-workers had changed many times, creating further delays.

"Doesn't matter to us," Phil had reassured me. "We're not letting anyone take you away from us."

Because I was twelve, I had to sign consent to the adoption and select my name. "I've been a Rhodes all my life," I told the Courters, "and I don't want to lose that."

"We'd like everyone to know you are our daughter," Phil said, "but we won't force it." He left the paper in my room. "We'll never change our minds about adopting you, but you can change yours. Let us know when you have made your decisions."

For the most part, we were getting along better and better. Phil was easy, but Gay was always on my case when it came to food. Usually, I was starving by four o'clock, so on the way home from school I would beg Gay to stop for a burger. She relented when she was cooking something like curry or a casserole, because she knew I would not even taste foods when she combined them in some disgusting way. I would eat vegetables only if they were canned, and I hated the bright green crunchy ones she steamed and claimed were healthier. At least Gay did not spice my portions and stopped wincing when I dumped steak sauce over every meat. I knew she was trying; and yet—for some reason— that irked me too.

"I'm preparing all of your favorite recipes," Gay called out as I headed for the portable phone. "Roasted chicken, cauliflower with cheese sauce, pickled cucumbers, and freshly baked blueberry muffins." I did not respond. "Want to lick the bowl?" she asked after she poured the batter into the muffin tin.

"I'm on the phone," I said, even though I had not yet dialed. I dragged out the call and came to the table reluctantly. The food smelled delicious, yet I did not want to give Gay the satisfaction of winning—although I did not know why I felt that way. I sat down as though I suspected there was a tack on my chair.

Phil lifted a slice of white meat. "Hand me your plate," he said to me.

"I'm not hungry." I stared Gay down. A little thrill went through me as I saw her twitch. I knew she was thinking about how to respond to my rejection of her menu.

Gay's jaw tightened. "No alternate dinners," Gay said to me, then turned toward Phil. "She likes everything that's being served."

"Fine," I retorted in relief. "May I please be excused?" I went to my room and did not emerge for the rest of the night, even though my stomach rumbled and my mind churned, trying to understand why I would rather annoy Gay than eat her food.

The next day Gay picked me up from school. "Want to stop at Wendy's?"

"Are you going out or something?" I asked.

"Nope. You won't like what I'm cooking tonight."

"What is it?"

"Sweetbreads."

"That doesn't sound so bad."

"It's a cow's pancreas gland."

I figured she was grossing me out as revenge for not eating her chicken dinner. While we were ordering at the drive-through, Gay said, "I called Beth Reese today."

"About the adoption?"

"Nope."

Her cheerfulness was troubling. If she was sending me back, she would have spoken to Beth Reese. "Ashley, I've been bending over backward trying to cook for you, but from now on, I am serving the sorts of meals that Phil and I prefer. I will try to make a plain version for you, but I won't care if you eat it. You may have all the alternate dinners you want."

Once we were home, I unpacked my sandwich while Gay started her preparations. She peeled carrots as if she was enjoying skinning their flesh. "Are you mad at me?" I asked.

"No."

"What did you talk to Ms. Beth about?"

"Why you didn't eat any of your favorite foods last night." Gay put down the peeler. "I love feeding my family, yet you resist my nurturing because all those other mothers—especially your birth mother—failed to care for you. I cannot force you to accept my love through food, kisses, or any of the ways I know." She melted butter in a sauté pan, then tossed in pieces of the gnarly meat. "So I won't frustrate myself trying."

I reached for my burger. It was cold. I ate it anyway and tried to decide once again whether I had won or lost.

Did I really want to stay with the Courters? Some days I felt as if I had been born into their family; other times I felt like a guest who had stayed too long. Yet I was more afraid of an unknown place. This could be the best deal anyone would ever offer me.

Finally, I decided on a name: Ashley Marie Rhodes-Courter. Gay's cousin, Neil Spector, was going to be our attorney for the finalization. We went to Tampa to sign the consent forms at his office.

"Will Neil also be my attorney after the adoption?" I asked.

Phil raised his eyebrows. "Why? Are you planning to sue us?"

"No, but I want to sue the Mosses for what they did to me—and Luke."

"It will be their word against yours," Phil said.

"They should pay for what they did to us!" I seethed.

"Cutie-pie, let it go," he added.

Gay whispered, "Why don't you talk about that with your therapist?"

Neil ushered us into a conference area to review the paperwork with us. He glanced from the Courters to me and was probably wondering why we did not seem happier about the occasion.

Gay told me she was going to Tampa to review my whole file. "I want to fill in the blanks in your life before they store your files."

"We've got the kid, what else matters?" Phil asked.

"Ashley has had so many questions about her past. Maybe I'll find some answers in those boxes."

That evening she came home waving a thick manila envelope. "Your new worker dragged out three file storage boxes. I found all sorts of information on your birth family, foster homes, schools. . . ." She grinned mischievously. "When I lifted out the last section of files in one case, I noticed this!"

She handed me the envelope. I gasped when I opened it and found my hospital newborn photo, family snapshots, even professional baby portraits. "I didn't know that I had any baby pictures!"

"I'd recognize those dimples anywhere," Phil said like a proud papa.

He made copies, and soon my framed baby pictures sprouted up next to those of Blake and Josh.

Before going to school one morning, I came in to ask Gay something while she was sipping tea in bed. She pointed to the photo of me as a bald baby in a sky blue dress. "Sometimes I pretend you were my baby," she said.

I looked at the picture, then at Gay. "Gotta run." I started out the door, turned around, bent over, gave Gay a peck on the cheek, and rushed from the room.

The Courters bustled about with legal preparations and plans for three adoption parties. To honor the people who had helped make my adoption possible, they were hosting a luncheon near the courthouse. Mary Miller and the Guardian ad Litem Program staff headed the guest list, which also included Martha Cook, who had been my pro bono Attorney ad Litem. Next, we were going to The Children's Home for a smaller dessert party, which only served to remind me that I could get sent back there any-time. The Courters also planned a gathering in their home for friends and family over the weekend.

When Gay asked what sort of cake I wanted, I said, "I don't care." And I really did not. I did not want them to make a big deal because I expected that all the celebrations would just add to future bad memories.

"From now on, you'll have two birthdays: your adoption day and your regular one," Gay announced. Then she asked, "What would you like for your adoption day gift?"

"I want to have my ear cartilage pierced like Ms. Sandnes."

"I'm not mutilating you the minute I get you," she snapped.

"Tess's mother let her have her belly button pierced!"

"Lucky Tess," she said in a snide voice.

The closer the fateful day came, the grumpier I felt. That morning I did not dress until the last possible minute. Gay was annoyed that everyone—including my godparents, Adam and Lesley Weiner, and their three young daughters—was waiting on me. Josh carried the professional video camera to capture every "precious" moment. At the luncheon I could barely swallow more than a soda. Gay had told me to write a poem to thank everyone. She had my poem printed and waiting on every place setting.

Phil stood up and welcomed the guests, and then Gay made a few remarks. She concluded, "Thanks, everyone, for giving us our daughter! Now here's Ashley."

I stayed in my seat. Gay flapped her copy of my poem in my face. "You're supposed to read it," she hissed.

I looked out and saw the expectant faces of the Merritts and Ms. Sandnes, Mary Miller and Martha Cook, The Children's Home staff, the Weiners and other Courter friends and family. I was more furious at Gay's prompting than nervous. Snatching the paper, I spoke in a monotone:

You have helped me so much over these past few years,
I just can't thank you enough, you wonderful dears.
You came through for me even when I was blue.
You even found me a great family!
Who knew?

You've gone to great lengths to please little ol' me
You really cared, and that I now see,
Words cannot express my deep gratitude.

You've made me one happy little dude
What I say is true, I hope you don't mind
But you guys are definitely one of a kind!

I was trembling as I spit out the last forced sentence. Thinking I was overwhelmed with emotion, Phil stood and put his arm around me protectively. "We'd better not keep the judge waiting."

I squirmed away and went to the restroom to avoid saying good-bye to those who were not coming to the adoption proceedings. Gay followed me into the bathroom. "Ashley, are you all right?"

I flushed and came out. "Yeah, sure."

"I'm nervous too," Gay said.

I pushed in front of her without responding. The car was hotter than a sauna, and it didn't have time to cool off before we found a parking lot near the courthouse. The downtown buildings radiated heat like giant toasters in the midday July sun, making my dress stick to my legs. At first the frigid courthouse felt as refreshing as an icy bath, but by the time we took the escalator upstairs, I could not stop shaking. Soon we were called into Judge Florence Foster's chambers. I could not wait for it to be over, but there was a delay. Clayton Hooper—the same caseworker I'd had at the Hagens and now my most recent adoption worker—was late. I stared into the distance while everyone chatted as if this were a cocktail party. I sucked in my cheek and chewed on the side of my lip.

"Hey, everyone, sorry I'm late," called Mr. Hooper as he breezed in without explaining where he had been. He reached over and patted my head. "Where's that sunshiny smile of yours, Ashley Marie? This is the happiest day of your life!"

"The judge is waiting," a bailiff said, and opened the door for us all to enter.

I expected that we would go into a TV-style courtroom, but we went from a public hallway to a private one and then into a corporate-style conference room with a polished table in the middle. Judge Foster sat at one end. Neil Spector was in charge of the seating plan, and I was told to take the chair between my almost-parents. I stared across at Mary Miller, Mary Fernandez, and Beth Lord. I wanted to crawl under the table and sit on the other side because I felt that is where I really belonged. They had known me longer than the Courters, so in my mind, they were more like family. I glanced at Phil and Gay, who were listening to the legal gibberish. Mary Miller was smiling, and so were Beth Lord and Mary Fernandez. They wanted me to move on to another life, but I was ready to call the whole thing off.

Gay's father—he liked it when I called him "Grampy"—coughed. He was signaling Josh to get a shot of one of the Weiners' daughters, who was making a monkey face, but Josh remained focused on the judge as she turned to speak directly to me.

"Nothing in life comes easy," Judge Foster began. "If it does, you should be suspicious."

Now I realize that the judge was trying to connect with me by understanding that I had overcome many hardships, but—at that moment—I believed she sensed that my new family was too good to be true. Gay could morph into a Mrs. Moss as soon as nobody was checking on us, and I had glimpsed how furious Phil could become during the episode in the Washington subway. What would he do if he got angry with me again? It was only a matter of time before this happy-family farce would be over. I looked anywhere but at the judge, hoping there was some way to leave the room without causing a scene.

I tuned back in as the judge was complimenting the Courters on their willingness to take me. Then the judge asked me, "Do you want me to sign the papers and make it official, Ashley?"

Because of my age, I had to consent to the adoption. There was a long silence. I could hear Gay's short little breaths. Grampy coughed again.

I muttered, "I guess so." Three little words and it was done.

Gay blotted her eyes, reached over, and tried to kiss my cheek. I arched away and rubbed my grazed cheek as though it were tainted.

I headed to the door, but Phil nudged me toward the judge. We took a few stilted photos with the judge. Mary Miller presented me with a bouquet, which required more photos, and then it was back out into the pounding sunlight. I wished I could melt into the pavement rather than have to get into the Courters' van and pretend that this was a happily-ever-after occasion.

We stopped at The Children's Home for the dessert celebration. I had been to these productions for other kids—kids who were sent back—so what was the point? My old friends stood around awkwardly and left the room as soon as they had finished their cake. Luke, who was normally a total terror, sat docilely and sipped a soda.

For the last time, Mary Fernandez asked me how I felt. I said, "This is horrible for Luke."

"Today's your day, Ashley," she said, but my feeling of doom did not recede.

Not long after the adoption, the strangest thing happened: I started tasting new foods. While we were in Tampa shopping, the Courters decided to have sushi.

"Do you want to have a burger before or after?" Phil asked.

"I'm not hungry yet," I said, sulking.

At the sushi bar the young, handsome chef automatically served me a piece of yellowtail. Wanting to impress him with my sophistication, I popped it in my mouth. It tasted both sweet and tangy, and the texture was silky. "It's really good!"

I saw Gay and Phil exchange a shocked glance. I dared myself to try a piece of tuna roll from Phil's plate. "May I taste your soup?" I asked. He pushed it in front of me, and I ate it—seaweed and all.

"Still want a burger?" Phil asked when we were in the car.

"Nope." A few miles down the road I blurted, "I can't believe I ate raw fish!"

As the adoption made me feel more secure, the tautness in my stomach relaxed, and I found that I was interested in new foods. I realized that I could find something I liked at almost any restaurant, whereas before I had often left hungry.

School started again in a few weeks, which was a relief because my quarrels with Gay had intensified. She hassled me about everything, and sometimes I enjoyed provoking her.

On the Halloween just before my thirteenth birthday, Tess came over. We fashioned low-cut, tight costumes and elaborately made up our faces. "What are you going as?" Gay asked.

I strutted on high heels and placed my hand on my hip in a provocative pose. "A hooker."

"You can't go out like that!" Gay shrieked.

"What about Tess?" I felt humiliated in front of my friend.

"I'll take her home and see what her mother thinks of her choice. But if you don't modify that outfit, the only trick you are getting is to stay here."

I gave her the silent treatment. "Those blank stares may work on other people, but I've lived with you long enough to know what you're up to," she said.

"You're an unreasonable—" My voice became shrill, but I censored myself. I had never cussed at Gay to her face and did not know what would happen if I did.

"And you're acting like your mother!"

I recoiled as if I had been punched and gasped for breath. Gay looked like she wished she could suck the words back in. As soon as I caught my breath, I found beads and scarves to make the outfits more discreet, and we went out as gypsies.

I did not know then that the Courters had withheld something that Gay had found along with my pictures in the files: letters from my mother, Aunt Leanne, and Dusty.

Gay waited until after the adoption to contact Leanne. My aunt was thrilled to hear about me and told Gay how she and Lorraine had tried hard to parent me when I was a baby. Leanne was married with two sons. My uncle Sammie was also married and had been eager to find Luke and me. Gay asked her whether she should contact my mother. Aunt Leanne explained that my mother had a steady job and a new boyfriend. "She would love to hear how Ashley's doing."

"I'll write her," Gay replied.

"Well, you be careful," Leanne warned. "My sister can't always be trusted."

Mary Fernandez and Mary Miller also urged caution. The therapist told Gay that it was important for me to have integrated more of the Courter family's values before I identified with my mother again; and my guardian, who had dealt with my mother for several years, distrusted her. Phil was also negative and insisted she use our attorney's return address. Gay kept the correspondence secret from me for quite some time.

Every time I visited Luke at The Children's Home, I was haunted by the thought of where I would be without my new family. I used to think of the campus as a haven, but now I saw it as a holding pen where my brother would stay until he turned eighteen or could find another family. But still I couldn't get along with Gay.

My friend Brooke agreed that Gay had no sense of what girls our age were wearing and had terrible taste in clothes. She never got manicures and did not own a single pair of heels or jeans! Then Tabitha pointed out that her family's rules were far stricter than mine were. Sure, I had to set the table, but her mother used dainty china every night and she had to hand-dry the plates. She reminded me to be grateful, and reluctantly, I sometimes agreed with her.

Gay's father, Grampy Weisman, lived only a few miles away. I loved driving up to his house because his front door was guarded by gigantic lion sculptures—exactly like the ones I had fantasized would protect me. Grampy sometimes noticed how cranky I was with Gay. At first I thought he would take his daughter's side. "You come to me if she's too tough on you," he said. "I'll calm her down." His lips crinkled into a smile. "Now, where's your latest report card?" He gave it the once-over. "Okay, Ash, here's the cash." He handed me a hundred dollars for being on the honor roll.

"There's an honor roll breakfast, and Gay and Phil can't make it. Would you like to come with me?" Grampy beamed.

In January, Gay picked me up at school. "We're going to have to go to Washington again." She sighed as though it was going to be a drag.

"What are you filming?"

"Actually, the invitation is for you." She handed me a fax from the director of the Dave Thomas Foundation, who had arranged for me to attend a White House event.

"Will I meet President Clinton?"

"I'm not sure, but the First Lady will be there."

Gay and I flew to Washington together. She seemed to know everyone in the line that snaked through the security checkpoints. Once inside, we stopped at the women's restroom in the East Wing. A sitting area featured portraits of previous First Ladies. Gay snapped photos of me in front of many of them. Even the paper towels were imprinted with the White House logo, and I took a few for my friends.

As I walked up a marble stairway, a trio of musicians was playing classical music. "Are you okay?" Gay asked, noticing my face blushing from excitement.

"Just hot," I said to avoid having to explain that it was as if my childish fantasies about accidentally being lost in foster care, while I was really meant for another, grander life, had come true.

The occasion was an announcement of a program for children who were aging out of foster care. One girl described how she slept on gurneys in hospital emergency rooms at night while attending college during the day. I wondered if Luke would end up that way.

On the way out Gay introduced me to Michael Piraino, the CEO of the National Court Appointed Special Advocates Association. Guardian ad Litem volunteers like Mary Miller are often called CASAs for short in many parts of the country. "I see you're representing the Dave Thomas Foundation here," he said. "Awesome!"

"That's my kiddo," Gay bragged.

"What did you think of Mrs. Clinton's announcement?" Mr. Piraino asked me.

I probably should have given him a polite reply, but I was thinking about Luke and the other Children's Home kids who might never be adopted. "Children need families, not programs," I said.

"How old are you?" he asked.

"Thirteen," I mumbled, thinking I might have offended him.

"We're going to be hearing a lot more from you," he said, smiling gently.

Gay added, "Ashley was in foster care for nine years, and she wouldn't have been adopted if it wasn't for her child advocate, Mary Miller."

"It only takes one caring person, right?" He winked at me.

I did not know that Gay had been in touch with my mother until she handed me an envelope toward the end of March, during my seventh-grade year. "I found out how to contact Leanne," Gay explained, "and then I wrote to Lorraine." I was furious when I found out that Gay and my mother had been writing letters behind my back. I felt that Gay had horned her way into my most private relationship without my permission. "What did you tell her?"

"How well you are doing in school, that you have braces—that sort of thing."

"Did you say that you're a bestselling writer and Phil makes films for television?"

"Not exactly. I didn't want her to be intimidated. It was more general—like how many other children we have. I enclosed recent photos of you and offered to send regular updates. I promised that we would always love you and treat you as our own child." Gay swallowed hard. "I said that we would allow you to contact her—or any of your biological family—when you asked to."

"So why didn't you tell me?"

"I wasn't sure if she would even reply." I noticed that my mother had addressed the envelope to *The Parents of Ashley, in Care of Neil Spector.*

"Doesn't she know where we live?"

"No, Phil didn't think that was wise."

The envelope contained a card picturing a redheaded girl on the front. Inside, my mother wrote that she had remarried on Valentine's Day. She also mentioned that she played softball for a team called the Pride, which seemed like a meaningful coincidence because my Little League team's name was also the Pride! She signed the letter, *All my love, Lorraine.*

I felt as if I had gulped down five Cokes in a row. I hurried to write back. *My new "parents" are nice people,* I began. I could not resist boasting about all the traveling I had done and my visit to the White House. I told her that I thought the coincidence of our teams' names was bizarre. As a P.S., I wrote, *I love you always and I call my "parents" by their first names. No one can take your place.*

My mother's next letter included photos of her wedding. Aunt Leanne had been her maid of honor, and Uncle Sammie had given her away. She told me that she wanted to see me and that I would always be the most important person in her life.

A series of letters, photos, and packages went back and forth through April. I started daydreaming about being with my mother again. I kept these feelings secret from the Courters, and I did not dare tell Luke that I had two mothers—while he had none.

Gay and Phil read all my mother's letters and checked

the outgoing replies to make certain I did not reveal any private information, which I would not have done anyway. On one level, I had never stopped loving my mother; on another, I still distrusted her. Her first letters had made me feel elated; some subsequent ones made me squirm. She wrote that her husband, Art, desired a child, yet she did not want anything to alter the relationship we had begun to rebuild.

I thrust that letter at Gay. "I don't think she should have another baby! I'll be fourteen years older than the kid!" I huffed. "What makes her think she won't screw it up the next time?"

"My guess is that she's asking for your forgiveness, not your permission."

Gay and I stared at each other without speaking. We were thinking the same thing: My mother was already pregnant. Gay handed the letter back. I crumpled it and tossed it toward the wastebasket, but I missed.

"I'm not sure I did the right thing by contacting your mother," Gay said.

"Are you going to forbid me from writing?"

"No, Ash, we would never do that. But every time you get a letter, you go on a little high, then you crash, like too much sugar at a birthday party." She paced her office and stared out at the water. The dusk sky looked molten, as if it might explode in the west. "Let's talk it over with your therapist."

At my next therapy session we showed the March and April letters to Dr. Susan Reeder. I watched as the therapist reread the closing of the most recent letter: *I love you. I love you. Please find comfort in that. I miss you. Please write soon. All my love, Lorraine. P.S. How's Luke? Tell him hello and I love him, too.*

The doctor turned to me. "How do you feel about this?"

I was quiet for a few seconds. How many times had I heard those three little words from my mother? In her way, she meant them, but they still felt hollow. Even so, they were precious to me.

"It's tough keeping the secret from Luke."

"Do the letters upset you?" the therapist asked Gay.

"Yes. Every time a letter arrives, Ashley is off-kilter for a few days. Her mother has been writing for less than two months, and look what tension it has caused." Gay paused, and the office filled with the constant low drone of the air conditioner. "Also, her mother wants to meet with her."

"Do you want to do that?" Dr. Reeder asked me.

"Not now." I could not imagine my mother and Gay in the same space.

"How would you feel about limiting the letters?"

Gay jumped on this. "Why not center them on holidays, like birthdays, Easter, Christmas, even . . . Mother's Day. There's probably something every month."

"Is that okay with you?" the therapist asked me.

"Sure," I agreed, and Gay left the room.

Before Gay sent my mother the letter outlining the new plan, she gave it to me to edit. "Promise you'll tell me if something happens," I asked.

"Like what?"

"With my mother, you never know."

Just before Mother's Day, Gay asked me if I wanted to send my mother a card. "Why? I never think of her that way."

"Well, I'm thinking of her, and I'm grateful that she had you," Gay said.

In June, I went to stay with my godparents, the Weiners, in South Carolina and attend an arts camp where they taught. One night I called home and said, "I'm sick."

"What's wrong?" Gay asked.

"Homesick," I admitted. "I never felt this way before, maybe because I never had a home to be sick for."

Gay laughed, but I was not joking. I missed my room, my bed, Phil's scrambled eggs, and even Gay's chicken nuggets.

A few weeks after I started eighth grade, Gay was making notes in her date book when she looked up. "Oh, today's Lorraine's birthday."

"I know," I replied. I had never forgotten the date.

"Even though she hasn't written you very much, I've called her a few times. She always sounds grateful for the news," Gay said, "but she keeps asking when she can talk to you." She studied my reaction. "Are you ready to call her?"

"I guess." I nibbled at the corner of a hangnail while Gay dialed and asked Lorraine if this was a good time. She handed me the phone and went to the far side of the room.

My mother's voice was smoky, like a jazz singer's. "Hey," she said. I imagined her in tight jeans and high-heeled sandals. "How are you?"

"Great! I made All-Stars in softball this summer." I paced around Gay's office as I chattered on. "I'm in the program for gifted students." I continued to describe some of our recent trips. "Oh, and I got a lot of clothes in L.A."

"My, you've changed," she replied. "You sound like a stuck-up Valley girl."

I leaned against the back of the couch to steady myself. Gay sensed something was wrong and walked over to me. I held the phone so she could hear, but it was my turn to speak and I had nothing more to say. Without another word to my mother, I handed the phone back to Gay and stomped out of the room. Gay hung up and followed me.

"What did she expect?" I shrieked. "I wasn't going to stay seven forever!"

Gay just listened as I vented. "What's wrong with trying to do well in school and sports? What's wrong with having a nice lifestyle? I can't believe that she sounded"—I hunted for the right word—"jealous of her own daughter!"

A few weeks later my mother asked Gay what I wanted for my fourteenth birthday. Gay mentioned that I had treasured all the gifts she had ever given me and that I still had the music box. When Gay told her that Mrs. Moss had kept my dolls and Easy-Bake oven, my mother said, "I never liked that woman!" Then my mother dropped the bombshell: She was expecting another baby—a girl—the day before my birthday.

Gay broke the news as gently as she could.

"She knew she was pregnant when she wrote that bull about how her husband wanted a baby, didn't she?" I exploded. Gay nodded. "They should take this one away from her in the hospital."

Autumn was born a few days earlier than expected, and I was relieved that we would not have the same birth date. My mother sent me another Easy-Bake oven for my birthday along with some other gifts. I was way too old for the toy but baked one cake to show Gay how it worked. Using my allowance, I bought my mother and the baby some Christmas gifts. Late in January my mother sent me a gift certificate and some pictures of the baby. "My mother is going to ruin her life." I told Gay I did not want to keep the pictures.

I looked over at Gay, who was grooming one of the cats. Her hair covered half her face, and the lamplight made her hair glow. She looked like she had been painted by Rembrandt. I blurted, "Do you realize I've lived with *you* almost as long as I ever lived with *her*?" I groaned. "Or anyone," I added. "I haven't seen my mother in six years."

"Let me know when you want to," she replied.

My reddening face revealed both my exhilaration and my embarrassment. "Won't you feel weird?"

Gay sighed. "When a man's beloved wife dies, he mourns her forever—even if he marries again for companionship. Your mother is a hard act to follow. She will always be the love of your life."

I could not believe Gay was admitting that she knew she would always come second.

There was a long silence between us. "Look, Ashley, you need to make peace with what happened with your mother before you can feel secure with anyone else. I have read the records. Like most people, she has good and bad points."

"So why didn't you offer this before?" My voice wavered.

"We've talked about it in a general way, but I hoped you wouldn't push it too soon because . . ." Gay measured her words. "She holds the power to hurt you, and I haven't figured out how to protect my daughter— well, *our* daughter—from any more pain."

In June, I prepared to attend the arts camp in South Carolina for the second time. As I was packing to leave my adoptive parents and return once more to the state where I was born and where my relatives still lived, the curiosity about my mother that I had kept at bay for the past several months was renewed. I still didn't feel ready to see her, but I knew that I wanted something to happen. When Gay was helping me with a suitcase, I suggested as nonchalantly as possible, "Hey, why don't you visit my mother while I'm at camp? Use your Guardian ad Litem vibes and tell me what you think." I studied her expression to see if she approved. "And give her some parenting tips while you're at it."

I did not say anything else about it, although I was fairly certain Gay would do it. When the Courters arrived for my showcase performances, I showed them around the theater. During a lull Gay said, "I visited your mother."

"Is she okay?"

"She's doing well, Ash," Gay replied in a reassuring voice. "She's living with Art, who's a few years younger."

"What kind of place is it?"

"A simple apartment. Not much furniture, but nice and clean." Gay laughed. "When I arrived, Lorraine said, 'I thought you would look like either Princess Diana or Janis Joplin.'"

"Definitely not Princess Di!" I said. "What did you wear?"

"My batik-print skirt, so I guess I was closer to Janis Joplin, without the voice or the Mercedes-Benz." Gay chuckled again. "I wasn't sure if I liked being compared to two dead female icons!" She waited for me to ask the *B* question. When I didn't, she paused a moment and then took the plunge. "Autumn is now eight months old."

I skipped over my half sister and asked, "What did my mother want to know about me?"

"What you looked like. I brought your recent albums, and she showed me one she had kept, including pictures from when you lived with your grandfather in South Carolina. We don't have most of those pictures, so Phil made copies."

"Does Autumn look like me?"

"Maybe your eyes, but there isn't much more of a resemblance. You do have many of your mother's facial expressions, though."

"What did she say about me?"

"We talked a lot about what you were like as a baby. She said you were very precocious, especially in toilet training and speech."

"Does she want to see me?" I asked.

"Very much so. She asked when she could."

"And what did you tell her?"

"That you were waiting to hear how our visit went." Gay's eyes darted—a signal that meant she was holding something back.

"Tell me everything." I sucked in my breath.

"Well, she became a little belligerent and asked me what I was going to tell you about getting together with her. I said that as far as I was concerned, you could see her whenever you wanted. Then she said that would be immediately." Gay sighed. "I said that I wasn't sure about that. Then she became even more defiant and asked, 'When is Ashley going to get over it?'"

"What? How can I just get over it?" I bristled as Gay continued.

"I said, 'Ashley will never get over it.' I explained to her that you were terribly hurt when she couldn't get her act together, that you had believed all of her promises." Gay took another long breath. "Your mother went on: 'I know all about hurt. My own mother abandoned me in a park, and I also grew up in an orphanage.' So I told her that she should have known how much you wanted—and needed—her."

I could hear the echo of my mother's whine when trying to explain herself to Mary Miller the last time I had seen her. She had not changed her tune after all these years.

"Anyway, she moaned about how she tried to get you back, but 'they' made it impossible. Just as I was tempted to ask her about the dirty drug tests, Art interjected. He said, 'I understand what the kid is going through,' and then he told me about some difficulties in his own family. That stifled your mother's pity party. She ended by saying that she signed the papers because her attorney believed that would give you and Luke a better life. She claimed she did everything out of love."

"She really doesn't know what she did to me, does she?"

"Her guilt makes her blind to your feelings."

"What feelings?" I said sarcastically. "I have no feelings."

That night I thought a lot about what Gay had told me. I remembered aching for my mother when I was in foster care, desperate to climb on her lap, smell her musky perfume, have her stroke my hair and call me "Sunshine." I did not want to hear her jabber on about Autumn. Just thinking my half sister's name made me grit my teeth. I was torn between resenting that she had taken my place and worrying that my mother might neglect her. I tried to imagine what it would be like to sit across from my mother, and I decided that is all I wanted. I needed her to see me—how great I had turned out without her help. I wanted her to know about how well I was doing in school and all my accomplishments. I was even secretly proud of my adoptive parents, who were far superior to her in education and status. Then I remembered her Valley girl put-down.

We heard little from my mother for six months, and just like the year before, she did not acknowledge my Christmas gifts until late in January. It seemed as though gaps in time were a tradition with her. I wondered if she routinely thought about me and my welfare, or if she just randomly remembered that she had other children and then had a little woe-is-me moment for herself.

Her next letter to Gay said that she and Art had separated. *I guess I need a mom,* she wrote. *Would you like to adopt me?*

That really felt creepy to hear. I said, "We'd be sisters!" Then I worried whether Autumn was safe alone with my mother. "If my mother ever calls, tell her I'm willing to meet her," I said.

But the arrangements weren't made until my sophomore year in high school. By that time, I was almost sixteen. We met at a restaurant north of Tampa, which was about halfway between our homes. I had asked both Phil and Gay to come for support. My mother arrived with Autumn, who was almost two, and a friend named Brenda. As I crossed the parking lot, my mother rushed over with outstretched arms. We hugged. I breathed in a familiar smokiness that mingled with a soapy sweetness.

Phil delivered our sandwiches to a corner table. He smiled at Autumn when she looked in his direction; other than that, he said nothing. Gay made small talk with my mother and Brenda. I kept glancing from my mother to Autumn. The three of us have the same almond-shaped eyes with coffee centers, I realized. My mother and I share muscular shoulders, and our lower center teeth cross at the same point. Her skin—and Autumn's—is more sallow; mine is bisque white. We all have round cheeks, although Autumn's face is oblong, while my mother's and mine are heart-shaped.

"How was school this year?" my mother asked me.

"I did okay," I said modestly, to avoid another insult.

"Honor roll," Gay crowed. "She's in all the highest classes."

"I finished high school before you were born," my mother retorted. "Not a GED—a real diploma."

I felt as if I were walking on broken glass. "That's great." I glanced from my mother to Gay to Phil. My mother was trying to act polite and sophisticated. Gay was artificially cheerful. Phil's face was blotchy, a sure sign that he was upset. I wondered what the other diners would think if they knew why we were all meeting. Here we were—my adopted parents, my birth mother, my half sister, and a stranger my mother needed for support—courteously sitting across from one another. Beneath my calm, my emotions were stewing. I felt resentful . . . abandoned . . . alone . . . sad . . . scared . . . and furious.

Autumn reached for the potato chips on my plate. I handed her one, and then she started to climb on my lap. I lifted her into my arms and was surprised at how chunky she was. She pulled my loose hair and wound it around her sticky fingers. I realized that when I was her age, I had lived with my mother. A year later they had taken me away.

Almost as if she were reading my mind, my mother said, "Everything's different now—I go to church, have a good job, and I'm sober."

I glanced at Phil. Disapproval wafted from him when my mother said, "I tried to get you back." I could almost hear him thinking, *Yeah, right.*

I sipped my soda to quiet my churning stomach. "What was I like as a baby?"

"You spoke early, and, my, what came out of your mouth!" When Phil heard about the time my car seat fell out of the moving car, his face paled. He excused himself to go to the restroom. I felt sorrier for him than I did for my mother. She seemed like a former neighbor or babysitter who just happened to know about my childhood.

Autumn wiggled down from my lap and reached toward my mother. "Mama!" Her flailing arm knocked over my mother's drink. Brenda mopped the spill. Autumn said, "Ash-wee, carry me."

I walked her around while my mother refilled her beverage. Autumn stroked my face with her gummy hands, and unexpectedly, she poked her finger in my mouth, which was slightly open. I nibbled her finger playfully. Autumn started screaming.

"Oh, I'm so sorry!" I said just as my mother reappeared. I handed over her crying child. Gay saw my distress and came over. "I didn't think I bit her that hard," I whispered to Gay.

My mother kissed the boo-boo as if it were a big deal, even though there was no mark. Autumn gulped and sniffled in my mother's arms.

"How about some pictures?" Gay asked. She handed Phil the camera.

My mother and I posed with and without Autumn until Phil said it was time to go.

When we left, Phil asked how I felt. "I'm glad I did it, though I have no desire to see them again."

By the second half of eighth grade, I had started spending more and more time with Brooke. She was a year older than me and had exotic looks that made her a guy magnet. Her parents would not let her date yet, so she would ask me to go to the movies with her and sit a few rows in front of her and her boyfriend, Seth. One time she did not want to leave Seth after the movie was over, and they continued to make out in the back of the theater until the usher threw them out. When I dragged Brooke outside, Gay—who had been waiting for more than a half hour—was seething.

"What took so long?"

"The movie ran later than we thought," I replied.

"No, it didn't. I went in and checked."

"I thought you would be at the Kmart entrance." Admitting a mistake in foster care had just brought further punishment, so I never backed down.

"Whatever," Gay snarled between gritted teeth. "No movies for a week."

Brooke begged me to get Gay to change her mind. "I *have* to see Seth!" A few days later she asked, "Could you arrange an overnight at your house on Friday?"

"Probably."

She explained her plan. "Your parents sleep upstairs and go to bed early. Mine are in the next room and stay up late." The idea was for us to wait until Phil and Gay went to bed, sneak out onto the pool patio, leave through the screen door, get on our bikes, and ride to the intersection, where Seth would be waiting with his car. "We can go down to the beach and hang out for a while."

"I don't know . . ."

"And he's bringing Rudy Mason," she said, "for you!"

I had never met Rudy, but I knew he was a senior and one of the stars of the basketball team. I was both excited and terrified.

Gay and Phil agreed to the sleepover. I hurried through dinner and clearing the table. "Why don't I finish up the kitchen myself tonight while you watch the news?" I suggested in my sweetest voice. "Gay, shall I make you a cup of tea?"

She seemed surprised. "That would be lovely," she said, and sat on the couch.

Phil had had a glass of white wine with dinner. There was enough in the bottle for one more. I carried the tea and the wine into the bathroom. I shook out the pills that Brooke had suggested I use to get them to fall asleep early. I crushed them with the bottom of the pill bottle and then pounded them into finer particles with a scissors handle. Next, I stirred the powdery remains into the beverages. The grains dissolved easily in the hot tea, but they clouded the wine.

The front door opened and closed. "Hi," Phil called. "I think she's in the kitchen."

Assuming Brooke had arrived early, I cracked the bathroom door. "I'm in here," I called in a loud whisper.

"What's up?" The voice was not Brooke's. Tabitha had stopped by to return a CD she had borrowed.

She saw the tea and wine on the bathroom counter. "What's going on?"

I closed the bathroom door behind us and told her as little as possible.

"That's not cool at all," she said. "I'm out of here!"

"Bye!" she called to my parents in the living room.

I handed Gay the tea. Very casually, I said to Phil, "Thought you might like another glass of wine."

"Thanks, cutie-pie," he said. "What's with Tabitha? I don't think she was here more than thirty seconds."

"Oh, she's jealous that Brooke is coming over. Those two don't get along."

"Three's a crowd," Gay added, and turned back to the news.

"I'm going to take a shower," I mumbled.

Just as I soaped up my hair, I heard banging on the bath-

room door. Phil shouted, "Ashley, open this door at once!"
I pretended I did not hear him.

Gay yelled, "What did you put in our drinks?"

How had they known so quickly? Had Tabitha called
them? Phil's pounding increased. "Either you open the
damn door or I'll break it down!"

I stepped out of the shower and wrapped a towel around
me. I turned the lock and jumped back in time to avoid the
door slamming into me.

Phil pinned me against the linen cabinet. "What did you
put in our drinks?"

"N-nothing," I insisted. "Maybe the water was bad."

"What about my glass of wine?" His neck flamed scarlet.

Gay said, "We both tasted something bitter. I chased
down Tabitha, and she admitted that you put"—she
choked—"pills in our drinks."

"Did not!" I tried to wriggle away. Phil held my shoulders firmly while I clung to the towel to keep it from slipping. The shower was still running. Gay pushed past us and
turned it off.

"He's hurting me!" I protested to Gay.

Phil allowed me to squirm so the cabinet's handle did
not press into my back. "What was in the drinks?"

"Nothing!" I insisted.

"We have a lot of medicines in this house," Gay said in a
raspy voice, "and chemicals and poisons. How long do we
have? Do we need to call an ambulance?"

"No." I felt as if my limbs were melting. Phil's grip kept
me from falling.

"Then we'll have to call the police," Gay continued in a
slow, deep voice.

I dropped my head. "It was just Advil."

"How many?"

"Only a few," I whispered.

"Why?" Phil asked in panting breaths.

"Just to make you tired sooner." Tears flowed as if a faucet had been twisted on full blast. "Now I've ruined everything!"

Gay's mouth looked as if a gash had sliced her face. My heart was skipping beats, pounding inside my chest. Even though it was Phil who was restraining me, I was more terrified of what Gay would do to me.

"What are you talking about?" Phil asked. He loosened his grip.

I collapsed to my knees on the floor. "This is the end of my placement!"

"Placement?" Gay sputtered. "We have adopted you." Her anger seemed to expand as she moved closer to me. "You're our daughter, so cut the poor-orphan-me crap. We never had anywhere to send our sons, so why should you be different?"

But I was different—or at least I had felt different. I glanced up at Gay. She was fuming, but I was certain that she wasn't going to hurt me or . . . I swallowed hard at the next thought: She wasn't going to ditch me, either.

Gay exhaled. "Now go get dressed, and then we will deal with your idiotic behavior."

I was so ashamed, I stayed in my room for the entire weekend. I lay in bed feeling feverish as I tried to rewind what I had done and find a way to make it so that it had never happened. Every time I got to the part where I mixed the crushed pills in their drinks, I would run to the toilet and vomit.

Gay held cold washcloths to my forehead while I wretched. I could not believe she was being so kind; meanwhile, Phil had not come near my room.

Sunday evening Gay came to tuck me in. "Did you ever do anything horrid when you were my age?" I asked.

"Oh, there were some stupid pranks," she admitted. "Once, we had a slumber party, and we were going to make plaster face masks. When we tried to remove one of my friend's masks, we started to yank her eyelashes out."

"That's awful!"

"My mother had to clip her lashes with sewing scissors." I laughed. "It wasn't funny then." Gay's voice deepened. "That was an unintentional mistake. What you did was far worse. You'll need to talk to your therapist about it."

"Okay." I managed to focus on her expression and saw compassion, not resentment. I would do whatever it would take to regain their trust.

Gay flipped off the light. I turned my face upward for the inevitable kiss. Her lips brushed my tear-chapped cheek. "Love you, sweetie," she said.

I clutched her arm. She froze. Then I kissed her back. "Love you, too," I said.

12

Now they will have to listen to me

"Are you serious?" Tess was filling me in on the latest gossip while I gave myself a pedicure. The television news was playing in the background. Suddenly, the anchor-woman said, "Charles and Marjorie Moss." I looked up, saw their mug shots, and dropped my brush. It missed the bottle and landed on the carpet.

"Gay!" I shouted. "Come see this!"

Just then the other phone line rang. Gay picked it up. "Really? That must be what Ashley just got excited about." She mouthed *Mary Miller* to me and jotted down some notes. When she hung up the phone, she braced herself on the counter. "Mary says that Mrs. Moss was arrested on twenty-five counts of felony child abuse and nine counts of felony child neglect for abusing the children she and her husband were allowed to adopt after their foster home was closed. Mr. Moss was also arrested for failure to prevent or report it."

"See! I tried to tell everyone, but nobody would listen." I reached for a metal post that supported the ceiling and spun around, lifting my feet off the floor as I thought about the Mosses in their respective jail cells. "They're gonna get it now!"

Exactly eleven years to the day that my mother was first arrested, the newspapers featured the Moss arrest. I studied the Mosses' mug shots. To me, they looked like Mr. and Mrs. Potato Head. But I knew how quickly they could morph into something else: a brownie-baking mom, a fascist guard, or self-crowned foster parents of the year. Dress Mr. Potato Head up in plastic droopy eyes and thin-pursed lips, and you could replicate Mr. Moss's blank stare in front of the television while his wife was torturing a child. I read the caption next to their photos in the *Tampa Tribune* and shouted, "I knew they would try to blame the kids! It says: 'The attorney for the couple accused of child abuse says the teenage children are making up the allegations.'" My long-suppressed simmering ire erupted into a full boil.

The story reported that the Mosses were accused of abusing their adopted children over the past four years and that Mrs. Moss was accused of beating the children using her hands, feet, a wooden paddle, and a two-by-four board. Most of their children were in state custody again. "They're probably glad to be out of that house of horrors, but now they're back in foster care." I sighed. "And one of them is Mandy."

Phil read from the article, "It says here that their attorney said 'These people were the epitome of good foster parents' and that 'their reputation has been totally damaged.'"

"What about *my* reputation?" I shouted. "They told everyone I had been lying!"

"It mentions that they were investigated three times before, but the charges were never substantiated," Gay said. "Weren't you questioned when you were there?"

"Yes, several times." I turned to the *St. Petersburg Times* story. It concluded by saying that the Mosses were in the process of adopting a ninth child.

"I need to do *something* to help those kids. If I tell the police what happened, it will be cooperation."

"You mean 'corroboration,' cutie-pie," Phil said with an uneasy chuckle.

"And could you call the newspapers, too?" I tossed in.

Phil rubbed his chin. "And tell them what?"

"That there are more of us out there who've got a lot to say about the Mosses!"

Gay agreed to call the newspapers. A reporter from the *St. Petersburg Times*, Wayne Washington, was interested in the information we offered. That afternoon he drove out to the Mosses' trailer, and he spoke to both Mary Miller and Mrs. Merritt. The article that appeared the next morning called the Mosses' mobile home "a living hell for children." It quoted Mrs. Merritt: "This isn't something that fell through the cracks because they didn't know." It also included Gay's comments about my cruel punishments.

"She's still locked up!" I crowed when I learned that Mrs. Moss remained in jail on $635,000 bail with thirty-four charges of felony child abuse and neglect, but I was disappointed to learn that Mr. Moss was free on bond and that he had been charged with only six counts of felony child neglect. According to Mr. Washington's article, "He did nothing, an arrest report said, as his wife maliciously punched the children, pulled them into a bathroom and held them under hot water, deprived them of food, threatened them with a gun, denied medical care, and beat them with a wooden paddle."

"The article said they put one kid—I wonder if I knew him—in juvenile detention, so nobody will believe him." I paused. "But I've never been in any trouble, so they might listen to me."

"I don't want you involved in a criminal case," Phil said.

"I *need* to do this!"

"Why?" he asked.

"For me, for Luke, for Mandy, for the other kids they hurt. And"—I took a deep breath—"to keep them from getting more children. I don't want this to blow over like the other investigations. They aren't fit to take care of gerbils, let alone children."

Detective Shannon Keene, who was handling the Moss case, arranged for me to be interviewed by our local authorities. The next day Deputy Tina Brooks met me at my parents' office after school. The deputy's daughter was in my class, and we had worked on a project together.

"Do you have proof that Ashley lived with these people?" Deputy Brooks asked Gay.

Gay handed her the list of my placements that she had found in my files, which showed the eight months I had lived with the Mosses.

I answered the deputy's questions—surprising myself with how fresh the memories still were, even though it had all happened seven years earlier. A few days later I had to go to the Citrus County Sheriff's Department, where they videotaped my statement. I thought I would be frightened to talk to these law enforcement authorities and looked for a place to concentrate my attention; however, the more I spoke, the easier it was. All I was doing was telling the truth, and nothing I said was going to get me into further trouble.

We received transcripts of my session as well as those of some of the other children interviewed. Just in case Gay or Phil ever thought I had been exaggerating, I pointed out that the other children's comments were nauseatingly familiar. For instance, I had testified: "I was sleeping on a top bunk and I can recall a couple of occasions when I was taken by my hair and just thrown on the floor." One of the other victims told the authorities that she had been pulled by her hair into the bathroom. Mrs. Moss used to punish Luke by dunking his head in the bathtub, and one of the adopted kids claimed Mrs. Moss held her head underwater for several minutes until she had trouble breathing.

I gave a detailed description of the squatting punishments, and another child explained how Mrs. Moss forced her to squat for hours at a time. Hitting was a common punishment. I testified that Mrs. Moss beat me with the spaghetti spoon. One of the new victims revealed that Mrs. Moss beat her for putting a movie in the wrong case and struck her in the face for not sweeping the patio correctly. The Mosses kept another child home from school until her bruises disappeared.

After the second article appeared in the *St. Petersburg Times,* Gay received a call from a woman who said that two of her children, Gordon and Heather, had lived in the Moss home the same time I was there. "Gordon remembers Ashley," the woman said. "They've told me all the same stories, and I complained to the department, yet nobody would listen."

Gay told her that the reporter wanted to hear from other children who were in the Moss home, and she agreed to contact him.

Wayne Washington called to talk to me about what I remembered. "Will your parents allow me to interview you directly?" he asked in a mellifluous voice.

Gay got on the phone and set an appointment for him to visit our home. When he arrived, I showed him to Gay's office.

"Wow!" Mr. Washington said when he took in the sweeping views of the Crystal River. "This is where the manatees come in the winter, right?" I nodded. "Not exactly like your foster home, is it?"

Mr. Washington was even more thorough than the deputies had been, and I gave him many details. After he left, I asked Gay, "Do you think he believed me?"

"Of course he did."

I grinned, then dashed off to do my homework.

A few weeks after Wayne Washington interviewed me, he called Gay to verify some facts and told her that he had copied the Mosses' foster care licensing file.

"I didn't know you could do that," I said to her.

"Apparently, it's public record, and it substantiates what you described. He told me that we should look at it"—Gay paused meaningfully—"before too long." She cleared her throat. "He said that it refers to a report that is critical of how they treated Luke. And there's a mention that the report should be destroyed."

I gasped. "Is the report there?"

"No, Mr. Washington only found the reference to it. The licensing file also says that Mrs. Moss stated that she no longer allowed the children to taste her home-cooked hot sauce."

"Remember when we were in Cousin Neil's office and I wanted to sue the Mosses? Phil said it would be their word against mine. Now here's the proof!"

"You have a right to be angry," Gay replied, "but don't let it eat you up inside."

Phil already gave me his Dalai Lama lecture. "We've been through the whole forgiveness thing and none of that changes the fact that they keep hurting children."

I often went to the movies with my friends on Saturday nights, but nobody was available one weekend. "Why don't you come with us?" Gay suggested. "We're going to see *Erin Brockovich.*" I wrinkled my nose at the title. Gay played the guilt card. "We haven't seen a movie as a family in a long time, and I'd like to take Grampy. He hasn't been out of the house in a while."

"I wanted to buy some shoes."

"You can shop first and meet us at the movie at seven," Gay added, putting on the pressure.

Later that afternoon she dropped me off at the mall. I saw some kids I knew in the food court and hung out with them. When I checked my watch, it was six thirty and I still had not bought the shoes. By the time I got to the theater, it was ten past seven.

Phil was waiting out front holding my ticket and scowling. "Where were you?"

I held up my shoe bag. "Took longer than I thought."

"You had more than two hours to buy shoes!" Phil rarely got upset—and ten minutes should not have been a big deal—but he had been embarrassed in front of Gay's father.

Gay passed me the popcorn bucket and shot me a disappointed look. When the movie started, I focused on the story. Julia Roberts played Erin Brockovich, a woman who was running out of money after a car accident. When her attorney could not get her a settlement, she convinced him to hire her as an assistant. She stumbled on some medical records mixed in with his real estate files and discovered that a corporation was hiding contaminated water that was making people sick. Eventually, she helped file a class-action lawsuit that won a lot of money for the victims.

"That was better than I expected!" I announced when we exited the theater.

Phil clicked the car door opener, but I was too charged up to sit down just yet.

"Why can't we have one of those class-action suits for all of the kids who lived with the Mosses?" I pumped the air with my fist in excitement. "There must be dozens of them, plus Luke and me, as well as the adopted ones who are back in foster care."

"In the movie they sued a huge corporation that could afford to pay millions. The Mosses live in a trailer," Phil said. "Where would the money come from?" He came around and opened the van door on my side, ushering me inside.

"Has any kid ever sued the Department of Children and Families?" I asked as I reluctantly climbed in.

Gay turned around from the front seat. "One of my former guardian kids was in a class-action suit, but it was unsuccessful," she said somberly.

"I want to talk to a lawyer and see what he thinks!" I insisted.

"Most of the time nobody wins." Phil's voice sounded tired. "Anyway, you don't have to worry about the future, kiddo." He turned on the ignition. "You'll always have us."

That did not satisfy me. "Who will Mandy and those other kids have?"

At my insistence, Gay called Karen Gievers, the attorney who had handled the class-action suit involving one of Gay's guardian children.

"She told me that she's working with some other lawyers on a class-action suit against the state of Florida on behalf of all the state's foster children. They're hoping to change some of DCF's practices, but there would be no individual financial benefit for you," Gay explained. "She wanted to know if you would like to participate."

"Of course!" I could not believe it was actually happening. "Will she include everyone who was in the Moss home?"

"The problem is that someone would have to locate all

those children; next, someone would have to act on their behalf since they don't have parents."

"What about Luke? We know where he is."

"I've called Mary Miller to see whether she wants to represent Luke. I'll also call Heather and Gordon's parents."

"What about the Mosses? Can't we sue them separately?"

"I told the lawyer that Phil and I didn't want you to dredge it all up again only to be called a liar." Gay's voice lifted a little. "You know what Ms. Gievers said?"

"That you should have trusted me the first time!"

"We've always believed you—we were just worried about proof. However, Ms. Gievers said that I am a better mother than a lawyer. Once she studies the files, she will know if there is a case against the Mosses or not."

The summer before my freshman year, a group of lawyers filed a class-action lawsuit in the U.S. District Court in West Palm Beach on behalf of thirty-one Florida children, referring to most of the plaintiffs by their initials, although they used my whole name. A few weeks later the attorneys decided that anyone who had been adopted or had returned to their biological parents should be excluded from the class. I was disappointed, but Luke was still in it. Ms. Gievers suggested that we file individual lawsuits on my behalf soon because of statute of limitations laws.

"That's not what I had in mind, and it won't help Mandy or the others."

"No," Gay said, "but if they hear about your case, they can still come forward and have their own."

That same week—almost six weeks after the arrest of Charles and Marjorie Moss—Wayne Washington's most extensive article about their home appeared in the *St. Petersburg Times.* It began:

> *It was half a lifetime ago, but that's not so long when you're only 14. Ashley Rhodes-Courter says she remembers clearly her time in the foster home of Charles and Marjorie Moss. She remembers the day she learned what living in that home would be like. Nauseated, Ashley was hurrying to the bathroom when she threw up on the floor. Marjorie Moss didn't clean up the vomit. Instead, Ashley said, she held her face in it. "You know, like you would do with a dog you were training."*

There were two photos of me, one of Heather, the Mosses' mug shots, and a view of their seedy trailer. The article said that the department had known about the hot sauce and the other inappropriate punishments seven years earlier but had merely offered the Mosses "counseling and reminders of its policy against the use of corporal punishment." In addition, the department allowed the Mosses to adopt eight of the children.

Gay looked up from the newspaper. "I wonder if we still could get hold of that licensing file or if it has gone missing."

The reporter had interviewed one of my teachers who said I was "a once-in-a-lifetime kind of student" and "a determined, focused girl."

Phil beamed as he read aloud. "'Now, some of that

determination and focus are aimed at the Mosses and the system that allowed them to take in children. In addition to serving as a plaintiff in the lawsuit against state officials, she gave a statement to police to support the case against the Mosses.'"

Wayne Washington quoted me in the final paragraph: "'They used us to get money,' she said of the Mosses. 'They used us to look like better people in the community. My whole goal is to make sure they never get children again.'"

"Is there any mention of the class-action suit?" I asked.

"Yes, Erin, there is." Phil chuckled and pointed to quotes from Karen Gievers.

"Has anyone found Mandy yet?" I asked.

Gay shook her head. "We're trying. All I know is that all of the Mosses' adopted kids have the same guardian."

"So ask him."

"You know he can't tell us anything because of confidentiality."

"I hate that confidentiality crap!" I snapped. "It just protects the workers, not the kids."

After the incident with Brooke, I felt as though I had broken through a wall—one I had carefully constructed over many years. I still had to navigate the fallen bricks so I would not trip up again. I know the Courters were angry and distrustful of me for much longer than they let me know, but they did not punish me for what I had done. For the first time, I let myself appreciate Gay's generosity. She was always trying to please me—sometimes too hard—but her intentions were kind, and only someone who loved me would have tolerated how mean I had been to her in both little and large ways. Once Phil recovered from his initial outrage, he was the same as ever—gentle, understanding, and always offering to help me with homework, drive me somewhere, make me a snack, or play a game of pool or basketball. I finally noticed that they were always *there:* waking me up, tucking me in, ready to listen, checking whether I needed anything.

I was harder on myself than they were, and I resolved to prove their faith was justified. Before, I had held something back so that when they discarded me, I would not be so wounded. But with my parents by my side, who had proven their love for me, I felt safe enough to allow sunlight to sweep the shadows from my life. So many wonderful events were unfolding that I believed that I had been given a second chance.

One of my first opportunities was being asked to give the keynote speech for the National Court Appointed Special Advocates Association, the CEO of which I had met at the White House. Gay helped me write the speech that explained everything Mary Miller had done for me as my Guardian ad Litem, and Phil edited a video clip that illustrated my journey through foster care.

I loved drama and giving speeches at school, but I was worried about speaking before a huge crowd. One of Gay's friends, Lou Heckler, is a professional motivational speaker. She arranged for him to be my speech coach. When the time came, I stood behind the lectern gazing across more than a thousand pairs of eyes that were intent on me, but I was confident—at least at the beginning—because I had memorized my speech down to the pauses and emphases that Mr. Heckler had suggested.

"I like to think that my story has three parts," I began. "First is the time when I felt like I was lost in the system. Second is when my CASA, Mary Miller, came into my life. And third is when she helped find a family for me."

When I started to describe the horrors at the Moss home, my urge was to rush and get the address over with more quickly, but Mr. Heckler's voice in my head was like a conductor keeping the beat. "But the worst moments were the really cruel punishments" [pause] "like having to run laps in the hot sun" [pause] "crouching in awkward positions" [pause] "being hit with a spoon until my bottom was raw" [pause] "and even food was withheld." I took a long breath. "Luckily, I was the kind of kid who knew how to stay out of trouble, so I learned to avoid the worst of the punishments. Unfortunately, my brother had much worse things done to him" [pause] "like having his head dunked in the bathtub until he nearly drowned and having hot sauce poured down his throat."

The audience gasped in unison, then groaned when I told them how Violet Chavez had let me go back for the weekend. They applauded when they heard how Mary Miller rescued Luke after he was sent to the Mosses a second time, and they cheered when I announced that the Mosses had been arrested.

Then I drove home the point about the difference Mary Miller had made in my life, even though I had not appreciated her when I was younger. "I'd like to say that my guardian and I became best friends, but by then I was used to caseworkers who came and went—all sorts of therapists, counselors, and people with different titles who said they would do things but never did." I held up my hand and counted on my fingers. "By the time I met Mary Miller, I'd already had eight foster mothers, a biological mother, my grandfather's girlfriend, not to mention shifts of counselors in the shelter, and though Mary was nice enough, I didn't expect her to make a difference." I took a long pause. "Why should I? Nobody else ever had.

"I want to make certain that no other child has to endure one more day with those sadistic people. I now have a lawyer who is helping put together a class-action lawsuit on behalf of all the children who suffered in that home. Maybe you can figure out that I saw the movie *Erin Brockovich* recently! My mother says it is okay for me to have a lawsuit, but I can't wear the sort of suits Julia Roberts did!"

The unanimous laughter broke the tension. My confidence soared. These people were actually listening to a teenage girl, and they believed me! Hopefully, it also would help them pay attention to the kids they served.

"I never realized what it would take to be found, but I'm certainly glad Mary Miller did," I said in my conclusion. "Volunteers like you make a huge difference, and I want to thank you on behalf of the thousands of children that court-appointed advocates serve every year."

Tears welled up in my eyes. "Even though she isn't here, I'd like to thank Mary Miller. And thank all of you. Please don't stop until each of your children has a permanent family forever!" The audience rose as one long wave and clapped.

Afterward I received dozens of requests to speak all

over the country. When I delivered a similar speech to the Florida Guardian ad Litem Program, Mary Miller *was* present. At the end I handed her a bouquet. Both of us cried as we hugged each other, each realizing how much we had overcome together.

Back when I was still living at The Children's Home, Mary Miller had asked me, "If you could do anything you wanted, what would that be?"

I did not mind this question as much as her probing about my feelings. I blurted out, "I want to travel all over the world." I remember looking around the confines of the campus, thinking I would be lucky to ever get out of Tampa again. During my first few years with the Courters we had been all over the country and on a cruise. After Josh graduated from Hampshire College, he and his girlfriend joined us in Cambridge, England, where the Courters had arranged to exchange homes with a British family the summer before I started high school.

Josh's girlfriend bought me the British edition of the latest Harry Potter book the day it was released. On a whim I asked Gay, "Do you know J. K. Rowling?"

"I don't know everyone!" she said with a laugh.

"I bet you could arrange for us to meet her while we're here," I persisted.

"I don't think so, sweetie."

From England, we went to France. On our last evening in Paris, we took a *bateau-mouche* to watch the millennium lights on the Eiffel Tower. I went over to the bench where Phil and Gay sat holding hands and I snuggled between them. "Do you realize that three summers ago the most exciting moment of my life was welcoming guests to The Children's Home?" I grabbed Gay's left hand and Phil's right and held them in my lap. "My parents!" I sighed theatrically. "In Paris!"

One day soon after the trip, Gay came across a contest announcement in *USA Today*. "You've got to see this." She waved the paper at me. "Look! It's an essay contest about how the Harry Potter books changed your life. Check out the prize."

Even though I was intrigued, I pretended not to be. "What is it?" I said without looking in her direction.

"Breakfast in New York with J. K. Rowling!"

"Remember I once told you how similar Hogwarts is to The Children's Home?" I began. "They have cottages and a house cup, like the one we had for the Murphey Awards. And he's also an orphan who was abused by relatives." My excitement mounted. "I'll write about that."

The next day I read Gay my first draft. "Hey, kiddo," Gay said enthusiastically, "you can write!"

"You think so?"

I knew that was the sort of encouragement any parent would give, so when the day to announce the Harry Potter contest prizes passed, I did not mention it to anyone. I had never thought I would win anyway. The next day the publisher called to tell me I was one of the ten winners!

A limo met us at the airport. It was so long, it could barely maneuver in the congested streets of Manhattan. As Gay chattered about the events we would attend, I shut her out and concentrated on absorbing every minute. I expected Ms. Rowling would just shake my hand, but she was down-to-earth and whispered some encouraging words about my life and future, and then she hugged me. "It's been a privilege to meet you." I smiled so hard, my cheeks ached for hours. Once again, I experienced that surreal feeling of having a dream come true.

After reading my winning essay, the public relations people for Casey Family Services asked me to be a presenter at their postadoption services conference and also to address a Senate reception.

Hundreds of guests stood around the packed rotunda in the Russell Building on Capitol Hill. While the presenters made the introductory remarks, the room reverberated with chattering and clinking glasses. I figured that nobody would pay attention to me; yet, the minute I began, there was a hush. Since many of the guests had legislative power to make reforms, I suggested that they find a foster child who needed a permanent home and help make it happen in less than six months. Then I concluded with a quote from Molière: "It is not only what we do, but also what we do not do, for which we are accountable."

The silence made me think I had said something offensive until the echoing applause encouraged me to believe that some of the dignitaries might remember my story and work to protect children from a failing foster care system.

The Harry Potter contest and the Senate reception had made big ripples in my ninth-grade fall. The rest of the time I was busy balancing the workload from several honors classes, drama rehearsals, and varsity basketball practice. I had been thrilled to make the team as a freshman, but the coach demanded rigorous sessions; and after weeks of running several miles a day, doing sprints, and jumping exercises, I had to add physical therapy for my knees to my schedule. Most of all, I liked hanging out with Tess and some new friends from the team. There wasn't much to do in our small town, but we were content going to the mall, getting our nails done, going to football games, and gossiping about guys.

One day in early December, I came home from basketball practice and Gay said, "Check the answering machine."

On it was a message from a member of Hillary Rodham Clinton's staff inviting me to attend a Christmas party at the White House! The day after my essay appeared in *USA Today,* the First Lady, who has a special interest in foster care and adoption, mentioned my essay on Rosie O'Donnell's talk show. I had sent her a note, never expecting an acknowledgment—and certainly not an invitation.

Gay and Phil were busy on the day of the party; however, Gay's sister, Robin Madden, a pediatrician in Maryland, was delighted to be my guest. Grampy bought me the airline ticket for my Hanukkah gift. I was going back to the White House, and this time the president of the United States greeted me—and I have the pictures to prove it!

When I celebrated my fourth Christmas with the Courters, I enjoyed hanging the familiar decorations. My friends and I had many activities planned, and I could not wait for Josh and Blake to come home for the holidays. For the first time, I felt that I fit right in.

The Courters had warned me that lawsuits could drag on for years. They had also told me not to expect victory or financial compensation. I was more concerned about what was happening in the Mosses' criminal case. When we heard nothing, I asked Gay to contact the assistant state attorney.

"Mr. Sinacore said that he can't use your testimony—or Luke's—because the statute of limitations had passed," she reported.

I was furious. "I spoke out about these people so many times, but they said I was lying! Shouldn't they be counting from way back when I started to tell?"

Gay sighed. "He did say you and Luke had given the best interviews."

"They'll try to discredit the other kids," I said between gritted teeth. "They'll claim they had behavior problems or collided to make it up."

"Colluded." Gay grinned. "It means to plot or conspire."

"Yeah, whatever." I was not in the mood for a vocabulary lesson.

Almost a year after the Mosses were first arrested, a new reporter from the *St. Petersburg Times* informed me that Mrs. Moss pled guilty to one count of child neglect and gave up parental rights to her adopted children. Her sentence? Probation for only five years! Mr. Moss also relinquished rights to his adopted children but received no further punishment.

I was dumbfounded. "Is that all?"

"The assistant state attorney believed that the children had been mistreated, but he thought that it was going to be tough to prove," the reporter explained. "Would you like to comment?" he asked.

"The Mosses need a nice, long time-out in jail to think about what they did," I responded.

I was even more irate when I read the article, which quoted the Mosses' attorney as saying he thought it was a very fair agreement and that the charges were "pretty outlandish." He also added that several witnesses had "credibility problems."

"Credibility problems!" I snorted. "I told you they would say that! That's why I wanted to testify!" I growled in frustration.

Phil continued reading aloud, "The article goes on to say that the Mosses' attorney said, 'Marjorie Moss always got the worst of the worst . . . We felt that Mrs. Moss probably did the best she could.'" Phil hugged me. "Oh yeah, that really describes my daughter—top student, athlete, White House guest."

Mrs. Merritt stuck up for us by saying, "That's all? That's all she gets? Five years' probation? That is an insult to those kids."

The reporter quoted me, too: "Kids are always taught there are going to be consequences for what they do, but this case is completely contradicting to that because they are getting a slap on the wrist."

"Read the part about the time-out!" Gay said with a chuckle. My quote made it into the article.

Phil complied: "Here it is! 'I think they deserve a little time to think of what they have done. A little time-out.'"

I made the naughty-naughty gesture with my finger. "At least it also mentions my lawsuits." I exhaled. "Maybe Mandy will see it this time, and she can sue the Mosses."

My lawsuit was not as glamorous as the ones I had seen on television. Boxes and boxes started arriving as the Department of Children and Families complied with Karen Gievers's requests to see all the evidence. As I shuffled through the volumes of papers, I noted the signatures of people who I had never met but who had been in charge of a facet of my care during some moment in time. I remembered only a few of the names and wondered if they knew who I was. There were also the histories of all my foster families, as well as the caseworkers' personnel files. Nothing was in order.

"How am I ever going to make sense of this?" I asked Gay. It took hours to sort through what caseworkers in two states were writing to one another while I was at my grandfather's. The Mosses' licensing file was filled with reports calling them "model" foster parents and recommending they get more children. The praises of caseworkers who should have known better infuriated me so much that I had to walk away to calm down.

It turned out that the Mosses were not the only villains in my story. I did not recall that other placements had been almost as crowded. Ms. Gievers told me that foster parents are not supposed to have more than five children in a home, including birth children. The O'Connors had crammed one small bedroom with five toddlers, some even sharing the same bed. The Hineses' file noted they had too many children and needed a waiver for Luke and me, which might have been one reason they sent me to the other home. The Ortizes had at least fourteen children at one point when their official capacity was two. When I returned from South Carolina the first time, I lived in the Pace home, which was packed with at least ten children, mostly preschoolers.

In addition to the legal irregularities, I was also unaware of many other troubling aspects of my care. It was not until Gay had all the documentation in chronological order that she realized that years had gone by without a judge reviewing our case and that we had originally been sent to South Carolina without a court order, which then made it difficult to retrieve us when our safety became a concern. Gay pointed out that I was officially missing for nine months. By piecing together scraps of information—including photographs that showed me spending Christmases and Easters in South Carolina looking quite different in size and having different hair lengths—Gay figured out that I was with Adele during the paperwork gap. It appears that the records had been doctored to conceal the errors.

"In all my years as a guardian, I have never seen such shoddy social work!" Gay grumbled. "Why were so many of the homes grossly overcrowded? How could they even consider Sam Rhodes as a placement when his own children had grown up in foster care? He was violent and a substance abuser! Caseworkers, licensing people, even supervisors knew of the Mosses' abuse, and they all looked the other way," she ranted. "Remember when they first investigated the home and Mrs. Moss forced you to recant? Well, that same night someone else called the abuse hotline and said you children were afraid to tell the truth in front of Mrs. Moss. For some reason, the child protection supervisor decided it wasn't necessary to check up further." Gay rearranged a few more documents. "Then, a week later, someone from the school again contacted the hotline, but the worker assured the caller that you were okay and the child protection team didn't follow it up!"

The more upset Gay became, the calmer I felt. It was as if she were lifting a heavy weight off my back. "Look at this!" She showed me evidence of yet another time the department officials met to discuss the inappropriate discipline in the Moss foster home.

"If my mother had forced Luke or me to drink hot sauce, paddled us, or not fed us, we would have been placed in foster care, wouldn't we?" Gay nodded. "Then she would have had to go to court, sign a case plan, and attend classes to get us back."

"I know," Gay said gently. "It's hard to understand why the Mosses weren't at least held to the same standard as parents."

"What gets me is that the state paid them a lot of money to take care of us, but they wouldn't give my mother a cent," I added.

"I'm still floored that the department kept noting that they were overcapped but didn't remove any kids. Plus, they were allowed to use 'inappropriate discipline techniques' because they were frustrated and overwhelmed." Gay tossed her head as if to try to clear it. "Supposedly, they just clarified their discipline policy with the Mosses," she said facetiously.

Then Gay's voice deepened and slowed—always a

bad sign if I had done something wrong, but now it was soothing. "Phil and I felt that the process of becoming licensed adoptive parents was exhaustive and intrusive, but we put up with it because we understood the state must protect children who already were victims of abuse and neglect." Gay slapped some of the Moss papers on the floor, where she had been rummaging through their box. She stood, stretched, and rubbed her temples. "I'm shocked at how many red flags their licensing workers overlooked."

"You mean when they first became foster parents?"

"Yes. Anyone with half a brain would have realized that Marjorie Moss was probably too troubled to care for needy kids."

"In what way?" I asked, looking for more validation of my feelings.

"First of all, according to her foster parent licensing file, Mrs. Moss's mother was a strict disciplinarian who whipped Mrs. Moss on three occasions when she was a child. You'd think that would make a person more compassionate, but sometimes it just makes it worse. Guardians are taught about the cycle of abuse—how those who are demeaned eventually take revenge on those who are weaker." Gay caught my apprehensive expression. "Don't worry, Ashley, you'll be fine. You are going to break that cycle."

"How can you be sure?"

"You are going to have advantages—and education. You'll be around better role models. Mrs. Moss had several violent, failed marriages." Gay studied the files. "And one of her sons who lived on their property was a convicted felon?" She groaned. "That's another reason they shouldn't have had foster kids."

When Phil came home, Gay told him what she had learned about Mrs. Moss's background. "I'll never understand how anyone can be cruel to anyone, especially *our* child!" he said. "You know I wasn't in favor of this lawsuit, but maybe it will change practices so they don't allow people like this to become foster parents in the first place—or at least get rid of them at the first sign of trouble."

"Their blunders are unbelievable," Gay said. "Some of the workers, who were supposed to see Ashley monthly, ignored her for long periods. Others falsified their time sheets. One even worked a second job when he was supposed to be visiting children and was arrested on drug charges. Another worker was accused of soliciting. Administrators sent her to South Carolina without the proper judicial order, and you already know they left that telltale note about destroying some of Luke's files." She took a long breath. "There was even more. The Mosses were not the only foster parents with a blighted record, and Sam Rhodes was not Ashley's only caregiver involved with violence. Mrs. Pace was charged with aggravated assault against her husband with a motor vehicle even before Ashley lived there."

Phil turned to me. "What do you think of all this?"

I shrugged. "I was too young to remember."

"What about the Pottses?" Gay acted as if she were tiptoeing through a long, dark hallway.

"I've told you about that creepy movie!"

"What if I told you that Boris Potts really *was* a creep?" Gay began slowly.

"In what way?" My breath caught, and I felt like I was slipping underwater.

"He was arrested shortly after you left."

"For what?"

"Pedophilia."

"You mean molesting kids?"

Gay nodded.

"Well, he never touched me!" Most of my memories of the Pottses were rather pleasant—except for that film. Then again, I was a chatty kid, so he might have been afraid to pull anything with me for fear I would tell someone.

The next day I combed the files for more details. Three years before I lived with Mr. and Mrs. Potts, a relative reported that their son, who allegedly had been charged with attempted murder, was living in their home while a foster child was there. The same relative also reported that Mr. Potts had a pornographic movie collection.

Instead of closing the Potts foster home, the department merely asked the Pottses for an explanation about each of the accusations. They told the authorities that their son had moved out and that he had been charged with *only* false imprisonment and spousal battery. Regarding the filthy films, they said they watched the Playboy Channel after their foster child was in bed. It was like questioning a criminal who says he is not guilty and then closing the case based on his word.

I wanted to talk to Gay about it, but I was afraid that she would get the notion that Mr. Potts had sexually abused me and I was repressing it. I remembered so much—surely I would have recalled if he touched me. The paperwork, though, was sickening. Mr. Potts had driven other foster children to family visits and medical appointments. After he had transported a baby girl, they found blood in her diaper. The incident was categorized as an "injury to the vaginal area, but no known perpetrator." The report also noted that the Pottses were the only transporters of that child.

Something else was strange. The Pottses had been foster parents for many years and had received a license for two children. For the first time, I was in a home that was below capacity. Why, if they had room for Luke, was I there alone? In the Pottses' licensing file, a caseworker noted, *The current placement, A. R., has been with the family two plus months. Mrs. Potts reports she is "perfect."* And yet I was sent elsewhere. There was no evidence that any worker checked on me during the five months I was there, even though they were already investigating Mr. Potts for molestation. The officials must have decided it would be prudent to remove a female foster child from his home, because not long after I left, Boris Potts was charged with committing a felony offense of lewd, lascivious assault on a child under sixteen, plus one count of sexual battery.

"You have a way of finding photos of criminals online, don't you?" I asked Gay.

"Who are you trying to find?"

"Some of my foster parents."

"Mr. Potts?" she said as if she had been expecting the request. She handed me a printout from another file. "I found him on a sex offender page. Mary Miller and I ran background checks on all your foster parents for Karen Gievers."

I stared at the old man's face. His mouth drooped like a hound dog, and his expression was more worried than scary. "That's the foster father who gave me all those gifts," I said. "I thought he was just being nice."

After Gay called a Hillsborough County detective, she reported to me. "I asked him whether any of Mr. Potts's victims had lived with him, and he said that one had been their foster child—before you were there—but the other cases involved children Mr. Potts had transported." Gay's skin was the color of an eggshell, and her expression was so tight, I thought her lips might crack. "I'm glad they took you out of there," she said. "The saddest part is that they sent you to live with the Pottses' daughter, and even if you had wanted to, you couldn't have confided in her."

I wanted Karen Gievers to represent Luke, too. Because he was still in foster care, he needed an adult to bring the legal actions on his behalf. Mary Miller, who had now been his Guardian ad Litem for six years, agreed to fill that role.

Both Luke and I had separate negligence lawsuits against the Mosses as well as against the state. Ms. Gievers also contemplated filing additional lawsuits in federal court under the civil rights statutes because the case-workers in question were not merely stressed or poorly trained; many were sloppy, a few were downright incompetent, and others may have willfully neglected their duties. Mary Miller pointed out that since the Mosses, Mr. Potts, Sam Rhodes, and Mrs. Pace had all had criminal charges brought against them before or shortly after they cared for us, almost half of our foster parents had been people of questionable character. Ms. Gievers, Gay, and Mary wanted someone to take responsibility for this. After all, someone had selected these families to care for us, someone had supervised them, and everyone had acted with the understanding that they were accountable for the kind of care we received.

Ms. Gievers developed a list of the individuals most responsible and filed a federal civil rights suit against them. It asked for relief due to the defendants' "reckless disregard and deliberate indifference to and violations of plaintiff's constitutionally protected due-process rights to be safe, and free from harm and cruel and unusual punishment while in the custody and control of the Florida foster care system." The puppeteers who had pulled the strings of my lost childhood became defendants—but the case dragged on for several years, and I admit it was not at the forefront of my thoughts as I enjoyed life in high school.

In the meantime, the class-action suit, which still included Luke, proceeded until U.S. District Judge Federico A. Moreno decided that the dependency court already protected foster children. The attorneys appealed, but the U.S. Supreme Court declined to consider the case.

Gay told me, "The ruling says that Florida's laws 'provide sufficient protection' for children in state care."

"When did I ever have 'sufficient protection'?"

"You still can make a difference—like when you give your speeches."

"Could the courts or someone force me to stop?"

"Not a chance!" Phil said with a hearty laugh. He placed his arm around Gay's shoulders.

As I looked from him to Gay, I felt a surge of something I could not quite define swell inside me. If I had been the type, I would have hugged them both. I did slide closer to them. I recall being once again struck with the realization that they would be there for me. They had let me pursue my legal rights, even though they initially had doubts about going that route, and they always had a fresh way to solve my problems. There was a time I didn't think I needed anyone; now I wondered how could I need these people so much.

The class-action lawsuit didn't have the Hollywood ending I'd wanted. But my cases against the Mosses and the state were still alive, and we received notice that Mr. and Mrs. Moss were going to give their depositions. The Courters said I did not have to be there, but I wanted to hear what they would say—under oath—with me sitting across from them.

We drove to Tampa on a cloudy morning in April. Instead of the courtroom I had envisioned, we were crammed into a dreary conference room in a court reporter's office. At first I avoided looking at the Mosses, and then I dared a sideways glance. They appeared older and much more drab than the goblins in my nightmares.

Ms. Gievers interviewed Mr. Moss first. She tried to determine the extent of the Mosses' assets. Mr. Moss admitted they had received more than $265,000 in tax-free subsidies, plus Social Security checks for some of the children they had adopted. When the questions turned to

Mandy and her brother, I perked up. I had not known that their mother, who had tried to give them away in a bar, was actually the sister of Mrs. Moss's daughter-in-law. Those poor kids had traded one hell for another—and now they were back in foster care limbo.

Mr. Moss admitted whipping two of the children he adopted, but not any foster children. I was shocked when he divulged that they currently had joint custody of a seven-year-old boy, even though a condition of Mrs. Moss's probation prohibited her from caring for any more children. When Mr. Moss was asked if he had seen me since I had been removed from their home, he said I had called three or four times wanting to visit. I gaped in amazement as he declared that he had picked me up from a home in Brandon and had taken me to spend the weekend with them.

Seeing my reaction, Ms. Gievers called for a break.

"How could he say that?" I hissed in the hallway. "Not only would I never have made such a call, but I never lived anywhere near, Brandon!"

"Calm down," my lawyer said. "But I'm glad you told me that."

After lunch Mrs. Moss swapped seats with her husband. Until that moment, she had not said a word, but when she began to answer questions, she spoke in the same deceitful voice she had used to con caseworkers. When asked about the squatting, she said that when children stood in the corner for time-outs, they would scratch the drywall. "And my solution to that was to face the corner, arms like—well, sometimes they would go down on their knees—however they'd want to stand there. That's not me making them squat. They're doing whatever, as long as they're facing

279

that corner and they're quiet. They got time to think, that's what the corner is for."

She emphatically denied telling an investigator that she sometimes punished with hot sauce or that she had paddled another child.

Ms. Gievers asked, "Do you remember putting children into an empty garbage can and beating them while they were in the can?"

"No." Mrs. Moss's lips turned into a snide grin, an expression that used to precede some of her meltdowns. As a reflex, I bit my cheek.

Ms. Gievers checked her notepad and asked, "Do you recall—" Seeing Mrs. Moss's smirk, she asked, "Is there something funny about children being abused?"

Mrs. Moss tried to cover her blunder. "That did not happen."

Ms. Gievers looked her straight in the eye. "What do you recall about Ashley?"

"She was very, very smart." Mrs. Moss glanced in my direction, and then her voice became smooth as syrup. "I remember her, me, and Mandy going shopping. And they matched up and dressed alike and we had a good time."

You are making that up! I wanted to scream; instead, I continued to chew my cheek. I was furious that she could still twist everything, but what hurt the most was that she could still make me feel helpless. A wayward teardrop slipped down the side of my nose. Phil handed me his folded handkerchief.

Mary Miller caught Gay's eye. Gay followed her gaze, then covered her mouth as if she was going to cough. Mr. Moss had been sitting slightly behind us on our left. We had been concentrating on Mrs. Moss and Ms. Gievers. Phil noticed what was happening first and nudged me to turn and look at Mr. Moss, who grunted. I realized he was snoring. Not only had Mr. Moss fallen asleep, his dentures had slid out of his mouth! Mary and Gay had lost it and were laughing behind cupped hands. The Mosses' attorney tapped her client on the shoulder. He startled awake. His wife motioned him to replace his teeth.

After that, I listened dispassionately as Mrs. Moss gave a made-for-television version of their lifestyle that included trips to the circus and Ice Capades, dinners out on Fridays, and pizza every Wednesday night. She contradicted reports she had given to a deputy about how she punished us, confused the names of the children, and made up a story about burning wrapping paper to cover her threats to destroy our Christmas presents. She claimed she read us bedtime stories, wrote us poems, put our baby songs in individual life books. When Ms. Gievers asked where these books were, she insisted that she had sent them along with us.

"What about Ashley's Easy-Bake oven and her dolls?" my attorney asked.

"I don't remember anybody asking me about an Easy-Bake oven or dolls," she said hesitantly. "These kids sit around and they go over it and over it and over it." After hours of questioning, her inner shrew finally emerged. "And they read it in the paper." Her voice became as shrill as fingernails on a blackboard. "Then one kid picks up what the other one says and it just goes on and on."

Ms. Gievers's voice was firm. "Let's stop a minute, Mrs. Moss."

"The kids wanted to do it—and they did!" Mrs. Moss continued anyway.

"The only article that has ever appeared in the newspaper didn't appear until after you were arrested and charged criminally in 2000, correct?"

"The kids picked up on these reports. And the people that come in asked the same questions."

Karen Gievers softened her voice. "Did you ever stop to think that the report sounded similar because you kept doing the same things to the children?"

Mrs. Moss was defiant. "But I didn't, and that's why I know how they did this!"

Ms. Gievers shook her head. "Do you have any idea of the harm that you caused the children?"

Mrs. Moss's attorney interrupted. "Object to the form."

"I haven't caused harm because that stuff is not true! I think y'all are causing more harm by playing along and letting them say this stuff and encouraging them. I know that's where your money comes from, but I don't think that is a fair thing to say."

Ms. Gievers paused on purpose. "And tell us, again, the total amount of money that you and Mr. Moss got?"

"I have no clue," Mrs. Moss said.

"More than a quarter of a million, correct?"

Next, Ms. Gievers asked about the overcrowded home. With every answer, Mrs. Moss was getting testier, until her attorney interjected, "We're bordering on harassment."

Ms. Gievers apologized and asked, "Do you recall telling Ms. Miller that you had Ashley's Easy-Bake oven and her radio and dolls?"

"If I had them, I would have given them to her. I

sent her off with thirty-six outfits and God knows what else."

Then why did I have to scrounge in Lake Mag's charity closet? I seethed silently.

As she concluded, Ms. Gievers looked at a note that Gay had passed to her. "Have you had any contact with Mandy?" she asked.

"No." Mrs. Moss stated she had not seen her in two years.

I left the room feeling claustrophobic and exhausted. "How could she tell so many lies?" I shrieked when the car door closed.

"They'll catch up with her when they match what she said today with what's in the licensing files," Gay said.

My lips felt moist. "Do you have a tissue?"

Gay turned around. "Your mouth is bleeding!"

"I bit my cheek."

Phil kept his eyes on the road, but I could see him shaking his head. "I knew we never should have let her do this," he mumbled to Gay. "I'm so sorry, Ashley."

I looked at the blood spots on the tissue and then started laughing. "It was worth it to see Mr. Moss's false teeth fall out!"

After realizing the scrutiny that the Mosses had to endure during their depositions, I was concerned that their lawyer would try to trap me during mine and then they would have grounds to say I was lying. My head pounded as I tried to recall the tiniest details about my time in their home nine years earlier.

"Don't worry," Ms. Gievers said in her gravelly voice that sounded maternal when she was on your side, aggressive when she was not. "When the Mosses' attorney asks a question, just wait a second in case I want to object. If I don't say anything, then tell the truth. If you don't recall, just say that. Don't volunteer more than you've been asked."

We walked into the airy conference room that overlooked Tampa Bay, which was an improvement over the crowded location for the Mosses' depositions. Ms. Gievers arranged her papers and then placed a bottle of Crystal hot sauce on the table as a silent reminder of why we were there. A few minutes later Mr. and Mrs. Moss and their counsel entered the room and sat opposite us. I was not sure where to look; and then I settled on a point above their attorney's head. When I gathered the courage to glimpse at the Mosses, their faces seemed carved out of lifeless plaster.

The initial questions were simple, but even when I was asked more specific ones, my worries faded because the incidents I was asked to recall were as vivid as the day they happened. After a break the Mosses' attorney questioned me about how I felt about my mother, about Grandpa being shot, and about other problems in foster care. The deposition concluded with my return weekend to the Moss trailer. "Was it your sense, at that point, that Mrs. Moss was trying to intimidate you?" she asked.

"I felt that way," I answered.

At last my turn was over. Gay and Phil would be in the hot seat next. During lunch Phil asked, "How do you feel?"

I shrugged. "Nothing," I replied, because the emotion was so complex. I sipped my soda and wondered if Dorothy felt this way when she dumped the bucket of water on the Wicked Witch of the West and watched her archnemesis melt.

As the cases proceeded to trial, the judge asked both sides to try to reach an agreement through mediation. Karen Gievers explained that at mediation the parties agree that everything discussed at that time will be confidential. This helps develop a trusting atmosphere because what the people say cannot be rehashed in a trial or harm other aspects of the case. Mostly, I wanted some acknowledgment that I was right and the Mosses were wrong—that they lied and I told the truth—but I knew that no amount of money was going to repair the damage they had done.

One of my attorneys, Gay's cousin Neil Spector, learned that the Mosses had few assets left. He told me that in Florida, creditors cannot take your home, and the Mosses had mortgaged most everything else they owned, probably to pay their bail bonds and legal fees. When the state offered a settlement in the Moss case, Karen Gievers suggested to the Courters that they accept it on my behalf and continue mediations in the other two actions, which they did. I did not attend these meetings, which dragged on for both the remaining negligence case against the state and the civil rights case against the caseworkers in federal court.

The Courters reported everything to me. The initial offers insulted them more than me. "I hope we go to trial," I said, "because even if I don't win anything, I'd like to be heard."

Karen Gievers was still trying to gather testimony from

Mandy, Toby, and the rest of the adopted Moss children. After some wrangling, the judge said he would allow Ms. Gievers to write each child a letter, which the department had to deliver by a certain date. All of a sudden, the department's counsel asked us to return for yet another mediation.

"They sound serious this time," Ms. Gievers said, "because if we settle, they won't have to send those letters."

"Would you mind if we accept the next reasonable offer?" Phil asked me.

"You are asking me to sell out Mandy. We were sisters— at least for a while."

"We must look out for your best interests," Phil said.

"But it was never about money for me."

"At this point we can't even find Mandy and the others, and even if we do, we don't know if they will want to sue." Gay sighed. "Besides, there's no guarantee you would win in a trial, and even if you did, it could get bogged down in appeals, which might result in any judgment being reduced or even a whole new trial."

"I'd like to know you had something for college," Phil added.

"Karen Gievers has several kids who won very large verdicts but are virtually homeless because they couldn't collect," Gay said.

"Like Mandy will be!"

"We can still try to find her, and she could still have her own lawsuit," Phil said.

"Do what you want!" I replied in a huff.

Phil and Gay returned from the next mediation and told me that it was over.

"Over?" I stared at them blankly. "Just like that?" I thought back to all my files in all those boxes and what they had revealed to me about just how horribly my case had been handled. It wasn't just about the Mosses—although they had triggered my quest for justice; it was the workers who refused to believe me, being moved without explanation, the separations from Luke, not being allowed to live with Adele again and . . . Thinking about all these things together brought back a familiar feeling. It wasn't about being reunited with my mother anymore, but still I could not suppress an almost overwhelming sense of longing. They could have done so much more for her—for us. I pulled myself back to reality. No lawsuit was going to make my fantasy of a different life with my mother come true.

Phil misunderstood my stricken look. "I thought you understood that this might happen."

"How could all our work just fizzle out in one afternoon?"

"They *really* didn't want to send those letters," Phil said.

"So I'll never go to court?" I fluttered my hands like a bird with a broken wing.

"Everything ends sometime, and now you have a sure thing," Gay replied.

My hands fell to my sides. "But we were getting so close to Mandy."

Even though I did not feel it immediately, I was relieved that the lawsuits were over and that I did not ever have to face the Mosses or any of the workers again. More and more invitations to give speeches poured in. I accepted as many as I could fit into my school schedule, including keynote addresses at several large conferences for judges, social workers, and foster parents. I spoke at the Wendy's International convention in Las Vegas to more than three thousand guests just before a fund-raising auction for the Dave Thomas Foundation for Adoption. Although Mr. Thomas had died by then, I fondly remembered how kind he was to me on my twelfth birthday and how he told me that everything was going to be all right. I only wished he could have been there to see how far I had come. At least I could honor him for helping so many children.

During Christmas vacation of my junior year, Gay was looking for a movie to watch when she discovered the videotape from my adoption day four and a half years earlier. She popped it in before I could object. When Gay saw me wiping her kiss off my cheek, she said, "Okay, we won't be showing this at family gatherings."

"We've all come a long way," Phil agreed.

"It's funny"—I gave him a crooked smile—"in those days I didn't need anyone; but now I sure do."

I cannot say that, even today, Gay feels like my real mother. She is different from my biological mom, with whom I have those powerful memories that always acted like magnets connecting me to her no matter how much time passed or what circumstances intervened. But now, more than love or an unfulfilled longing, I feel pity for my biological mother. Her own mother abandoned her. Nobody helped her, and her life has been hard. Even though she could not take care of me, she did care about me. If my mother had received a fraction of the money the

Mosses—or any of my foster parents—were paid, she could have established herself in Tampa and made a home for us. I expect I will see my mother again in some friendly way, yet I do not have the same desire to be with her.

I am still resentful of Mrs. Moss. The state had paid her to shelter children who were already wounded, and she broke them further—some permanently. In addition, I cannot help but hold a grudge against those in authority who were incompetent, negligent, or looked the other way when the system's foster parents were harming us. So many children in my position have no voice, but I will not be silent. I will continue to speak out about the importance of getting children into permanent homes more quickly.

Broken promises crippled me for many years. As the Courters kept their pledges to me, my faith in others expanded. Day after day, they were there for me; until one day, I not only felt safe, I did not want to leave. Maybe that is one definition of love.

13

Sunshine found

I journeyed alone for almost ten years before I found home. Adoptions are like very delicate gardening with transplants and grafts. Some are rejected immediately. Mine took hold, rooted, and bloomed, even though there were inevitable adjustments to the new soil and climate. Yet I have not forgotten where my roots started.

I still do not know who my biological father is. Recently, I came across the name and address of the most likely candidate. In a moment of courage, I telephoned him and left a message. He returned my call while I was out and told Gay that he very well might be my birth father. He offered to undergo DNA testing if I wished. I was too nervous to try again, although I later sent him my high school graduation picture. When he received it, he was so struck with my resemblance to members of his family that he called again. We had a long talk, but we have not confirmed paternity. My mother also dated his brother, which complicates the situation.

A few years after meeting my mother for lunch, I attended a drama camp at Duke University. Gay and Phil came to see my final performance. On the way home, we visited my uncle Sammie and his wife, Aunt Courtney. Their children's chocolate eyes, red hair, and freckled faces mirrored mine.

"Yep! You're a Rhodes, all right," my uncle said.

Aunt Leanne stopped by, and we fell into each other's arms. I felt more warmth toward her than I had to my mother the last time I saw her. Side by side, we went through some of the family albums. As I turned a page, an envelope fell out. Aunt Leanne reached for it, but the picture of a tiny baby in a box had already slipped into view.

"Do you remember Tommy?" she asked.

I felt as if my spine had turned to ice. The baby in the box . . . the secret I wasn't supposed to tell . . .

"He was born when you were almost two," Aunt Leanne whispered. "He lived for only forty-eight days."

The gray, doll-like baby transfixed me. "Why did he die?"

"SIDS," Aunt Courtney said. "He was premature and his lungs hadn't developed well, so that's probably why."

"It was a horrible time." Uncle Sammie sighed and left the room. Then I heard him on the phone. "Guess who's sitting in our kitchen? Ashley!" When he came back in the room, Uncle Sammie announced, "Your grandpa is coming over. We don't see him much, but he always asks about you."

"Where's Adele?" I asked.

"She's been quite ill." Sammie said that they had not been in contact for many years.

When my grandfather arrived, he did not have much to

say, although I could tell he was pleased to see me again.

Uncle Sammie asked if I wanted to revisit some of the places where I had lived. Aunt Courtney, Gay, Phil, and my cousins piled into Phil's van. We drove past the house where Dusty had grown up, the trailer Dusty and my mother had rented, and the apartment where Tommy died.

"Do you remember any of this?" Phil asked.

"No, nothing," I said. I was still numb from the startling news that I had had another brother, something I remembered as a kid, but had somehow forgotten.

We parked alongside a small country cemetery and marched over clumps of ruddy earth to the Grover graveyard. "Your brother was named Tommy Grover, after him." Uncle Sammie pointed to the tombstone for Dusty's father, Thomas.

"He was only thirty?" Gay asked after doing the math.

"His own father shot him—supposedly over a card game," Uncle Sammie replied. "Those Grovers were always trouble."

"Was there a family feud or something?" I asked.

"You might say that. Luke's grandma didn't want us Rhodeses to get you, because the Lord knows we tried," Aunt Courtney said.

"Leanne called social services for years, but they wouldn't tell her nothin'," Sammie added.

"Where's Tommy buried?" I asked.

"I thought there was a marker for the baby," Uncle Sammie said.

"Used to be next to his grandfather." Aunt Courtney paced the Grover section looking down.

I felt dizzy in the hot Carolina sun and leaned against Phil for support. He steered me back to our van.

Shortly after we returned to my uncle's house, the phone rang. Aunt Courtney handed it to Aunt Leanne, who took the portable outside. After she hung up, there was a muffled discussion between Aunt Courtney and Gay. Gay announced that it was time for us to leave, and before I knew what was happening, my reunion was over.

"What was the deal with the phone call?" I asked when we got on the road.

"Lorraine heard you were going to visit the family, so she started driving up from Florida yesterday," Gay said. "They didn't want you around when she arrived."

"Why?"

"I'm not sure. They said she was about an hour away and they wanted us gone."

Later that evening Aunt Leanne called Gay and told her that my mother's car had broken down and that the police had arrested her.

My heart fluttered wildly. "What about Autumn?"

"Your uncle is going to get her."

"Find out if she's okay!" I insisted. "Don't let them put her in foster care!"

Gay stayed in touch with Aunt Courtney and Uncle Sammie, who cared for my sister during this crisis. I continued to e-mail Uncle Sammie and had some contact with Aunt Leanne. My mother also e-mailed me, and we had several telephone conversations around that time.

When I was in my last year of high school, a letter for me from a federal prison arrived in care of the school. Dusty Grover had read an Associated Press article about me that mentioned the name of my school, which is how he knew where to reach me. He wrote me a long letter and included another for Luke. He said he had been trying to contact us for many years. In his correspondence Dusty gave a different spin on various episodes. He claimed he was never violent to my mother and loved Luke and me very much. He told one story that I found especially curious.

He described how Lorraine and Leanne made plans to go to Florida to visit Luke and me. When he asked whether she was bringing us any presents, she said she did not have the money. So he claimed he bought me an Easy-Bake oven, and other things for Luke. So my precious oven—always a symbol of my mother's love for me in my mind—may have been bought by him! I suppose he really did care for me.

Currently, Dusty is serving time in a federal prison for bank robbery and will not be released for many years. Although we are not blood relatives, I still think of him as my first father. After our reunion at Uncle Sammie's, my grandfather was sent to jail for selling drugs. His former girlfriend, Adele Picket, passed away after a long illness. Mrs. Moss was arrested again for child neglect. She had violated her probation by caring for another child. She did not receive any additional jail time.

My uncle Sammie and his family have been very kind to me. They have visited us twice and even flew down for my high school graduation, where they became reacquainted with Luke. My mother now has a good job and is divorced from Art. I have been getting to know her and Autumn again. It has been important for me to have caring biological family in my life.

Karen Gievers and Mary Miller worked out a favorable settlement in Luke's case. He continued to live at The Children's Home for five years after I left. The Hudsons and the Merritts remained his friends. Then—at last!—a champion came forward for Luke. A former navy officer was working on his B.S. degree in special education when he saw Luke's listing on Florida's adoption website. He went through extensive training and jumped through many bureaucratic hoops to become his adoptive parent. However, by then Luke had been in the system for fourteen of his fifteen years.

During a trip to London, Luke admired the royal horses and asked to have riding lessons. He showed a natural aptitude for jumping and loved competing, but nothing comes easy for my brother. He is now eighteen and struggling to overcome all the setbacks he has had over the years.

I am still in contact with Mary Miller, my Guardian ad Litem, to whom I owe so much and appreciate far more now than I did when I was a child. She still volunteers to represent children in the court system. Martha Cook, the attorney who handled our termination case pro bono, is now a family court judge in Tampa. Coincidentally, she finalized Luke's adoption.

Ms. Sandnes received her master's degree in social work, became a licensed counselor, and still works at The Children's Home as the counseling services manager. She married her former Lykes colleague Mr. Todd, and they have two adorable sons. Every time I return to The Children's Home, Mr. Irvin greets me with a broad smile. Those kids are blessed to have a staff member who cares as much as he does.

Blake and Josh have been supportive and have helped me through the times when a girl needs big brothers.

Karen Gievers was hired by most of the Mosses' adopted children—including Mandy. I learned that Mandy was married and had a baby, but not much else.

Before I went to college, I packed the boxes that pertained to my foster care history. When I reviewed the spreadsheet that listed everyone in South Carolina and Florida who had been responsible for my case, I was amazed by how many there were. I counted:

73 child welfare administrators
44 child welfare caseworkers
19 foster parents
23 attorneys
17 psychologists, psychiatrists, and therapists
5 Guardian ad Litem staff
4 judges
4 court personnel
3 abuse registry workers
2 primary caseworkers
1 Guardian ad Litem

Out of these 195 people, only Mary Miller and Martha Cook were unpaid volunteers—yet they are the two people who made the greatest difference in my life.

I completed the first draft of this book on the sixth anniversary of my adoption. Thunder boomed as I returned home after picking up pizzas for our celebration. The skies started to brighten as I unwrapped an elegant wooden box. The top had a decoupage portrait of a nineteenth-century princess twisting a pearl necklace, which Phil had altered by substituting my face. I laughed aloud, then opened the box. It was a music box. And it played "You Are My Sunshine."

Something very tight and very deep inside me snapped. Tears spurted unexpectedly. I looked across the table directly into the shining eyes of my parents. Gay and Phil—my mother and my father—were crying with me. Then we laughed at one another's bawling. The late-afternoon light streamed through the mist on the Crystal River, and I felt something I had never known before: Home.

"Home is not where you live, but where they understand you."
—Christian Morgenstern

This book is a memoir of my journey though a troubled childhood—
one where I often felt abandoned, neglected, and trapped in a failing
foster care system—to my eventual arrival at a secure and loving
home. In re-creating events described, I relied on my memory as well
as extensive research, which included review of court records, legal
depositions, social service files, other govern-ment records, newspaper accounts, and photographs. I also conducted personal interviews
and traveled to former foster homes and other places I lived. I have
changed names and identifying details—including, in some instanc-
es, locations—of some persons portrayed, including those in my biological family, my foster families (with the exception of Marjorie and
Charles Moss, who have been the subject of prior news coverage), and
anybody who was a minor during the time of my story, except for my
adoptive brothers and myself. A few characters are composites.

I have happily identified, by their real names, many wonderful
people, including some very special teachers, who were positive
influences.

Many of the adults who cared for me did a decent job; a few literally
saved my life. But there were some rotten apples who not only abandoned, neglected, or abused me, but also defiled their legal, moral,
and ethical duties. I don't know which is worse: parents who don't care
for their children, biological fathers who don't support their offspring,
or professionals who violate their professional standards, as well as the
public trust, by neglecting those under their care and control.

Because of my civil suits, much of my story has already been made
public. I hope that the other children who lived with me in the Moss
home—particularly the one I call Mandy in this book—will let me
know how they are doing. I only wish I could have done more for

them. I think that one of the reasons people have been so interested in having me speak and write about my story is because most children's voices are suppressed or ignored. I represent thousands, probably tens of thousands of children who have been lost in the system. We are a chorus of voices that need to be heard.

I could not have written this book without the extensive help of my brilliant and talented adoptive mother, Gay Courter. She organized the materials, researched the legal aspects, and uncovered some of the mysteries of my past. There is no way this book would have come together without her hard work and endless devotion to the project. Gay, who is a bestselling author, also guided me through the grueling task of producing a readable book as she helped me relive some painful periods of my life. I expected to regurgitate my story; I did not expect to rediscover my fractured childhood and reassemble it, like a puzzle.

My adoptive father, Phil, was also an essential part of the process. He helped immensely with the research; in particular, reading huge blocks of court documents and making notes. He also read every draft of the manuscript and offered his insights, dedication, and unwavering love.

Someday I would like to know for certain who my biological father might be. I hope that he would be proud of me.

I have recently been in touch with members of my biological family, and I am grateful for their warmth and kindness. My biological mother and I are building an adult friendship, and I plan to be there for my little sister in any way I can.

I want to thank the following people for bringing me home:
Judge Martha Cook, Mary Miller, and the staff of the Thirteenth Judicial Circuit Court Guardian ad Litem Program in Hillsborough

County, including Joel Valdes, Alyce Krepshaw, Wayne Coleman, Angie Smith, and Laura Ankenbruck. They are the true heroes of my story, even though they worked behind the scenes on my behalf and I knew only Mary Miller personally.

My legal advisers—Karen Gievers, Frank Bach, Neil Spector, Roy Wasson, Bob Glenn, Edwin Krieger, and Donald Linsky—helped give me a voice and secure my future.

Carol Paine and Susan Sampson connected my adoptive parents to me. Victoria Hummer, Marie Brzovich, Beth Reese, Barbara Luhn, Beth Lord, Sharon Ambrose, Sharon Williamson, Joe Kroll, Jann Heffner, Maureen Hogan, and Susan Reeder helped with my adoption and transitions.

Also thanks to Sandnes Smith Boulanger, who was always there for me and gave me someone to trust. Todd Boulanger was blunt and honest, but had a way of lightening any situation with a warm smile. Irvin Randle always made me feel good about myself with his welcoming hugs, encouragement, and jokes about my feet. Mary Fernandez and Bruce Wesolowski put up with me in therapy, even though some of the hours we spent together were like ripping stitches out. Thanks to the many others—from the office staff to the administrators to the recreation staff—at The Children's Home, who helped me survive campus life. I also want to thank my cottage sponsors, Mr. and Mrs. Thomas Gaffney, whose scholarship prize in fifth grade convinced me that I would go to college.

I am indebted to all my teachers, guidance counselors, and school administrators, especially Mrs. Trojello, Ms. MacDonald, Ms. Worthington, Mr. Johnston, and Ms. Beeler, who took me under their wings and made such a huge impact on my life. A few very special teachers, whose names I do not know, tried to protect me by reporting abuse.

In addition, a special thanks to Rita Soronen, Denny Lynch, and others at the Dave Thomas Foundation for Adoption for the special role they have played in my life.

I also want to thank Jessica Brown, Joanna Carter, Katie Connolly, Glori Helms, Cyndal Houts, Jill Bailey, Becky Smith, Erick Smith, and all my friends who have helped me through tough times.

For assistance during the writing of this book, I cannot thank my adoptive mother, Gay Courter, enough. I would also like to thank my agent, Jöelle Delbourgo; my adoptive father, Philip Courter; Elizabeth Law; Kiley Fitzsimmons; Jennifer Weidman; Cindy B. Nixon; Jeannie Ng; Sarah Flynn; Esther Mandel; Lynn Mills; Jonellen Heckler; Pat Gaudette; Kathryn Olney; Sharon Smith; and Dr. Montague Chancey for their editorial wisdom.

I want to recognize my platform-speaker mentor, Lou Heckler, who gave me the confidence to tell my story to large audiences.

All of Phil and Gay's extended family have accepted me as their own, especially Grampy Weisman, who has been so generous to me.

Finally, thanks to my family: Phil, Gay, Blake and Josh, who I now know will be there for me as I will be there for them— forever.

When I was a junior in high school, Gay showed me an announcement for a *New York Times Magazine* essay contest that asked high school students to describe a moment in their lives in which they learned something about themselves. The experience had to be true. I immediately was reminded of my adoption-day videotape. I blurted, "I'll write about my adoption day." I paused for a moment, then told her why I would title it "Three Little Words": "Everyone will assume the words are 'I love you'—but what I actually felt and said that day was far from that."

Three Little Words

I never thought three little words would have such an impact on my life, even though they weren't the words I was supposed to say. Every time I see the videotape, I cringe. It was one of those memorable occasions that families treasure, but this is one "treasure" I would rather bury.

It was July 28, 1998, my adoption day. I had spent almost ten of my twelve years in foster care; I was now living in my fourteenth placement. Some homes had lasted less than a week; few more than a year. So why would this one be any different? Before this placement, I had been in residential care (the politically correct name for an orphanage). Do you remember the movie *The Cider House Rules*, when the orphans try to smile in just the right way so they will be picked by the couple shopping for a child? While it was not supposed to be so obvious at The Children's Home of Tampa, prospective parents did act as though they were looking at puppies in a pet shop. For more than two-and-a-half years, I watched the few lucky dogs pack up their belongings, wave goodbye and exit the gate. I also saw them return—even after being placed with a family—with their tails between their legs. People made promises about "forever families," but often something went wrong. I don't know what families expected. Nobody is perfect, and children who have already been rejected by their parents—or at least feel they've been—are hoping that someone will love them no matter how they behave. I had been living with my new family for eight months. Everything seemed to be going well, but would that change after the papers were signed? And just because it was "official," did that mean they would not send me back if I didn't live up to their expectations?

My parents have two biological kids who are grown; so they thought raising a daughter might fill their empty nest. I loved my new waterfront house, with my own room and a bathroom I didn't have to share. For the first time, I could have friends over, and my all-star softball team came to swim after our games. Overnights are forbidden in foster care, but now I hosted and went to slumber parties. I could use the phone anytime I wanted, and lots of the calls were for me. I had my first pet, a kitten named Catchew that slept on my bed. There were no locks on the refrigerator or scheduled mealtimes. I could help myself to as many boxes of macaroni-and-cheese, bowls of ramen noodles or grilled-cheese sandwiches as I wanted.

When I did something wrong, my pre-adoptive parents docked my allowance or cut back on TV or telephone time. In one foster home, I was beaten with a paddle, denied food, forced to stand in awkward positions, swallow hot sauce and run laps in the blistering sun. Other times, I was removed to a new home with a new set of rules and promises. Nobody really lives happily ever after, do they? So when was this picture-perfect story going to fall apart? Before or after the "finalization"?

You can see how terrified I am on the videotape as we enter the courthouse. My eyes seem to be searching for a way out as I am led into Judge Florence Foster's chambers. On one side of the conference table are the people from my old life; on the other, those who represent my new one. I am placed between Gay and Phil, who are about to become my new parents. Across the way are two representatives from The Children's Home, both therapists. They are happy for me, but that is their job. Mary Miller is smiling and holding a bouquet. She had been my volunteer Guardian ad Litem for four years and did the most to help me get a family.

"Our" side is also represented by Gay's father, Grampy Weisman; one of my new brothers, Josh, who is home from college and acting as the cameraman; and my new godparents, the Weiners, who have brought their three small daughters. The proceedings are delayed because the Department of Children and Families representative is late. He also held up the adoption by neglecting the paperwork for months. While the others chat, I am biting my lip and biding my time. Finally, the representative arrives, and my attorney, Neil Spector, who is also Gay's cousin, begins the proceedings. I wait for my cue. But what am I supposed to do? Act as if this is the happiest day of my life? How can it be, when I am petrified that everything is a big fat lie?

After some legal jargon, the judge turns to me. "Nothing in life comes easy," she begins. "If it does, you should be suspicious." She may be trying to comfort me by saying that she knows I've overcome many hardships to get where I am. Instead, she just reinforces my fears that life with my new family is too good to be true. Because of my age, I have to consent to the adoption. After talking to my parents, the judge asks me, "Do you want me to sign the papers and make it official, Ashley?"

On the tape, it looks as if I am trapped center stage in the spotlight. Do I have a choice? I stare straight ahead, shrug my shoulders and mumble, "I guess so." In three words, it is done.

P. S. Almost five years later, I am still with my family. I didn't know then what I know now: some people can be trusted.

After I won first prize and the essay appeared in the newspaper, I received calls from agents, editors—even movie producers—wanting me to tell or sell my story. I had dipped into my files that had arrived for the lawsuit but did not know how the fragments stitched together. My memories were like tangled chains without a beginning or ending. Some were raw feelings, like a tendon cut loose from bone. I knew there was much more I had to find out before I could write my story, and that journey has helped make sense of my convoluted past. My anger toward the Mosses and my mother has dissipated, maybe because I understand each of them better. Most of all, my traveling companions are my "real" parents. We learned about my childhood together; and in some ways, it was if I grew up with them by my side.

One of my few baby pictures. Just before my adoption, Gay found it with many other baby pictures buried in my case files.

Luke and me, ages two and four, respectively, when we were living at the Hines foster home. Researching my lost childhood, I revisited the Hineses, and they gave me an album that covered the time Luke and I lived with them.

Chicken pox! Me and two other children in the bathtub.

A birthday party—not mine—in the Ortiz home. I'm third from
the right on the couch.

I'm playing house at my grandfather's home in South Carolina.
He built us a playhouse outside our trailer. Adele hung a
clothesline for me to dry my dolls' clothes.

A friend and I posing in swimsuits on the Mosses' patio before
going to the beach.

I'm in the cramped girls' bedroom at the Mosses'.

Luke and me outside of his cottage at The Children's Home. When we moved there, Luke and I had been apart for six months. He would cling to me whenever he saw me, and sometimes the staff would have to drag him away.

Children in Waiting
— 4th Edition —

o I'd love a family rich or mid as long as they want a loving kid, If they love me and care for me, that's all I want in a family. By Ashley

Adoption Directory

My drawing won the contest, and was on the cover of *Children in Waiting*, a catalog of faces and biographies of children available for adoption. Later the Courters, who first saw my photo in this book, told me that they had hoped this drawing was mine.

I'm at my first Murphey Awards ceremony at The Children's Home. I participated in many events and won several awards. Members of the Tampa Bay Buccaneers football team presented the trophies that year.

Here I am meeting Phil and Gay Courter for the first time in September 1997. They were much older than the parents I had hoped for, but they were the only ones who had ever wanted me. I was relieved to have Ms. Sandnes at my side.

Grampy Weisman, Phil, me, Judge Florence Foster, and Gay pose after my adoption on July 28, 1998. I had just uttered my fateful three little words. I felt the adoption was all a sham, and thought the Courters would unadopt me at any moment.

Here I am with my Guardian ad Litem, Mary Miller. She is the volunteer who rescued me from foster care and helped me get adopted. Thinking she was just another in a long line of workers, I did not appreciate all that she was doing for me at the time.

Here I am with J. K. Rowling at the breakfast for the Harry Potter essay contest winners in New York. J. K. Rowling told me how proud she was that I had overcome so much already, and predicted I would go far. I've taken her encouraging words to heart.

Here, I'm meeting President Clinton in December 2000. After Hillary Rodham Clinton mentioned my Harry Potter essay on television, I wrote to her. In response, she invited me to an amazing Christmas party at the White House.

This is one of the first 'Courter holiday pictures' with all of our cats featured. Every year we take a family photo; some funny, some serious. It's difficult getting everyone to agree on a theme or place, but I treasure each one.